CAMBRIDGE TEXTBOOKS IN LIN

General Editors: W.SIDNEY ALLEN, B.COMRIE
C.J.FILLMORE, E.J.A.HENDERSON, F.W.HOUSEHOLDER
R.LASS, R.B. LE PAGE, J.LYONS, P.H.MATTHEWS,
J.L.M.TRIM F.R.PALMER, R.POSNER

SOCIOLINGUISTICS

SOCIOLINGUISTICS

R. A. HUDSON

LECTURER IN LINGUISTICS
UNIVERSITY COLLEGE LONDON

CAMBRIDGE UNIVERSITY PRESS

CAMBRIDGE
LONDON   NEW YORK   NEW ROCHELLE
MELBOURNE   SYDNEY

Published by the Press Syndicate of the University of Cambridge
The Pitt Building, Trumpington Street, Cambridge CB2 1RP
32 East 57th Street, New York, NY 10022, USA
296 Beaconsfield Parade, Middle Park, Melbourne 3206, Australia

First published 1980
Reprinted 1981, 1982

Printed in Great Britain
at the Alden Press, Oxford

Library of Congress Cataloguing in Publication Data

Hudson, Richard Anthony
Sociolinguistics.

(Cambridge textbooks in linguistics)
Bibliography: p.
Includes indexes.
1. Sociolinguistics. I. Title.
P40.H8   301.2′1   79-51824

ISBN 0 521 22833 6 hard covers
ISBN 0 521 29668 4 paperback

To Gay, Lucy and Alice

CONTENTS

Contents

Contents

Contents

PREFACE

I have written this book in the hope that it will do a number of different things, from informing and stimulating the newcomer to providing a theoretical framework within which the findings of sociolinguistics may be related to the theory of language structure (so-called 'theoretical linguistics'). If there is a bias in my selection of topics to cover, it is in favour of those topics which will be of most interest to students of language or linguistics, but I hope that others coming from sociology, social psychology and anthropology may be interested to see how the relations of language to society look to one whose training and research has been almost exclusively in structural linguistics. As a theoretical linguist myself, I have felt free to criticise the tradition within which I work, and the writing of this book has made it clear to me that there is much to criticise in this tradition. At the same time, I have tried to pick out the many positive contributions that a sociolinguistic viewpoint can make to the study of language.

My thinking on sociolinguistics is based on a course which I have been giving in London since 1970, on work with a number of stimulating graduate students, and on discussions with other sociolinguists (most of them British). It will be clear from the text and the references who has influenced me most, but I should like to mention in particular Bob Le Page, who first suggested the writing of this book and who spent a lot of time working through two quite different versions of it with me, discussing many of the theoretical issues and shaping my thinking on them. Other colleagues gave me helpful comments on various chapters – Thea Bynon, David Carmeli, Anne Holloway, John Holm, Joan Russell, Greg Smith, Adrian Stenton, Geoffrey Thornton and Peter Trudgill; and I had especially helpful and detailed comments from Geoff Sampson, Howard Giles and Jim and Lesley Milroy. I hope they approve of what I have done with their comments.

Preface

The book also owes a good deal to my family. My father John read the complete manuscript and his suggestions have certainly made the reader's task easier than it would otherwise have been. My wife Gay did more than her fair share of looking after our two small daughters, one of whom was born while the book was gestating, and the three of them between them kept my spirits up and my feet firmly on the ground. Finally, I have to thank the staff of the Cambridge University Press for their skilled assistance. I hope the result is a reasonably balanced mixture of fact and theory, and of enthusiasm and sobriety.

I

Introduction

1.1 Sociolinguistics

1.1.1 *A description*

We can define sociolinguistics as *the study of language in relation to society*, and this is how we shall be taking the term in this book. At the time of writing (1978), sociolinguistics has become a recognised part of most courses at university level on 'linguistics' or 'language', and is indeed one of the main growth points in the study of language, from the point of view of both teaching and research. There are now two major English-language journals devoted to research publications (*Language in Society* and *International Journal of the Sociology of Language*) and a number of introductory textbooks, apart from the present one (others are Burling 1970, Pride 1971, Fishman 1972a, Robinson 1972, Trudgill 1974b, Platt & Platt 1975, Bell 1976, Dittmar 1976, Wardhaugh 1976). Most of the growth in sociolinguistics took place in the late 1960s and early 1970s, however, so it can be seen how young the discipline is. This is not meant to imply that the study of language in relation to society is an invention of the 1960s – on the contrary, there is a long tradition in the study of dialects and in the general study of the relations between word-meaning and culture, both of which count as sociolinguistics by our definition. What is new is the *widespread* interest in sociolinguistics and the realisation that it can throw much light both on the nature of language and on the nature of society.

Like other subjects, sociolinguistics is partly empirical and partly theoretical – partly a matter of going out and amassing bodies of fact and partly of sitting back and thinking. The 'armchair' approach to sociolinguistics can be fairly productive, whether it is based on facts collected in a systematic way as part of research or simply on one's own experience. In particular, it allows the beginnings of an analytical framework to be worked out, containing terms such as LANGUAGE (a body of knowledge or rules), SPEECH (actual utterances), SPEAKER, ADDRESSEE, TOPIC and so on. And of course personal experience is a rich source of information on language in relation to society. However, it will soon become clear that the armchair approach is dangerous if it is applied to personal experience alone, for two reasons. First, we may be seriously wrong in the way in which we interpret our own experience, since most of us are not consciously aware of the vast range of variations in speech which we hear, and react to, in our everyday lives. And secondly, personal experience is a very limited base from which to generalise about language in society, since it does not take account of all the other societies, where things are arranged very differently.

However, the reason why interest in sociolinguistics has grown so rapidly over the last decade is not because of the achievements in arm-chair theorising but because of the empirical discoveries made in the course of systematic research projects. Some of this research has taken place in 'exotic' communities, and this has produced facts which many readers of this book will find stimulating because they are so unex-pectedly different from the kind of society which they already know. For instance, British people are generally surprised (and interested) to hear that there are societies where one's parents *must not* have the same mother-tongue (see below, 1.2.2). Other research projects, however, have been in the kind of complex, urban industrial society to which most readers will be accustomed, and this research too has provided some surprises, such as the discovery that differences between social classes are as clearly reflected in speech in America as they are in Britain, although the United States has an image of being much less class-conscious (the evidence for this claim will be discussed in chapter 5, especially 5.2.2).

It is important to recognise that much of the interest in sociolinguis-tics has come from people (such as educationalists) who have a *practical* concern for language, rather than a desire simply to understand better how this small area of the universe works. In particular, it became possible in the United States in the 1960s and 1970s to fund relatively large-scale research projects connected with the speech of underprivi-leged groups, on the ground that the findings would make possible a more satisfactory educational policy. Chapter 6 is largely devoted to the issues raised in and by this research, but the research reported in chapter 5 would probably not have been possible in a different social climate, and the same may also be true of that reported in chapter 4, though perhaps to a lesser extent. This practical orientation has led to a good deal of discussion of some theoretical issues – those with practical implications, including the ones aired in chapter 5 – but relatively little discussion (or at a less satisfactory level) of theoretical issues with less immediate practical consequences. This imbalance will no doubt strike the reader of this book, though I have tried to clarify theoretical issues of *both* kinds.

1.1.2 *Sociolinguistics and linguistics*

Throughout this book I shall refer to sociolinguists and linguists as separate people, but of course there are many sociolinguists who would also call themselves linguists, as well as the large number whose background is in sociology, anthropology or social psychology. The question of who is a sociolinguist and who is not, is neither interesting nor important; but it is important to ask whether there is a difference between sociolinguistics and linguistics and, if so, what it is. A widely held view is that there is such a difference, and that linguistics differs from sociolinguistics in taking account only of the *structure* of language, to the exclusion of the social contexts in which it is learned and used. The task of linguistics, according to this view, is to work out 'the rules of language X', after which sociolinguists may enter the scene and study any points at which these rules make contact with society – such as where alternative ways of expressing the same thing are chosen by different social groups. This view is typical of the whole 'structural' school of linguistics which has dominated twentieth-century linguistics, including transformational-generative linguistics (the variety developed since 1957 by Noam Chomsky). (It is also fairly typical, incidentally, of much foreign-language teaching in Britain.)

However, not all students of language would accept this view. Some would argue that since speech is (obviouly) social behaviour, to study it without reference to society would be like studying courtship behaviour without relating the behaviour of one partner to that of the other. There are two particular reasons for accepting this view. The first is that we cannot take the notion 'language X' for granted, since this in itself is a social notion in so far as it is defined in terms of a group of people who speak X. As we shall see in chapter 2, the problem is that this group will in all probability be defined, in a complete circle, as 'the group who speak X', especially when we focus on detailed differences between dialects and try to define 'dialect X' instead of 'language X'. This argument has been developed especially by William Labov (1972a: viii). The second reason is that speech has a social function, both as a means of communication and also as a way of identifying social groups, and to study speech without reference to the society which uses it is to exclude the possibility of finding social explanations for the structures that are used. This view is typical of J.R. Firth (e.g. 1950, 1964), who founded the 'London School' of linguistics, and whose followers include Michael Halliday (e.g. 1973) and Terence Mitchell (1975). An important recent discussion of the influence of language structure is Brown & Levinson (1978).

This book will argue that the findings of sociolinguistics are highly relevant to the theory of language structure – for instance, in relation to the nature of meaning (3.2) and the analysis of alternatives in a grammar (5.5). My preference is therefore for the second view, according to which linguistics ignores society at its peril. I point this out to warn the reader against possible bias, but it is also clear that there is a big difference between recognising that one *should* take account of the social dimension of language and knowing *how* to do so.

I shall refer throughout to 'sociolinguists' and 'linguists' as though they were separate individuals, but these terms can simply be used to reflect the relative amount of attention given to the social side of language, without taking the distinction too seriously. There is no denying that remarkable progress has been made in the study of language structure within the structural tradition, by people who would call themselves 'linguists' and not 'sociolinguists'. Moreover, it is clear that some areas of language, such as those covered in this book, relate more directly to social factors than others do. Those who concentrate on other areas, taking a more or less 'asocial' approach, we can call 'linguists', as opposed to 'sociolinguists'. However, although I am not arguing that the topics covered in this book are the only ones which should be studied, I do believe that all who study language, from whatever point of view, should be much more aware of the social context of their subject matter than is often the case, and the topics covered here seem most relevant in this context.

1.1.3 *Sociolinguistics and the sociology of language*

I defined sociolinguistics as 'the study of language in relation to society', implying (intentionally) that sociolinguistics is part of the study of language. Thus, the value of sociolinguistics is the light which it throws on the nature of language in general, or on the characteristics of some particular language. As we might expect, students of society have found that facts about language can illuminate their understanding – after all, it is hard to think of any property of a society which is as distinctive as its language, or as important for its functioning. 'The study of society in relation to language' (the converse of our definition of sociolinguistics) defines what is generally called THE SOCIOLOGY OF LANGUAGE.

The difference between sociolinguistics and the sociology of language is very much one of emphasis, according to whether the investigator is more interested in language or society, and also according to whether he has more skill in analysing linguistic or social structures. There is a very large area of overlap between the two and it seems pointless to try to divide the disciplines more clearly than at present. Much of what follows in this book could equally well have been written in a textbook on the sociology of language. On the other hand, there are some issues which such a textbook ought to include which this one will not, notably most of what is called 'macro' sociology of language, dealing with the relations between society and languages as wholes. This is an important area of research from the point of view of sociology (and politics), since it raises issues such as the effects of multilingualism on economic development, and the possible language policies a government may adopt (for discussion of these issues, see Fishman 1972a, 1972b, and also the following articles, all of which are reprinted in the very accessible Giglioli 1972: Fishman 1972c, Goody & Watt 1962, Gumperz 1968, Inglehart & Woodward 1967). However, such 'macro' studies generally throw less light on the nature of language than the more 'micro' ones described in this book, because the notion of 'language X' is usually left unanalysed. (There is a good discussion of the relations between sociolinguistics and the sociology of language in the introduction to Trudgill 1978.)

1.2 **Sociolinguistic phenomena**
1.2.1 *An imaginary world*
What, then, is there to say about language in relation to society? It may be helpful to start by trying to imagine a society (and a language) about which there is very *little* to say. The little world described below is completely imaginary, and most sociolinguists – perhaps all of them – would agree that it is highly unlikely that any such

world either does or even could exist, given what we know about both language and society.

In our imaginary world there is a society which is clearly defined by some natural boundary, impassable in either direction. The purpose of postulating this boundary is to guarantee, on the one hand, that no members of other communities join this one, bringing their own languages with them, and, on the other, that members of this community never leave it and take their language to another, thereby complicating the perfect coincidence between language and community.

Everybody in this society has exactly the same language – they know the same constructions and the same words, with the same pronunciation and the same range of meanings for every single word in the language. (Any deviation from such an exact identity raises the possibility of statements such as 'Person A knows pronunciation M, but Person B knows pronunciation N, for the same word', which would be a statement about language in relation to society.) An obvious problem is that very young members of the society, just learning to talk, must necessarily be different from everybody else. We might get round this problem by saying that child language is the domain of a branch of psychology rather than sociology, and that psychology can provide general principles of language acquisition which will allow us to predict every respect in which the language of children in this society deviated from the language of the adults. If psychology were able to provide the necessary principles, then there would be a good deal to say about language in relation to individual development, but nothing about language in relation to society. Needless to say, no psychologist would dream of claiming that this was possible, even in principle.

A consequence of the complete absence of any differences between members of this community is that language change is thereby ruled out, since such change normally involves a difference between the oldest and youngest generations, so that when the former all die only the forms used by the latter survive. Since change seems to affect every language so far studied, this makes the language of our imaginary community unique. The only way to allow for change in a totally homogeneous community is to assume that every change affects every member of the community absolutely and simultaneously: one day, nobody has the new form, the next day, everybody has it. (It is very hard to see any mechanism which could explain such change, short of community-wide telepathy!)

Another characteristic of the community we are considering is that *circumstances* have no influence on what people say, either with respect to its content or its form. There are no 'formal' and 'informal' situations, requiring different kinds of vocabulary (such as *receive* versus *get*) or different pronunciations for words (like *not* versus *-n't*) (see 2.4). Nor are there any 'discussions' and 'arguments', or 'requests' and 'demands', each requiring not only particular forms but also particular meanings. (For instance, in an argument you *attack* the other person's position, but in a discussion you *consider* it.) Nor are there any differences between the beginnings, middles and ends of conversations, such as would require greetings and farewells. None of these differences due to circumstances exist because if they did they would require statements about society – in particular, about social interaction; which is the topic of chapter 4. Indeed, if we discount any influence of the social context, it is doubtful if speech is possible at all, since spoken messages are generally geared specifically to the needs of the audience.

Finally, we must assume that there is no connection between the culture of the postulated community and the meanings which its language (especially its vocabulary) allows it to express. The language must therefore contain no words such as *cricket* or *priest*, whose meanings could be stated only with reference to a partial description of the culture, as will be argued in 3.2. To assume otherwise would be to allow rich and interesting statements about language in relation to society, since culture is one of the most important characteristics of society. Exactly what kinds of concepts the members of this community *would* be able to express is not clear – possibly they would only be able to assert logical truths such as 'If p and q, then p', since any other kinds of word are likely to involve some reference to the community's culture.

All in all, our blue-print for a community is an unpromising one. All the restrictions imposed on it were necessary in order to guarantee that there should be nothing to say about its language in relation to society, beyond the simple statement 'Such-and-such community speak language X'. However, it will be noticed that this statement is precisely the kind which is generally made by linguists (or laymen) about a language, and exhausts what they feel obliged to say about the language in relation to society. The purpose of this section has been to show that the only kind of community (or language) for which such a statement could be remotely adequate is a fictitious one – the kind, in fact, which Chomsky defined as the proper object of inquiry in theoretical linguistics (1965: 3).

1.2.2   *A real but exotic world*

We now turn to a real world, in which there is a great deal to be said about language in relation to society. It is the very exotic world of the north-west Amazon, described by A.P. Sorensen (1971) and J. Jackson (1974) (though we shall see in 1.2.3 that things are not so very different in the kind of society to which most of us are accustomed).

Geographically, the area in question is half in Brazil and half in Colombia, coinciding more or less with the area in which a language called Tukano can be relied on as a LINGUA FRANCA (i.e. a trade language widely spoken as a non-native language). It is a large area, but sparsely inhabited; around 10,000 people in an area the size of England. Most of the people are indigenous Indians, divided into over twenty tribes, which are in turn grouped into five 'phratries' (groups of related tribes). There are two crucial facts to be remembered about this community. First, each tribe speaks a different language – sufficiently different to be mutually incomprehensible and, in some cases, genetically unrelated (i.e. not descended from a common 'parent' language). Indeed, the *only* criterion by which tribes can be distinguished from each other is by their language. The second fact is that the five phratries (and thus all twenty-odd tribes) are exogamous (i.e. a man must not marry a woman from the same phratry or tribe). Putting these two facts together, it is easy to see the main linguistic consequence: a man's wife *must* speak a different language from him.

We now add a third fact: marriage is patrilocal (the husband and wife live where the husband was brought up), and there is a rule that the wife should not only live where the husband was brought up, but should also use his language in speaking to their children (a custom that might be called 'patrilingual marriage'). The linguistic consequence of this rule is that a child's mother does not teach her own language to the child, but rather a language which she speaks only as a foreigner – as though everyone in Britain learned their English from a foreign au-pair girl. One can thus hardly call the children's first language their 'mother-tongue' except by a stretch of the imagination. The reports of this community do not mention any widespread disruption in language learning or general 'deterioration' of the languages concerned, so we can assume that a language can be transmitted efficiently and accurately even under these apparently adverse circumstances, through the influence of the father, the rest of the father's relatives and the older children. It is perhaps worth pointing out that the wife goes to live in a 'long-house' in which the husband's brothers and parents also live, so there is no shortage of contacts with native speakers of the father's language.

What is there to say about language in relation to such a society? First, there is the question of relating languages as wholes to speakers, assuming for simplicity that it is possible to talk usefully about 'languages as wholes' (contrary to what we shall argue in 2.2). For any given language X, it will first be necessary to define who are its native speakers, but since this means referring to some tribe, and tribes are in fact defined solely with reference to language, there is clearly a problem. The solution is either to list all the long-houses belonging to the tribe concerned, or to specify the geographical area (or areas) where the tribe lives. (Most tribes do in fact have their own territory, which does not overlap with that of other tribes.) However, it will have to be borne in mind that about a quarter of the native speakers of language X will be made up of the married women who are dispersed among the other tribes, and similarly about a quarter of the people living in the area designated as 'language X territory' will be *non*-native speakers of X, being wives from other tribes. Indeed, any given long-house is likely to contain native speakers of a variety of languages, on the assumption that brothers need not be attracted to girls of the same 'other' tribe. In addition to the native speakers of language X, there will be people who speak it as non-natives, with every degree of fluency from almost native-speaker to minimal. Thus anyone wishing to write a grammar for language X will need to say precisely for whom the grammar is claimed to be true – just for the native speakers left at home in the tribal area, or for all native speakers including those dispersed among the other tribes, or for all speakers, native or non-native, in the tribal area.

Secondly, there is the question of discourse: how is speech used in social interaction? There are questions which arise out of the number of languages available: for instance, how do people get by when they travel around within the area, as they very often do? Are they expected to use the language of the long-house which they are visiting? Apparently not – the choice of language is based solely on the convenience of the people concerned (except for the rule requiring wives to use their husbands' language when speaking to their children). If the visitor does not know the long-house language, but someone there knows his, they will use the visitor's when speaking to him. What about language itself as a subject of conversation? Here too practical needs are put first, namely the need to know as many languages as possible in order to make it easier both to travel and (for young people) to find a partner. It is quite normal to talk about a language, learning its vocabulary and phrases from it, and this continues into old age; yet people generally do not know how many languages they can speak, and do not think of language learning as a way of gaining prestige. Perhaps this is what we might expect in a society where everyone can be expected to speak *at least* (i) his father's language, (ii) his mother's language (which she will certainly have taught her children with a view to their seeking partners among her tribe) and (iii) the lingua franca, Tukano (which may also be the language of his father or his mother). However, in addition to the aspects of discourse which are directly related to multilingualism, there are many other things to be said about the relations between speech and the social circumstances in this complex Amazonian society. For instance, there is a rule that if you are listening to someone whom you respect, you should repeat after him, word-for-word, everything he says, at least for the first few minutes of his talking.

Thirdly, there is the question of the relation of language to culture, on which we have little information in the reports on the north-west Amazon referred to above, but on which we can make some safe guesses. For instance, it would be surprising if any of the languages concerned lacked a word for 'long-house' or 'tribe', and we might reasonably expect a word for 'phratry' (though such higher-level concepts often lack names, as we shall see in 3.3.4). Similarly, we may predict that most concepts relevant to the culture will have words in each language to express them, and that most words in each language will express cultural concepts, definable only in terms of the culture concerned.

In the world of the north-west Amazon there is probably nothing that a linguist could satisfactorily say about any language without at the same time making some fairly complicated statement about it in relation to society. In particular, he could not say *which* language he was describing by referring to some pre-defined community who use it (in the way in which he might feel entitled to talk about, say, 'British English' or 'Birmingham English'). The main source of this complexity is the rule of 'linguistic exogamy', which might not be expected to be very wide-spread in the world. However, the other source is the amount of indivi-dual bilingualism (or, more accurately, multilingualism), which makes it hard to decide who is a speaker of a given language and who is not. This characteristic, of wide-spread multilingualism, is anything but excep-tional in the world as a whole, as an armchair sociolinguist can easily deduce from the fact that there are some four or five thousand languages in the world, but only about 140 nation states. At least some states must therefore contain a very large number of languages, and probably most contain a fair number, with an average between 30 and 35. In view of the need for communication with neighbouring communities and government agencies, it is fair to assume that many members of most communities are multilingual. It is worthwhile bearing this conclusion in mind in reading the next section, since it shows that the monolingual communities familiar to many of us may in fact be highly exceptional and even 'exotic' from a global perspective.

1.2.3 *A real and familiar world*

Readers are now invited to consider the world in which they themselves grew up. It is unlikely that any reader has had a background quite as linguistically exciting as the one described above, but most of us will certainly find that there is more to be said about our own sociolinguistic worlds than might be expected and much of it is surprisingly interesting.

In order to focus their thinking, readers may find it helpful to imagine themselves, reasonably fluent in Tukano, sitting in a long-house in the north-west Amazon, telling the residents about their language, in the way that travelling Indians in the area are presumably asked to do if they reach a long-house unfamiliar with their language. The kind of information they would be expected to provide would cover both very general and very specific matters. Who else speaks the language? Where do the speakers live? Do they speak any other languages? What do they say when they first meet a stranger? What is the word meaning 'phratry'? What are the meals eaten at different times of day called? Are there any special ways of talking to young children? How do you count? Is there any way of showing that you're quoting what somebody else has told you? How do you show that the thing you're referring to is already known to the addressee? Are there different ways of pronouncing any of the words according to where you come from? In answering every one of these questions, something will not only have been said about the language but also about one aspect or another of the society that uses it; and such questions could be multiplied by the inquisitive long-house residents until a complete description of the strangers' language has been provided.

The point of this exercise is to make readers aware of how much there is to say about their own language in relation to society. My hope is that, as they read this book, readers will keep their own background in mind and try to imagine what results would have been obtained if research projects comparable with those which will be described below were to be carried out in their language community.

1.3 Speakers and communities
1.3.1 *Conformity and individualism*

If sociolinguistics is about language in relation to society, we might expect a book on sociolinguistics to be mainly about large-scale social units such as tribes, nations and social classes. These will indeed be mentioned, and there will be a discussion of the relevance of some of them to language, especially in 5.4. However, society consists of individuals, and both sociologists and sociolinguists would agree that it is essential to keep the individual firmly in the centre of interest, and to avoid losing sight of him while talking about large-scale abstractions and movements. The individual speaker is important in sociolinguistics in much the same way as the individual cell is important in biology: if we don't understand how the individual works, to that extent we shan't be able to understand how collections of individuals behave either.

Moreover, there is an even more important reason for focussing on the individual in sociolinguistics, which does not apply to the cell in biology (or not to the same extent): we can be sure that *no two speakers have the same language, because no two speakers have the same experience of language.* The differences between speakers may vary from the very slight and trivial (in the case of twins brought up together, for instance) to total difference within whatever limits are set by universal characteristics of language. Unlike the individual cell, the individual speaker is presumably moulded much more by his experience (as a listener) than by his genetic make-up, and his experience consists in fact of speech produced by other individual speakers, each of whom is unique. What we shall try to do in this book is to look at society from the inside, so to speak, taking the view-point of an individual member talking and listening to other individuals, rather than observing it from the outside, as we might imagine some giant doing, who could see the community as a whole and could start to dissect it, but hadn't yet developed a microscope fine enough to see the individual speaker.

The uniqueness of each person's sociolinguistic past is not the only source of differences between speakers, however. We can imagine a person constructing a model of the community in which he lives (at a more or less unconscious level, presumably), in which the people around him are arranged in a 'multi-dimensional space', i.e. showing similarities and differences relative to one another on a large number of different dimensions or parameters. Some of these dimensions involve linguistic differences – such as how some particular phoneme or word is pronounced – and the model he builds up consequently covers linguistic parameters as well as variables of other types. The particular model which he constructs will reflect his own personal experience, so people with different sociolinguistic backgrounds will be led to construct correspondingly different models relevant to language and society.

However, the individual is not simply a 'social automaton', giving a true and accurate reflection of his past in his current model, in the way that a tape-recorder gives a record of its recent past. Rather, the individual *filters* his experience of new situations through his existing model, and two people could both hear the same person talking, but be affected by his speech in different ways. For instance, an Englishman and an American could both watch the same American film, but learn quite different facts from it about language – what for the American viewer counts as a new fact about how poor whites in the Deep South talk might count for the Englishman simply as a new fact about how Americans talk. From this point of view, we may expect differences in existing models to lead to differences in later models, even where the experience on which the changes are based is objectively the same in both cases. (For a similar view of the acquisition of language structure, see McCawley 1977.)

To complete this picture of the sources of differences between individuals, we can return to the multi-dimensional space to which we referred above. There is ample evidence that society is structured, from a sociolinguistic point of view, in terms of a multi-dimensional space, which we shall review in chapter 5. One need only think of the rather obvious ways in which people can be classified more or less independently according to the dimensions of age, region of origin, social class (or profession) and sex, to see an example of a four-dimensional space, each dimension of which is relevant to language. Once a person has constructed a model of how this multi-dimensional space looks from his point of view, he then has to *choose* where to locate *himself* in it. Language is only one part of the picture, of course, but a particularly important part because it gives the speaker a very clearly structured set of symbols which he can use in locating himself in the world. If we think of a child in an area where there are two different groups of children of roughly his age, and he belongs clearly to one of them, then he will most probably model his speech largely on that of others in the group he has joined, because that is the pattern he has *chosen*. In other words, at each utterance his speech can be seen as an ACT OF IDENTITY in a multi-dimensional space (Le Page 1977a, Le Page et al. 1974).

Against the background of the last few paragraphs, in which we have emphasised the scope for individual variation among speakers, we may be impressed by the amount of *agreement* that is often found among speakers, and which we shall also illustrate in chapter 5. It is important to point out that the degree of similarity generally found between speakers goes well beyond what is needed for efficient communication. For instance, contrary to what was predicted by Ferdinand de Saussure, father of the structural tradition in linguistics, it is not sufficient for a speaker to keep two adjacent vowel phonemes distinct from each other: his particular pronunciations of them must be *precisely* the same as those of the people he is taking as models. Similarly, his syntactic restrictions on the use of particular words will be more or less exact copies of the restrictions applied by other people (for example, all English speakers agree in restricting *probable* to use with a *that*-clause, in contrast with its synonym *likely* which can be used either with a *that*-clause or with an infinitive).

Perhaps the show-piece for the triumph of conformity over efficient communication is the area of irregular morphology, where the existence of irregular verbs or nouns in a language like English has *no* pay-off from the point of view of communication (it makes life easier neither for the speaker nor hearer, nor for the language learner). The only explanation for the continued existence of such irregularities must be the need for each individual to be seen to be conforming to the same rules, in detail, as those he takes as his models. As is well known, children tend to use relatively regular forms (such as *goed* for *went*), but *abandon* these forms later in order to conform with other people who have already abandoned them.

The two 'forces' which we have now considered, one leading to individual differences and the other leading to similarities between individuals, may be referred to for convenience as INDIVIDUALISM and CONFORMITY. The amount of variation actually found within any given community will depend on the relative strengths of these two forces, so that conformity will predominate in some communities and individual-ism in others. The terms FOCUSSING and DIFFUSION have been suggested by Robert Le Page for these two kinds of situations (1968a). Focussing is found where there is a high degree of contact among speakers and agreement on linguistic norms, and is typical of very closely knit small communities (such as the working-class networks in Belfast discussed in 5.4.3), or of societies where there is a highly standardised written language such as Sanskrit or French. Diffusion on the other hand is found where neither of these conditions holds, an extreme example being Romany, the gipsy language. Of course, there is no question of a clear distinction between focussing and diffusion; rather they are the names for the two ends of a scale on which any society, or part of it, may be located.

Interestingly, it has never been suggested that individuals can be more or less conformist so far as language is concerned, though it is of course conceivable that such differences exist. In order to show that they do, it would be necessary to find differences in, for instance, the extent to which individuals maintain irregularity in their morphology. It would not be enough to show that some individuals reject the model of their parents (as they clearly do), since this is probably because they are conforming to a *different* model (that of their peers) rather than to no model at all. There may also be individual differences in willingness to create new vocabulary or to use language metaphorically, in which case the 'creative' individual would be going beyond the accepted norms, and perhaps breaking them under special circumstances (e.g. in poetry). However, such creativity seems to take place against the background of a normal, conformist language system.

1.3.2 *The sociolinguistic development of the child*

Although we may assume that each speaker is unique in his experience of language, and on this basis develops a unique grammar, a number of generalisations can be made about the stages through which children may be expected to pass in their sociolinguistic development. However, it should be emphasised from the outset that the following generalisations must all be treated as tentative hypotheses rather than established research findings, since they are based on a very small body of research supported by anecdotal evidence.

The first generalisation concerns the linguistic models which the child follows. For many children, the pattern is as follows: first parents, then peers, then adults. William Labov has suggested (1972a: 138) that the child's models are his parents until he is 3 or 4, after which his peers replace his parents until he is about 13, when he (presumably) starts looking to the adult world towards which he is moving. However, the transition from parents to peers has been put at very different ages by different scholars, ranging from 4 to 6 (Hockett 1958: 361) down to below 2 (in various personal anecdotes and also Bolinger 1975: 334). On the other hand, it is clear that many children do take their peers rather than their parents as models sooner or later (though it is equally clear, from personal experience and from anecdotes like Labov (1972a: 307), that there are some who never do). Evidence for this claim is easy to find. For instance, many children of first-generation immigrants in British towns have accents indistinguishable from those of their non-immigrant friends, and could not possibly have acquired those accents by taking their parents as models.

More interestingly, and perhaps more surprisingly, there is the evidence of a phenomenon called AGE-GRADING (Hockett 1950), which is apparently found in many societies. Age-grading means that there are linguistic forms which are used only by children in the peer-oriented stage, and which are transmitted from one generation of children to the next without ever being used by adults. Such forms can be very archaic compared with adult speech forms – for instance, among black Americans, it is children who use forms nearest to the creole out of which the English of American blacks is widely believed to have developed (Dillard 1971). Similarly, most of us learned a whole range of oral culture as children – chants, poems, songs and so on – which we have now forgotten that we ever knew, and certainly never use in adulthood (I. & P. Opie 1959). On the other hand, some scholars have claimed that it is the peer-oriented stage which lays the basis for the adult language, in spite of these non-adult features which will later be abandoned:

> The blood-and-bone of many languages is transmitted largely through successive generations of four-to-ten-year-olds: the fires of childhood competition and the twists of childhood prestige do more to shape a given individual's speech patterns, for life, than does any contact with adults. (Hockett 1958: 361; cf. Labov 1972a: 138)

The picture we have just painted refers only to the models which the child adopts for his normal speech, but we must not forget that at the same time he is constructing the multi-dimensional model of his world, fitting into it all sorts of different types of speech, including of course speech such as his parents use, even if he does not use that speech himself. Another important source of influence is nowadays the mass media, particularly television, and here too the child must become aware of a range of speech forms, although they may affect his own normal speech only peripherally, if at all. As we shall shortly note, he may be able to 'switch on' some styles of speech in role play.

We now turn to a related question: at what age do children become aware of the social significance of different speech forms? They appear to be aware of different speech forms, and the fact that there are social differences between them, from an early age. Children brought up in a bilingual environment have been reported as being aware that two separate language systems were being used even at 18 months (Ronjat 1913, quoted in Weinreich 1953). Some anecdotes suggest that this may happen even earlier, though others put the age later. For instance, Robbins Burling reports (1959) that his son learned Garo (a tribal language of north-eastern India) from his nanny at the same time as he learned English from his parents, and that he was about 2 years 3 months before he realised that different people spoke different languages; only then would he work out who was likely to understand his Garo before speaking. Before this – by 18 months – he had noticed that many things had more than one word to express them, such as English *milk* and Garo *dut*, but he had not yet made the considerable abstraction to the existence of two separate systems. As for dialect differences, there is little evidence relevant to young children, but it seems a fair assumption that they are at least capable of being aware of such differences by the time they start to model themselves on their peers, and will be aware of dialect differences to the extent that the speech of their parents and of their peers is different.

Assuming that a child has learned that two different languages or varieties are different systems, each used by a different range of people, how long does it take him to become aware of the positive and negative prejudices that grown-ups have towards some of these varieties? And how long does it take the child to adopt these prejudices himself? Again the evidence is sketchy, and to some extent contradictory, but we shall see (6.2.4) that there is some evidence at least which suggests strongly that there are communities in which many children as early as age 4 have not only already become aware of such prejudices, but have adopted them themselves. On the other hand, this is clearly not the same thing as claiming that 4 year olds have fully developed adult prejudices, and we may safely assume on the basis of other evidence that their prejudices go on developing throughout childhood and adolescence. Indeed, there seems to be no reason for thinking that the process ever stops completely.

What about the child's own speech? How does this develop in relation to his social environment? The small amount of research again makes any generalisations very tentative, but it is clear that children from an extremely early age adapt their speech to its social context. As soon as they start to speak they speak differently to different people (Giles & Powesland 1975: 139), which is hardly surprising if we think of their speech as just one aspect of social behaviour, and remember that they behave differently towards different people from very soon after birth. Moreover, from a very early age – in the first year, before they have learned any of the adult forms – they use different noises for different purposes, such as asking for something or saying the equivalent of 'I say, just look at that!' (Halliday 1975). Similarly, a child of 23 months was reported as deliberately separating her syllables off to make them clearer when she was being misunderstood (Weeks 1971).

By age 3 the child of bilingual parents will probably be reasonably efficient at keeping his two languages separate from each other in his own speech, and any 3 year old may have started practising a range of roles such as baby, doctor or cowboy (Weeks 1971). The role of 'baby' is a particularly interesting one, as children get *better* at playing it, rather than worse, as one might expect from a naive view of baby-talk as a left-over from their own babyhood (Berko Gleason 1973, Sachs & Devin 1976). A 4 year old is already remarkably versatile. As Jean Berko Gleason puts it (1973), 'Four-year olds may whine at their mothers, engage in intricate verbal play with their peers, and reserve their narrative, discursive tales for their grown-up friends.' There is no reason to think that there is any end-point in the process of acquiring new styles of speaking, or of becoming more sophisticated in the use of the styles we already have.

1.4 Summary and conclusions

In the second section of this introductory chapter we considered three very different societies and showed that, although there was relatively little to say about language divorced from its social context (1.2.2), there is a great deal to be said about language in relation to society. If 'linguistics' is distinguishable from sociolinguistics only by virtue of its lack of social perspective, its subject-matter will be very restricted, and we may reasonably conclude that the study of language from an asocial point of view is scarcely worthwhile. Effectively, the 'socio-' of 'sociolinguistics' is redundant, and linguistics must include both the study of language in which social context has been taken explicitly into account (reported in later chapters of this book), and all the work done in descriptive, historical and theoretical linguistics, to the extent that this work has not been vitiated by its failure to take account of social context.

How pessimistic do we need to be about the chances of rescuing anything permanently valuable from past work in linguistics? It would certainly be wrong to dismiss the results of asocial linguistics as simply false. Rather, we can see it as incomplete, in the same way that linguists of the 1970s find earlier grammars incomplete because they had little to say about syntax and even less about semantics or pragmatics. If we are aware of the amount and kind of social information that might have been supplied as background to a grammar, we are in less danger of being misled into thinking of languages as neat, self-contained rule systems. Similarly, if we are aware that judgments of 'grammaticality', 'well-formedness', 'acceptability', 'Englishness', and so on, reflect not only the properties of the sentence concerned but also the social background of the judge, and in particular whether or not the judge is a linguist (Martin, Bradac & Elliott 1977), then we may worry less when linguists disagree among themselves about such judgments. At the same time, of course, it has to be recognised that the theories of language which have been developed over the last few decades are all likely to have serious flaws resulting from the asocial approach of their proponents, and the problem remains of identifying these flaws in order to decide which parts of the tradition are still acceptable.

The findings of sociolinguistics, as described in this book, challenge a number of widely held views. Chapter 2 proposes reasons for questioning the assumption that languages are discrete, identifiable entities, consisting of dialects which can further be subdivided until the individual is reached, as the locus of the 'smallest dialect'. Chapter 3 shows that 'knowledge of language' may not in fact be clearly distinct, or distinct at all (even unclearly), from 'knowledge of culture'. Chapter 4 indicates that speech is not clearly different in kind from other aspects of social behaviour, but that some aspects of language structure can be described properly only by reference to speech as social behaviour. Chapter 5, in some ways the core of the book, is about variability in the forms we use when speaking. It shows that there is no such thing as a homogeneous grammar, whether for an individual or community, but that a speaker makes extraordinarily subtle use of the variability available to him in order to locate himself in society. Chapter 6 deals with two separate issues. First is the use we make of this variability as *hearers*, in order to locate others in society, showing that we all have a very well-developed awareness of the social significance of differences in pronunciation (among other things). We might wonder whether this awareness should be included in the 'linguistic knowledge' we try to cover in a grammar. The last two sections of chapter 6 deal with the second issue, whether there is any sense in which we may justifiably talk of some people's language being 'inadequate', concluding that there is provided we take account of the social demands being placed on language. This conclusion requires a much more sophisticated approach to the distinction betwen 'description' and 'prescription' than so far exists in the study of language.

2
Varieties of language

2.1 Introduction
2.1.1 *Global and specific statements*

Our purpose in this chapter is to see how far it is possible to describe the relations of language to society in terms of 'global' linguistic categories such as 'language X' or 'dialect Y' and global social categories like 'community Z'. To the extent that it is possible, the relations concerned can be handled in terms of these global categories, and need make no reference to the individual linguistic items contained in 'language X' or to the individual members of 'community Z'. On the other hand, we shall see that it is not always possible to do so – indeed, it is doubtful whether it is *ever* possible – and that at least some linguistic items, such as items of vocabulary, are different from all other items with regard to the kind of person using them, or to the circumstances in which they are used. Similarly, as we saw in the last chapter, we may assume that every individual in a community is unique in his language. To the extent that different linguistic items have different relations to society (in terms of people and circumstances), it is obviously necessary to describe these relations separately for each item. Thus on the one hand there are statements about global categories, like whole languages, and on the other hand there are statements about individual linguistic items; and in each case the statement refers to speakers either as members of some community or as individuals.

The questions that arise are complex and surprisingly hard to answer, but they are most important to anyone interested in the nature of language in general or in the relations of language to society in particular. How should global linguistic categories like 'language X' be defined? How should particular instances of them be delimited? Indeed, do such categories correspond to any kind of objective reality in terms of which these questions make sense? Can distinct types of global category (e.g. 'language' versus 'dialect') be distinguished? How are global categories related to one another? What do they consist of (i.e. what are they categories *of*)? How should communities be defined and delimited for these purposes? Do communities defined on a linguistic basis have any kind of objective reality? And so on. It is still far too early to give definite answers to most of these questions, but it is possible to cast serious doubt on some widely accepted answers to them.

Briefly, we shall be able to show that things are much more complex than many linguists believe, though it may well be that readers with less professional commitment to linguistics will find that their current common-sense view of language fits the facts quite well. On the other hand, many lay people are prepared to ask the 'professionals' questions such as 'Where is real Cockney spoken?' and 'Is Jamaican creole a kind of English or not?', assuming that these questions are really meaningful, whereas we shall see that they are not the kind of question that can be investigated scientifically. Thus there may be some surprises in this chapter, both for the professional and for the lay reader, at least as far as the conclusions are concerned, though many of the facts on which these conclusions are based are unsurprising.

2.1.2 *Linguistic items*

The discussion will be easier if we have some technical terms to use, as we need to distance ourselves somewhat from the concepts represented by the words *language* and *dialect*, which are a reasonable reflection of our lay culture, called 'common-sense knowledge' (see 3.1.1), but not helpful in sociolinguistics. First, we need a term for the individual 'bits of language' to which some sociolinguistic statements need to refer, where more global statements are not possible. We have already used the term LINGUISTIC ITEM (2.1.1) and shall continue to use it as a technical term.

What is a linguistic item? The answer to this question concerns the theory of language structure, and people will give different answers according to which theory they think gives the best view of language structure. Those who accept some version of transformational-generative linguistics (as, for example, in Chomsky 1965) would probably say that linguistic items are (i) lexical items, (ii) rules of various kinds (for combining the pronunciations and meanings of these lexical items in sentences), and (iii) constraints of various kinds on these rules. In terms of this theory, we should expect to find sociolinguistic statements which refer to individual lexical items, rules and constraints. On the other hand, not all linguists would accept this answer. For instance, there is a respectable tradition in linguistics of referring to 'constructions' instead of rules (e.g. Bolinger 1975: 139), where a construction is an abstract pattern such as 'adjective + noun', and in terms of this tradition the answer would include constructions as well as (or even instead of) rules and constraints.

Fortunately there is no need to decide among these answers in this book, but it seems likely that a sociolinguistic approach to language structure could help to eliminate some of the candidates. For example, let us assume that sentences like 'The liquid was boiled' are preferred in scientific reports to those like 'We boiled the liquid', or 'The liquid was boiled by us'. In order to state this fact, we need to relate the first kind of sentence to the relevant social context, but how should such sentences be defined? If they can only be defined by referring to two separate rules (one for making the sentence passive, the other for removing its 'agent', in this case *by us*), then we may doubt whether the analysis is correct, since neither rule is a complete linguistic item. In contrast, the statement can easily be made with reference to the construction referred to (abstractly) as 'agentless passive'.

Later in this chapter we shall see evidence that different linguistic items in 'the same language' can have quite different social distributions (in terms of speakers and circumstances), and we may assume that it is possible for the social distribution of a linguistic item to be *unique*. In fact it is much harder to demonstrate this than to show differences between selected items, since we should need to compare the item suspected of being unique with every other item in the same language, just to make sure that no other has the same distribution. For example, it is easy to show that the distribution of the words used in England for *she* (*she, her, hoo, shoo*) is quite different from that for the words for *am* (*am, is, be, bin*) (see the maps in Wakelin 1978: 21, 23). What is not easy, is to show that none of these forms has the same distribution (i.e. is used by exactly the same speakers under the same circumstances) as any other word. There is, however, no known mechanism which could prevent items from having unique distributions, so it seems fair to assume that at least some of them do.

2.1.3 *Varieties of language*

If one thinks of 'language' as a phenomenon including all the languages of the world, the term VARIETY OF LANGUAGE (or just VARIETY for short) can be used to refer to different manifestations of it, in just the same way as one might take 'music' as a general phenomenon and then distinguish different 'varieties of music'. What makes one variety of language different from another is the linguistic items that it includes, so we may define a variety of language as *a set of linguistic items with similar social distribution*. This definition allows us to call any of the following 'varieties of language': English, French, London English, the English of football commentaries, the languages used by the members of a particular long-house in the north-west Amazon, the language or languages used by a particular person.

It will be seen from this list that the very general notion 'variety' includes examples of what would normally be called languages, dialects and registers (a term meaning roughly 'style', which we shall discuss in section 2.4). The advantage of having a general term to cover all these concepts is that it allows us to ask what basis there is for the distinctions among the latter – for instance, why do we call some varieties different languages and others different dialects of the same language? Sections 2.2, 2.3 and 2.4 will be occupied with precisely such questions, and will lead to the conclusion that there is *no* consistent basis for making the distinctions concerned. This leaves us only with the general term 'variety' for referring to things which the layman calls 'languages', 'dialects', or 'styles'.

This conclusion may seem rather radical, but the definition of 'variety' given above, and the examples given in the list, suggest even greater departures from the linguistic tradition. It will be noticed that it is consistent with the definition to treat all the languages of some multilingual speaker, or community, as a single variety, since all the linguistic items concerned have a similar social distribution – they are used by the same speaker or community. That is, a variety may be much larger than a lay 'language', including a number of different languages. Conversely, according to the definition a variety may contain just a handful of items, or even in the extreme case a single item, if it is defined in terms of the range of speakers or circumstances with whom it is associated. For instance, one might define a variety consisting of those items used solely by some particular family or village. Thus a variety can be much smaller than a 'language', or even than a 'dialect'. The flexibility of the term 'variety' allows us to ask what basis there is for postulating the kinds of 'package' of linguistic items to which we conventionally give labels like 'language', 'dialect' or 'register'. Is it because the items form themselves into natural bundles, bound together by a tight set of inter-locking structural relations of some kind, as has always been suggested by the 'structuralist' tradition of the twentieth century? The answer given in the following sections is again negative: the bundles into which linguistic items can be grouped are quite loosely tied, and it is easy for items to move between them, to the extent that bundles may in fact be muddled up. The extreme cases of this will be discussed in section 2.5.

In conclusion, discussions of language in relation to society will consist of statements which refer, on the 'language' side, to either individual linguistic items or varieties, which are sets of such items. There are no restrictions on the relations among varieties – they may overlap and one variety may include another. The defining character-istic of each variety is the relevant relation to society – in other words, by whom, and when, the items concerned are used. It is an empirical question to what extent the traditional notions of 'language', 'dialect' and 'register' are matched by varieties defined in this way. As we shall see in the following sections, the match is only approximate at best, and in some societies (and individuals) it may be extremely hard to identify varieties corresponding even roughly to traditional categories.

2.1.4 *'Speech communities'*

It may be helpful at this point to discuss the kind of com-munity to which varieties or items may be related. The term SPEECH COMMUNITY is widely used by sociolinguists to refer to a community based on language, but LINGUISTIC COMMUNITY is also used with the same meaning. If speech communities can be delimited, then they can be studied, and it may be possible to find interesting differences between communities which correlate with differences in their language. The study of speech communities has therefore interested linguists for some time, at least since Leonard Bloomfield wrote a chapter on speech communities in his book *Language* (1933: ch. 3). However, there has been considerable confusion and disagreement over exactly what a speech community is, as the following survey shows.

(1) The simplest definition of 'speech community' is that of John Lyons (1970: 326):

> Speech community: all the people who use a given language (or dialect).

According to this definition, speech communities may overlap (where there are bilingual individuals) and need not have any social or cultural unity. Clearly it is possible to delimit speech communities in this sense only to the extent that it is possible to delimit languages and dialects. (2) A more complex definition is given by Charles Hockett (1958: 8):

> Each language defines a speech community: the whole set of people who communicate with each other, either directly or indirectly, via the common language.

Here the criterion of communication within the community is added, so that if two communities both spoke the same language but had no contact with each other at all, they would count as different speech communities.
(3) The next definition shifts the emphasis entirely from shared language to communication. A simple form of it was given by Leonard Bloomfield (1933: 42):

> A speech community is a group of people who interact by means of speech.

This leaves open the possibility that some interact by means of one language, and others by means of another. This possibility is explicitly recognised in the definition given by John Gumperz (1962):

> We will define [linguistic community] as a social group which may be either monolingual or multilingual, held together by frequency of social interaction patterns and set off from the surrounding areas by weaknesses in the lines of communication.

(4) A later definition by Gumperz, however, introduces the requirement that there should be some specifically linguistic differences between the members of the speech community and those outside it (1968):

> the speech community: any human aggregate characterised by regular and frequent interaction by means of a shared body of verbal signs and set off from similar aggregates by significant differences in language use.

Unlike definition (2), this does not require that there should be just one language per speech community. The effect of putting emphasis on communication and interaction, as in these last two definitions, is that different speech communities will tend not to overlap much, in contrast with the earlier definitions where overlap automatically results from bilingualism.

(5) A relatively recent definition puts the emphasis on shared *attitudes* to language, rather than on shared linguistic behaviour. It is given by William Labov (1972a: 120):

> The speech community is not defined by any marked agreement in the use of language elements, so much as by participation in a set of shared norms; these norms may be observed in overt types of evaluative behaviour [see 6.2 below], and by the uniformity of abstract patterns of variation which are invariant in respect to particular levels of usage [see 5.4.1].

Rather similar definitions, referring to shared norms and abstract patterns of variation rather than to shared speech behaviour, have been given by Dell Hymes (1972) and Michael Halliday (1972). It will be seen that this kind of definition puts emphasis on the speech community as a group of people who *feel* themselves to be a community in some sense, rather than a group which only the linguist and outsider could know about, as in some of the earlier definitions.

(6) Lastly, there is an approach which may avoid the term 'speech community' altogether, but refers to groups in society which have distinctive speech characteristics as well as other social characteristics. It should be noted that the groups are those which the individual speaker perceives to exist, and not necessarily those which a sociologist might discover by objective methods; and the groups need not exhaust the whole population, but may represent the *clear* cases of certain social types (i.e. the 'prototypes', in the sense of 3.2.2). This approach has been advocated by Robert Le Page (1968a):

> Each individual creates the systems for his verbal behaviour so that they shall resemble those of the group or groups with which from time to time he may wish to be identified, to the extent that
> a. he can identify the groups,
> b. he has both opportunity and ability to observe and analyse their behavioural systems,
> c. his motivation is sufficiently strong to impel him to choose, and to adapt his behaviour accordingly,
> d. he is still able to adapt his behaviour.

This is the view mentioned in 1.3.1, according to which the individual 'locates himself in a multi-dimensional space', the dimensions being defined by the groups he can identify in his society. Unlike the 'speech communities' defined in (3), (4) and (5), these groups very definitely overlap. For instance a child may identify groups on the basis of sex,

age, geography and colour, and each grouping may contribute something to the particular combination of linguistic items which he selects
as his own language.

Our last quotation, by Dwight Bolinger, identifies these groups as
speech communities, and stresses the unlimited amount of complexity
that is possible (Bolinger 1975: 333):

> There is no limit to the ways in which human beings league
> themselves together for self-identification, security, gain, amuse-
> ment, worship, or any of the other purposes that are held in
> common; consequently there is no limit to the number and variety
> of speech communities that are to be found in society.

According to this view, any population (whether of a city, a village or
whole state) may be expected to contain a very large number of speech
communities indeed, with overlapping memberships and overlapping
language systems. Indeed, Le Page's proviso a ('to the extent that he
can identify the groups') raises the possibility that different members of
the population may be aware of different groups. If we take the position
that speech communities should have some kind of psychological reality
for their members (as in definition (5) above), then it follows that we
must identify different speech communities in the same population
according to the person whose viewpoint we are taking.

We have thus moved from a very simple definition of 'speech community' to a very complex one. How do we evaluate these different
definitions? One answer, of course, is that they are all 'correct', since
each of them allows us to define a set of people who have something in
common linguistically – a language or dialect, interaction by means of
speech, a given range of varieties and rules for using them, a given range
of attitudes to varieties and items. The sets of people defined on the
basis of different factors may of course differ radically – one criterion
allows overlapping sets, another forbids them, and so on – but there is
no need to try to reconcile the different definitions with one another, as
they are simply trying to reflect different phenomena. On the other
hand, the fact remains that they all purport to be definitions of the same
thing – the 'speech community' – and the tone of some of the definitions
given above (notably that of Labov in (5)) implies that it is a matter of
finding the 'true' definition ('the speech community is not defined by . . .
so much as by . . .'). Moreover, the word 'community' implies more than
the existence of some common property; after all, nobody would talk of
the 'community' of all the people whose names begin with the letter *h*,

or who have overdrawn bank accounts. To qualify as a 'community', a set of people presumably needs to be distinguished from the rest of the world by more than one property, and some of these properties have to be important from the point of view of the members' social lives. The question, then, is which of the definitions of 'speech community' lead to genuine communities in this sense.

It might be thought that they *all* do. Even taking the simplest of the definitions, according to which a speech community is simply the set of people who use a given language or dialect, it is hard to imagine such a community sharing nothing *but* the common language or dialect to set them off from other people – nothing in their culture, nothing to do with the area in which they live, and so on. As soon as the factor of inter-action comes in, of course, it goes without saying that there will be other shared characteristics in addition to the interaction. This answer has the attraction of resolving the apparent conflict between the definitions of 'speech community', but it leads inevitably to the conclusion that differ-ent speech communities intersect in complex ways with one another – for example, a community defined in terms of interaction may contain parts of several communities defined in terms of shared language varieties. It will be seen that this is in fact precisely the notion of 'speech community' as defined in (6), so we may take (6) as the most compre-hensive view which subsumes all the others, and therefore makes them unnecessary.

This conclusion may seem very satisfactory, since it reconciles con-flicting definitions with one another and replaces them all by a single definition. However, it raises a serious problem, since the notion 'speech community' thus defined is very much less easy to use for making generalisations about language and speech than the kinds of community defined by the earlier definitions. What would help the sociolinguist most in his work would be if he could identify some kind of natural speech community with reference to which he could make all his generalisations, and much of sociolinguistics has in fact been carried out on the assumption that this is possible. For example, the context of Labov's definition of 'speech community' given above is a discussion of his work in New York City, which he claims can be treated as a single speech community with reference to which a large number of generalisa-tions can be made. Indeed, he goes so far as to propose that this com-munity shares a single 'community grammar' (see 5.5.1). Our preferred definition of 'speech community' predicts that there will be no single set of people, such as all those living in New York City, with reference to which it will be possible for the sociolinguist to make all his generalisations: on the contrary, different claims will be true of differently delimited communities. It will be seen that this conclusion is amply supported by the facts and arguments of the following sections.

More seriously still, there is some doubt as to whether the notion of 'speech community' is helpful at all, or whether it is misleading. It implies the existence of discrete groups of people in society which the sociolinguist ought to be able to recognise, so that any given person either is a member of a particular group or is not. The first problem is that the definition in (6) states explicitly that these groups are real only to the extent that some speaker is aware of their existence, which leaves open the possibility that some groups may be very unclearly delimited by the speaker concerned. He may realise that some particular variety or item is used by 'northerners' or by children, but have little idea how to draw the line between northerners and southerners, or between children and grown-ups. The second problem, which we shall discuss in some detail in 5.4.3, is that in at least some cases it turns out to be better to analyse people's relations to each other in terms of networks of individual relations rather than in terms of groups to which they may or may not belong. In other words, it is possible that speech communities do not really exist in society except as prototypes in the minds of people, in which case the search for the 'true' definition of 'speech community' is just a wild goose chase.

2.2 Languages
2.2.1 *'Language' and 'dialect'*

We shall spend the rest of this chapter looking at the most widely recognised types of language variety: 'language', 'dialect' and 'register'. We shall see that all three types are extremely problematic, both from the point of view of finding a general definition for each one which will distinguish it from the others, and also from the point of view of finding criteria for delimiting varieties.

We first need to consider the concept 'language'. What does it mean to say that some variety is a language? This is first of all a question about popular usage: what do ordinary people mean when they say that some variety is a language? Having answered the question in this form, we may or may not wish to take 'language' as a technical term, and say how we propose to use it in sociolinguistics. We shall want to do so if we find that popular usage reflects some kind of reality to which we should like to refer in sociolinguistics, but if we come to the conclusion that popular usage reflects no such reality, then there will be no point in defining 'language' more explicitly in order to use it as a technical term.

One thing that is not in question is the importance of studying popular usage of the term 'language' simply as part of English vocabulary, along with 'well-spoken', 'chat' and other vocabulary which reflects the parts of our culture which are related to language and speech. It is part of our culture to make a distinction between 'languages' and 'dialects' – in fact, we make *two*, separate, distinctions using these terms, and we may draw conclusions from this fact about our culturally inherited view of language (in the same way that we can use vocabulary as evidence for other aspects of culture – see 3.2.1).

We may contrast our culture in this respect with others where no such distinction is made. For example, according to Einar Haugen (1966), this was the case in England until the term *dialect* was borrowed, as a learned word, from Greek in the Renaissance. In fact, we may see our distinction between 'language' and 'dialect' as due to the influence of Greek culture, since the distinction was developed in Greek because of the existence of a number of clearly distinct written varieties in use in Classical Greece, each associated with a different area and used for a different kind of literature. Thus the meanings of the Greek terms which were translated as 'language' and 'dialect' were in fact quite different from the meanings these words have in English now. Their equivalents in French are perhaps more similar, since the French word *dialecte* refers only to regional varieties which are written and have a literature, in contrast with regional varieties which are not written, which are called *patois*. The point of this discussion is to show that there is nothing absolute about the distinction which English happens to make between 'languages' and 'dialects' (and for readers familiar with some language other than English, this discussion will hardly have been necessary).

What then is the difference, for English speakers, between a language and a dialect? There are two separate ways of distinguishing them, and this ambiguity is a source of great confusion. (Haugen (1966) argues that the reason for the ambiguity, and the resulting confusion, is precisely the fact that 'dialect' was borrowed from Greek, where the same ambiguity existed.) On the one hand, there is a difference of *size*, because a language is larger than a dialect. That is, a variety called a language contains more items than one called a dialect. This is the sense in which we may refer to English as a language, containing the sum total of all the terms in all its dialects, with 'Standard English' as one dialect among many others (Yorkshire English, Indian English, etc.). Hence the greater 'size' of the language English.

The other contrast between 'language' and 'dialect' is a question of *prestige*, a language having prestige which a dialect lacks. If we apply the terms in this sense, Standard English (e.g. the kind of English used in this book) is not a dialect at all, but a language, whereas the varieties which are not used in formal writing are dialects. Whether some variety is called a language or a dialect depends on how much prestige one thinks it has, and for most people this is a clear-cut matter, which depends on whether it is used in formal writing. Accordingly, people in Britain habitually refer to languages which are unwritten (or which they think are unwritten) as dialects, or 'mere dialects', irrespective of whether there is a (proper) language to which they are related. (It would be nonsense to use 'dialect' in this way intending its 'size' sense, of course.) The fact that we put so much weight on whether or not it is written in distinguishing between 'language' and 'dialect' is one of the interesting things that the terms show us about British culture, and we shall return to the importance of writing in 2.2.2.

2.2.2 Standard languages

It is probably fair to say that the only kind of variety which would count as a 'proper language' (in the second sense of 'language') is a *standard language*. Standard languages are interesting in as much as they have a rather special relation to society – one which is quite abnormal when seen against the context of the tens (or hundreds?) of thousands of years during which language has been used. Whereas one thinks of normal language development as taking place in a rather haphazard way, largely below the threshold of consciousness of the speakers, standard languages are the result of a direct and deliberate intervention by society. This intervention, called 'standardisation', produces a standard language where before there were just 'dialects' (i.e. non-standard varieties).

The notion 'standard language' is somewhat imprecise, but a typical standard language will have passed through the following processes (Haugen 1966; for a somewhat different list, see Garvin & Mathiot 1956).

(1) *Selection* – somehow or other a particular variety must have been selected as the one to be developed into a standard language. It may be an existing variety, such as the one used in an important political or commercial centre, but it could be an amalgam of various varieties. The choice is a matter of great social and political importance, as the chosen variety necessarily gains prestige and so the people who already speak it share in this prestige. However, in some cases the chosen variety has been one with no native speakers at all – for instance, Classical Hebrew in Israel and Bahasa Indonesia (a newly created language) in Indonesia (Bell 1976: 167).

(2) *Codification* – some agency such as an academy must have written dictionaries and grammar books to 'fix' the variety, so that everyone agrees on what is correct. Once codification has taken place, it becomes necessary for any ambitious citizen to learn the correct forms and not to use in writing any 'incorrect' forms he may have in his native variety, which may take literally years of a child's school career.

(3) *Elaboration of function* – it must be possible to use the selected variety in all the functions associated with central government and with writing, for example in parliament and law courts, in bureaucratic, educational and scientific documents of all kinds, and of course in various forms of literature. This may require extra linguistic items to be added to the variety, especially technical words, but it is also necessary to develop new conventions for *using* existing forms – how to formulate examination questions, how to write formal letters, and so on.

(4) *Acceptance* – the variety has to be accepted by the relevant population as *the* variety of the community – usually, in fact, as the national language. Once this has happened, the standard language serves as a strong *unifying* force for the state, as a symbol of its *independence* of other states (assuming that its standard is unique and not shared with others), and as a marker of its *difference* from other states. It is precisely this symbolic function that makes states go to some lengths to develop one.

This analysis of the factors typically involved in standardisation has been quite widely accepted by sociolinguists (for more details and examples, see Garvin 1959, Garvin & Mathiot 1956, Hall 1972, Macaulay 1973, Trudgill 1974b: 149). However, there is ample scope for debate and disagreement about the *desirability* of certain aspects of standardisation. For instance, it is not essential either that standardisation should involve matters of *pronunciation* as well as of writing (Macaulay 1973), or that the standard language should be presented as the only 'correct' variety (a point argued by many linguists and sociolinguists, notably Trudgill 1975a; see also 6.2 below). Moreover, a policy suitable for one community may not fit another, so great care, sensitivity, wisdom and knowledge are needed for success in any standardisation programme (Kelman 1972).

The present section on standard languages is the only part of this book that deals in any detail with the large-scale issues of the sociology of language (see 1.1.3 for the difference between sociolinguistics and the sociology of language), but it has been included for three reasons. Firstly, it is relevant to the discussion of the second meaning of 'language' introduced in 2.2.1 (where 'language' = 'standard language'). Secondly, it is interesting to see that language can be deliberately manipulated by society. Thirdly, and perhaps most importantly, it brings out the *unusual* character of standard languages, which are perhaps the least interesting kind of language for anyone interested in the nature of human language (as most linguists are). For instance, one might almost describe standard languages as pathological in their lack of diversity. To see language in its 'natural' state, one must find a variety which is neither a standard language, nor a dialect subordinate to a standard (since these too show pathological features, notably the difficulty of making judgments in terms of the non-standard dialect without being influenced by the standard one). The irony, of course, is that academic linguistics is likely to arise only in a society with a standard language, such as Britain, the United States, or France, and the *first* language to which linguists pay attention is their own – a standard one.

2.2.3 *The delimitation of languages*

We now return to the question posed at the beginning of 2.2: what does it mean to say of some variety that it is a language? We can now clarify the question by distinguishing between the two meanings of 'language' based, respectively, on prestige and size. We have already given an answer on the basis of prestige: a language is a standard language. In principle this distinction is an absolute one: either a variety is a standard language, or it is not. (It is clear, however, that some languages are more standard than others; for instance, Standard French has been more rigidly codified than Standard English.) When we turn to the other distinction, based on size, the situation is very different, since everything becomes relative – for example, in comparison with one variety a chosen variety may be large, yet compared with another it may be small. The variety containing all the items used in Britain looks large compared with, say, Standard English or Cockney, but only small compared with the variety which consists of all the items used in any of the 'English-speaking' countries. This being so, the claim that a particular variety is a language, in the 'size' sense, amounts to very little. Is there, then, any way in which the distinction between 'language' and 'dialect' based on size can be made less relative? (To anticipate, our answer is that there is not.)

The obvious candidate for an extra criterion is that of *mutual intelligibility*. If the speakers of two varieties can understand each other, then the varieties concerned are instances of the same language; otherwise they are not. This is a widely used criterion, but it cannot be taken seriously because there are such serious problems in its application.

(1) Even *popular usage* does not correspond consistently to this criterion, since varieties which we (as laymen) call different languages may be mutually intelligible (e.g. the Scandinavian languages, excluding Finnish and Lapp) and varieties which we call instances of the same language may not (e.g. the so-called 'dialects' of Chinese). Popular usage tends to reflect the other definition of language, based on prestige, so that if two varieties are both standard languages, or are subordinate to different standards, they must be different languages, and conversely they must be the same language if they are both subordinate to the same standard. This explains the difference betwen our ideas on the varieties of Scandinavia and of China: each Scandinavian country has a separate standard language (indeed, Norway has *two*), whereas the whole of China only has one. (The effect of the Chinese situation is curious: a man from Peking cannot understand a man from Canton or Hong Kong when he is speaking his own dialect, but predictably can understand him fully when he writes the standard.)

(2) Mutual intelligibility is a matter of *degree*, ranging from total intelligibility down to total unintelligibility. How high up this scale do two varieties need to be in order to count as members of the same language? This is clearly a question which is best avoided, rather than answered, since any answer must be arbitrary. (It is worth noting that Gillian Sankoff has developed a system for calculating degrees of mutual intelligibility (1969), which clearly shows that mutual intelligibility may only be partial when applied to particular communities.)

(3) Varieties may be arranged in a DIALECT CONTINUUM, a chain of adjacent varieties in which each pair of adjacent varieties are mutually

intelligible, but pairs taken from opposite ends of the chain are not. One such continuum is said to stretch from Amsterdam through Germany to Vienna, and another from Paris to the south of Italy. The criterion of mutual intelligibility is, however, based on a relationship between languages that is logically different from that of sameness of language, which it is supposed to illuminate. If A is the same language as B, and B is the same language as C, then A and C must also be the same language, and so on. 'Sameness of language' is therefore a transitive relation, but 'mutual intelligibility' is an intransitive one: if A and B are mutually intelligible, and B and C are mutually intelligible, C and A are not necessarily mutually intelligible. The problem is that an intransitive relation cannot be used to elucidate a transitive relation.

(4) Mutual intelligibility is not really a relation between varieties, but between people, since it is they, and not the varieties, that understand one another. This being so, the degree of mutual intelligibility depends not just on the amount of overlap between the items in the two varieties, but on qualities of the people concerned. One highly relevant quality is *motivation*: how much does person A want to understand person B? This will depend on numerous factors such as how much A likes B, how far he wishes to emphasise the cultural differences or similarities between them, and so on. Motivation is important because understanding another person always requires effort on the part of the hearer – as witness the possibility of 'switching off' when one's motivation is low. The greater the difference between the varieties concerned, the more effort is needed, so if A cannot understand B, this simply tells us that the task was too great for A's motivation, and we do not know what would have happened if his motivation had been higher. Another relevant quality of the hearer is *experience*: how much experience has he had of the variety to which he is listening? Obviously, the more previous experience he has had, the more likely he is to be able to understand it. Both of these qualities raise another problem regarding the use of mutual intelligibility as a criterion, namely that it *need not be reciprocal*, since A and B need not have the same degree of motivation for understanding each other, nor need they have the same amount of previous experience of each other's varieties. Typically, it is easier for a non-standard speaker to understand a standard speaker than the other way round, partly because the former will have had more experience of the standard variety (notably through the media) than vice versa, and partly because he may be motivated to minimise the cultural differences between himself and the standard

speaker (though this is by no means necessarily so), while the standard speaker may want to emphasise these differences.

In conclusion, mutual intelligibility does not work as a criterion for delimiting languages in the 'size' sense. There is no other criterion which is worth considering as an alternative, so we must conclude (with Matthews 1979: 47) that *there is no real distinction to be drawn between 'language' and 'dialect'* (except with reference to prestige, where it would be better to use the term 'standard language' or just 'standard', rather than just 'language'). In other words, the concept 'language X' has no part to play in sociolinguistics – nor, for exactly the same reasons, can it have any place in linguistics. All we need is the notion 'variety X', and the obvious and unsurprising observation that a given variety may be relatively similar to some other varieties and relatively different from others.

2.2.4 *The family tree model*

A convenient way of representing the relationships among varieties is in terms of the *family tree model*, which was developed in the nineteenth century as an aid in the historical study of languages (for an excellent discussion, see Bynon 1977: 63). This model allows one to show how closely a number of varieties spoken at present are related to one another – that is, how far each has diverged from the others as a result of historical changes. For instance, one might take English, German, Welsh, French and Hindi as the varieties to be related. By building a tree structure on top of these varieties, as in Figure 2.1, one can show that English is most closely related to German, less closely to Welsh and French, and still less closely to Hindi. (For a fuller picture of the relations among these and many other 'Indo-European' languages, see Bolinger 1975: 446.)

Chinese has been added to show that it is not related *at all* to the other languages. If one includes two varieties in the same diagram, there is an

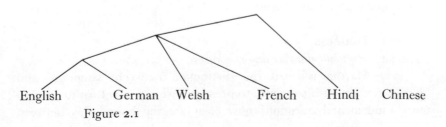

Figure 2.1

assumption that they are both 'descended', through historical changes, from a common 'ancestor' variety, which could be named on the diagram. Thus we could add the name 'Proto-Indo-European' to the node at the top of the tree, showing that all the varieties named at the bottom (except Chinese) are descended from this one variety. Similarly, we could label the node dominating English and German 'Proto-Germanic', to give a name to the variety from which they are both descended.

The main value of the family tree model for historical linguistics is that it clarifies the historical relations among the varieties concerned, and in particular that it gives a clear idea of the relative chronology of the historical changes by which the varieties concerned have diverged. From the present point of view, however, the advantage is that a family tree shows a *hierarchical* relation among varieties which makes no distinction betwen 'languages' and 'dialects'. Indeed, it is common in historical linguistics to refer to the varieties which are descended from Latin as 'dialects' of Latin (or 'the Romance dialects'), although they include such obvious 'languages' (in the prestige sense) as Standard French. If we had wished to add Yorkshire English and Cockney to our list of varieties, we would simply have added them below English, without giving them a different status from the others. The only change we would need to make in our interpretation of the family tree diagram, compared with the historical interpretation, is that the higher nodes would not represent *earlier* varieties from which the modern ones are descended (such as Proto-Indo-European), but *larger* varieties including all the items within the varieties below them.

Apart from the attraction which we have just noted, however, the family tree model has little to recommend it to the sociolinguist, since it represents a gross idealisation of the relations between varieties. In particular, it makes no allowances for one variety *influencing* another, which could lead in extreme cases to *convergence* – a single variety being descended from two separate varieties (see Traugott 1977). We shall see in 2.5 that this does in fact happen, and in 2.3.2 we shall introduce a better model, the 'wave theory'.

2.3 Dialects

2.3.1 *Regional dialects and isoglosses*

Having rejected the distinction between 'language' and 'dialect' (except with reference to prestige), we can now turn to an even more fundamental question: how clear are the boundaries between varieties? The hierarchical model of the family tree implies that the boundaries between varieties are clear at all levels of the tree. Is this so? In particular, is it possible to continue such a tree downwards, revealing smaller and smaller varieties, until one comes to the level of the individual speaker (the 'idiolect')? The answer must be no.

If we consider the most straightforward variety differences based on geography, it should be possible, if the family tree model is right, to identify what are called *regional dialects* within any larger variety such as English. Fortunately, there is a vast amount of evidence bearing on this question, produced by the discipline called DIALECTOLOGY, particularly by its branch called DIALECT GEOGRAPHY (see e.g. Bloomfield 1933: ch. 19, Chambers & Trudgill, forthcoming, Hockett 1958: ch. 56, Hughes & Trudgill 1979, Sankoff 1973a, Wakelin 1972; see also 5.4.2 below). Since the nineteenth century, dialectologists in Europe and the United States (and, on a smaller scale, in Britain) have been studying the geographical distribution of linguistic items, such as pairs of synonymous words (e.g. *pail* versus *bucket*), or different pronunciations of the same word, such as *farm* with or without the /r/. Their results are plotted on a map, showing which items were found in which villages (since dialect geography tends to concentrate on rural areas to avoid the complexities of towns). The dialect geographer may then draw a line between the area where one item was found and areas where others were found, showing a boundary for each area called an ISOGLOSS (from Greek *iso-* 'same' and *gloss-* 'tongue').

The family tree model enables a very important prediction to be made regarding isoglosses, namely that they should not intersect. This prediction follows from the strict hierarchy among varieties in the model, which allows only two relationships between any two varieties: either one is an ancestor of the other, or the two are 'sisters'. Now imagine a hypothetical state of affairs where a larger variety L contains two items x and y, neither of which is used by all the people who speak L. We can distinguish within L between varieties with and without x (+x and −x), and those with and without y (+y, −y), but all four possible combinations of these varieties actually exist: there are people who have both (+x, +y), others who have neither (−x, −y), and others who have just one or the other (+x, −y or −x, +y). What then are the relations between the varieties defined by x (+x, −x) and those defined by y (+y, −y)? For instance, what is the relation between the +x variety and the +y variety? Clearly neither is the ancestor of the other, since neither completely contains the other, but neither is the sister of the other, since each one partially contains the other. This kind of arrangement is thus incompatible with the family tree model.

There are many real parallels to this hypothetical situation. To take just one example, there are two isoglosses in southern England which intersect, as shown in map 2.1 (based on Trudgill 1974b: 159 and Wakelin 1978: 9). One isogloss separates the area (to the north) where *come* is pronounced with the same vowel as *stood*, from the area where it has the open vowel [ʌ], as in Received Pronunciation (RP), the prestige accent of England (see Gimson 1962: 83). The other isogloss separates the area (to the north-east) where the *r* of *farm* is not pronounced, from the area where it is. The only way to reconcile this kind of pattern with the family tree model would be to give priority to one isogloss over the other, but such a choice would be arbitrary and would in any case leave the subordinate isoglosses unconnected, each representing a subdivision of a different variety, whereas in fact each clearly represents a single phenomenon. Examples like this could be multiplied almost indefinitely (for another particularly clear example, see the map in Bolinger 1975: 349; and for a scholarly review, see Sankoff 1973a).

From such findings many dialectologists have drawn the conclusion that each item has its own distribution through the population of speakers, and that there is no reason to expect different items to have identical distributions (Bynon 1977: 190). This seems to be the only reasonable conclusion to draw from the data, though one might express reservations about the *extent* of difference between items; for example, the kind of pattern referred to above, with isoglosses intersecting in a chaotic way, is much less common in Germany than in France (Bynon 1977: 191, Matthews 1979: 47). But this leads to the further conclusion that isoglosses need not delimit varieties, except in the trivial sense where varieties each consist of just one item; and if we cannot rely on isoglosses to delimit varieties, what can we use? There seems to be no alternative, and we find ourselves in a similar position to the earlier one in our discussion of languages: there is no way of delimiting varieties, and we must therefore conclude that varieties do not exist. All that exists are people and items, and people may be more or less similar to one another in the items they have in their language. Though unexciting, this conclusion is at least true, and raises incidental questions such as what determines the amount and kind of similarity between people.

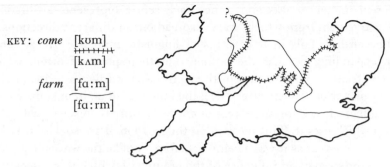

KEY: *come* [kʊm]
⟨++++++⟩
[kʌm]

farm [fɑːm]

[fɑːrm]

Map 2.1. Two intersecting isoglosses in southern England

2.3.2 *Diffusion and the wave theory*

An alternative to the family tree model was developed as early as the nineteenth century to account for the kind of phenomenon we have just been considering. It is called the WAVE THEORY, and is based on the assumption that changes in language spread outwards from centres of influence to the surrounding areas in much the same way that a wave spreads from the place where a stone is dropped into a pool. This view of language change is rightly accepted by most if not all scholars, both in historical linguistics (for discussion, see Bynon 1977: 192) and in sociolinguistics, where it has been developed especially by Charles-James Bailey (1973), Derek Bickerton (1971, 1973, 1975) and David DeCamp (1971b). (The theoretical work of these sociolinguists, based on the wave theory, will be discussed in 5.5.2.)

The wave theory explains why isoglosses intersect by postulating different geographical foci for the spread of different items. The isogloss between two items like *farm* with and without the /r/ shows where the influence of one item stops and the other takes over; on the assumption that one of the items represents an innovation, this means that the isogloss marks the furthest points which the influence of the new item has reached at the time when the dialectologist collected his data. There is no reason why innovations leading to any two different isoglosses should have started in the same place – or for that matter in the same period – so there is no particular reason why their isoglosses should not intersect. To return to the analogy, if two or more stones are dropped into a pool, there is no reason why they should fall in the same place, and there could be many different centres of influence from which ripples spread and intersect. Moreover, these centres may change with time, as different influences wax and wane. Each centre represents a different innovative item from which 'waves' spread out in different directions.

The analogy fails in that waves of linguistic influence 'freeze' and stop expanding, because the influence at their point of origin is no longer strong enough to sustain them. In other words, in terms of the theory of acts of identity (see 1.3.1), the influence of an item stops when individuals choose for some reason not to identify themselves with the group which uses it. This means that the location of an isogloss may be the same one year as it was a century before – unlike the waves in a pool – since the strength of influence of the group with which it is associated may still not be strong enough to make it move any further. Moreover, an item need not be an innovation in order to influence people, since its effects depend on the social standing of the group associated with it (what we called its 'speech community' in 2.1.4), rather than on its newness. It is quite possible for a relatively archaic form to oust a newer one after the latter has spread. For example, in some areas of the United States the pronunciation of words like *farm* with an /r/ is currently replacing the pronunciation without /r/, although the latter is in fact the innovation (as the spelling suggests) – we shall discuss an example of such an area in 5.2.2.

Because of these reservations it seems best to abandon the analogy of the stones dropping in a pool. A more helpful analogy would perhaps be one involving different species of plants sown in a field, each spreading outwards by dispersing its seeds over a particular area. In the analogy, each item would be represented by a different species, with its own rate of seed dispersal, and an isogloss would be represented by the limit of spread of a given species. Different species would be able to coexist on the same spot (a relaxation of the normal laws of botany), but it might be necessary to designate certain species as being in competition with one another, corresponding to items which provide alternative ways of saying the same thing (like the two pronunciations of *farm*). The advantages of this analogy are that there is no need for the distribution of species in a field to be in constant change with respect to every item, and that every item may be represented in the analogy, and not just those which are innovative.

In terms of this new analogy, a linguistic innovation is a new species which has arisen (either by mutation or by being brought in from outside), and which may or may not prosper. If it does, it may spread and replace some or all of its competitors, but if it does not it may either die out or remain confined to a very small area of the field (i.e. to a very small speech community). Whether or not a species thrives depends on how strongly its representatives grow (i.e. on the power and influence of its speech community): the bigger the plants, the more seeds they produce, and the better the chances of the species conquering new territory.

2.3.3 *Social dialects*

Dialects are not, of course, only distributed geographically, as has been implied in the discussion so far. There are two main sources of extra complexity. Firstly, there is geographical *mobility* – people move from one place to another, taking their dialects with them even if they modify them in the course of time to fit their new surroundings. Thus simply plotting speakers on a map may produce a more or less untidy pattern according to how mobile the population is (a problem which is generally avoided in dialectology by selecting as informants people who were born and bred in the place where they are now living).

The second source of complexity is the fact that geography is only one of the relevant factors, others being social class, sex and age (see 5.4.2). Dialectologists, therefore, speak of SOCIAL DIALECTS, or SOCIOLECTS, to refer to non-regional differences. Because of these other factors, a speaker may show more similarity in his language to people from the same social group in a different area than to people from a different social group in the same area. Indeed, one of the characteristics of the hierarchical social structure of a country like Britain is that social class takes precedence over geography as a determinant of speech, so that there is far more geographical variation among people in the lower social classes than there is amongst those at the 'top' of the social heap. This has in fact gone so far that people who have passed through the public school system (or would like to sound as though they had) typically have *no* regional traits at all in their language. This is a peculiarity of Britain however, and is not found in other countries such as the United States or Germany, where 'top people' show their region of origin through their pronunciation, though possibly in few other features of their language.

Because of the differences in sensitivity to regional and social distinctions between pronunciation and other aspects of language, it is normal to make a distinction between accent and dialect, with ACCENT referring to nothing but pronunciation and DIALECT referring to every aspect of language including pronunciation. This allows us to distinguish between the standard dialect (which ought to be called 'the standard language', see 2.2.2) and non-standard dialects, and also to make separate statements about pronunciation in terms of accents. Thus in Britain we may say that many people use a regional accent but standard dialect, and a select few use an RP accent with the same standard dialect. Great confusion results if the standard dialect, which is a matter of vocabulary, syntax and morphology, is referred to as 'RP'.

All I have done in this section is to introduce the terms 'social dialect' and 'accent', pointing out that there are linguistic differences between speakers which are due not only to geography but also to other social factors. The problems with delimiting regional dialects can also no doubt be paralleled for social dialects, and indeed we shall see that this is so in chapter 5. It would be hard to draw isoglosses for social dialects, since one would need to plot them on a many-dimensional map, but there is no reason to doubt that, could such a map be drawn, we should again find that each isogloss follows a unique path. Consequently we must reject the notions represented by both 'social dialect' and 'accent', for the same reason as we rejected the notion of a regional dialect, except as a very rough and ready way of referring to phenomena.

2.3.4 *Types of linguistic item*

One of the most interesting questions which this whole discussion of varieties raises is whether all linguistic items are subject to variation in the same way. In referring to the notion 'accent' we have already suggested that there may be a general difference between items of pronunciation and other items (morphology, syntax, vocabulary), in that pronunciation is less liable to standardisation. Given the special connection between standardisation and writing, and the fact that standardisation need not extend to pronunciation (2.2.2), it would not be surprising if this were so, though it may not be.

Pronunciation seems to differ from other types of item in its social function. For example, despite the manifest influence of the United States on Britain, its influence on British English is restricted almost entirely to vocabulary and appears to have had no effect at all on the pronunciation of even the most susceptible groups, such as teenagers (radio disc-jockeys and pop singers are complex and interesting exceptions). However, the difference between pronunciation and other types of item can have different manifestations, as in the case of some black middle-class children and adolescents in Detroit, who were studied as part of a project on 'urban dialectology' (the subject-matter of most of chapter 5). The writer of the report, Walter Wolfram (1969: 205) suggested that for these speakers syntactic and morphological items were those one would expect from the middle classes generally (for instance, there were few 'double negatives', which are common in lower-class speech in Detroit), but their pronunciation was much more like that of lower-class Detroit youths. He also suggests (1969: 204) that differences in pronunciation may be quantitative, while other differences are qualitative – i.e. class differences in phonology are a matter of *how often* particular items are used, whereas those in syntax and morphology are a matter of *which* items are used. However, the basis for this generalisation is extremely narrow, and it has not been confirmed by other research projects.

It may be, then, that pronunciation and other items play different roles in the individual's acts of identity to which we referred above. For instance, it could be that we use pronunciation in order to identify our origins (or to *imply* that we originated from some group, whether we really did or not – compare British people who acquire an RP accent late in life with the black middle-class Detroit youths who for some reason acquired a lower-class accent early in life). In contrast, we might use morphology, syntax and vocabulary in order to identify our current status in society, such as the amount of education we have had. At present this is conjecture, but there is enough evidence for differences between pronunciation and other areas of language to make it worth looking for general explanations. As already suggested, the difference may be simply an artefact of the standardisation process, so it is important now to look for evidence from societies not affected by standardisation. If such differences are found even there, then we may assume that we have discovered a fundamental, and rather mysterious, fact about language.

Is there any evidence for differences within what I have been referring to as 'pronunciation' (in order not to beg questions about the relations between phonology and phonetics)? For instance, is there any evidence to support the view that underlying representations (that is, the information given about the pronunciation of a particular word in the vocabulary, as opposed to the details we might give about its pronunciation in particular sentences) are less subject to variation from person to person than are the rules for pronouncing particular phonemes (a view suggested for instance by Chomsky & Halle 1968: 49)? There is little support for such a view, and it is generally recognised that differences in underlying forms (that is, lexical differences) are common. For example, those who pronounce the /r/ in *farm* may be assumed to have different underlying forms for this word (and all other words with /r/ before a consonant or at the end of the word) from the underlying forms of people who do not pronounce the /r/ (see 5.5.1). In fact, any kind of variation that one can imagine in phonology is actually found, and found on a large scale (cf. the surveys of variation in pronunciation in O'Connor 1973: 180, Trubetzkoy 1931, Wells 1970).

One might ask a similar question about aspects of language other than pronunciation. Is there any evidence, for instance, for the view that syntax is more resistant to variation than either morphology or vocabulary? It is certainly the case that examples of syntactic differences within a 'language-sized' variety are much less frequently quoted in the literature than differences in either pronunciation or morphology, which are in any case hard to keep separate; for example is the difference between *-ing* and *-in'* in words like *coming* a difference in pronunciation or in morphology? Moreover, differences in vocabulary are also much more frequently discussed in the literature of dialectology than are differences in syntax. It seems, then, that there is a difference between syntax and the rest of language which needs to be explained. (For more discussion of these types of variable item, see 5.3.1.)

It is important to be wary about this apparent difference, however. For one thing, the lack of references in the literature to syntactic differences could be due to the difficulty of studying such differences, since they occur relatively rarely in ordinary speech and are hard to elicit directly compared, in particular, with vocabulary items. Secondly, the apparent stability of syntax could be an illusion, because there are relatively few syntactic items (i.e. constructions) compared with vocabulary items, so that even if the same *proportion* of syntactic items varied the result would be a smaller number. Thirdly, even if there is a difference between syntax and the rest of language, this could again be an artefact of the process of standardisation. However, notwithstanding all these qualifications, there does seem to be a greater tendency to uniformity in syntax than in other areas of language, which is hard to explain. Could there be a tendency for people to actively *suppress* alternatives in syntax, while positively seeking them in vocabulary?

Evidence for such a view comes from two sources. Syntactic items are rather commonly diffused across 'language' boundaries into adjacent areas. (Features which are shared in this way, and cannot be explained as the result of a common heritage from a parent language, are called AREAL FEATURES; for a discussion of some such features see Bynon 1977: 244.) For example, three adjacent languages in the Balkans (Bulgarian, Romanian and Albanian) all have the rather unusual property of a suffixed definite article; thus in Albanian *mik* is 'friend' and *mik-u* is 'the friend'. This shared feature can only be explained by diffusion in the relatively recent past (at least since Latin, from which Romanian is derived). Features presumably spread across language boundaries as the result of bilingualism, and the prevalence of syntactic features among areal features may be due to the tendency among bilingual individuals to suppress the construction for handling some syntactic relation in one of their languages, thus leading to the spread of the syntactic feature used in the other language. The areal diffusion of syntactic features is otherwise rather hard to understand, since syntax generally seems to be relatively impervious to historical change.

Another piece of evidence for the view that we actively suppress alternatives in syntax is reported by John Gumperz & Robert Wilson (1971) from Kupwar, a small village in India, whose 3,000 inhabitants between them speak three languages: Marathi and Urdu, which are both Indo-European, and Kannada, which is not. (A small number also speak a fourth, non-Indo-European, language, Telugu.) As usual in India, the village is divided into clearly distinct groups (castes), each of which can be identified by its language. However, the different groups obviously need to communicate with each other, and bilingualism (or trilingualism) is common, especially among the men. These languages have coexisted in this way for centuries, but in spite of this contact they are still totally distinct in *vocabulary*. Gumperz & Wilson suggest that the reason for this is that the linguistic differences serve as a useful symbol of the caste differences, which are very strictly maintained; thus vocabulary has the role of distinguishing social groups, without which the demands of efficiency in communication would presumably have gradually eroded the differences in vocabulary over the centuries. As far as *syntax* is concerned, however, the three main languages have become much more *similar* in Kupwar than they are elsewhere. For example, in standard Kannada, sentences like *The postman is my best friend* do not contain a word for 'is', whereas in Urdu and Marathi they do; but in the Kannada of Kupwar there is a word for *is*, on the model of Urdu and Marathi.

47

This example is at least compatible with our hypothesis that alternatives in syntax tend to be suppressed, whereas those in vocabulary and pronunciation tend to be favoured and used as markers of social differences. There do not appear to be any examples of the converse relationship, in which vocabulary and pronunciation show less variation than syntax within a community.

A very tentative hypothesis thus emerges regarding the different types of linguistic items and their relations to society, according to which *syntax* is the marker of cohesion in society, with individuals trying to eliminate alternatives in syntax from their individual language (Wolfram's observation that syntactic differences tended to be qualitative rather than quantitative seems to support this view). In contrast, *vocabulary* is a marker of divisions in society, and individuals may actively cultivate alternatives in order to make more subtle social distinctions. *Pronunciation* reflects the permanent social group with which the speaker identifies. This results in a tendency for individuals to suppress alternatives, but in contrast to the tendency with syntax, different groups suppress different alternatives in order to distinguish themselves from each other, and individuals keep some alternatives 'alive' in order to be able to identify their origins even more precisely, by using them in a particular and distinctive proportion relative to other alternatives. Unbelievable though this may at first seem, it is certainly one way in which pronunciation variables are used, as we shall see in chapter 5.

The main reason for putting the above suggestions forward here is to show that it is possible to formulate interesting and researchable hypotheses against the background of the virtually unlimited view of language which we are developing, in which we have already seen that there is no place for the concepts 'language X', 'dialect X' or even 'variety X'.

2.4 Registers
2.4.1 *Registers and dialects*

The term REGISTER is widely used in sociolinguistics to refer to 'varieties according to use', in contrast with dialects, defined as 'varieties according to user' (Halliday, McIntosh & Strevens 1964; see also Crystal & Davy 1969, Gregory & Carroll 1978). The distinction is needed because the same person may use very different linguistic items to express more or less the same meaning on different occasions, and the concept of 'dialect' cannot reasonably be extended to include such variation. For instance, in writing one letter a person might start: 'I am writing to inform you that . . .', but in another he might write: 'I just wanted to let you know that . . .'. Such examples could be multiplied endlessly, and suggest that the amount of variation due to register differences (if it could somehow be quantified) may be quite comparable with that due to differences in dialect.

We can interpret register differences in terms of the model of acts of identity in much the same way as for dialect differences. Each time a person speaks or writes he not only locates himself with reference to the rest of society, but also relates his act of communication to a complex classificatory scheme of communicative behaviour. This scheme takes the form of a multi-dimensional matrix, just like the picture of his society which each individual builds in his mind (see 1.3.1). At the risk of slight oversimplification, we may say that one's dialect shows who (or what) you *are*, whilst one's register shows what you are *doing* (though these concepts are much less distinct than the slogan implies, as we shall see on page 51).

The 'dimensions' on which an act of communication may be located are no less complex than those relevant to the social location of the speaker. Michael Halliday (1978: 33) distinguishes three general types of dimension: 'field', 'mode' and 'tenor' ('style' is sometimes used instead of 'tenor', but this is best avoided as 'style' is used in a lay sense to mean roughly the same as 'register'). FIELD is concerned with the *purpose* and *subject-matter* of the communication; MODE refers to the *means* by which communication takes place – notably, by speech or writing; and TENOR depends on the *relations* between participants. Once again, a slogan may help: field refers to 'why' and 'about what' a communication takes place; mode is about 'how'; and tenor is about 'to whom' (i.e. how the speaker defines how he sees the person with whom he is communicating). In terms of this model, the two examples of letter-openings cited above would differ in tenor, one being impersonal (addressed to someone with whom the writer only has formal relations) and the other personal, but their field and mode are the same.

According to this model, register differences are at least three-dimensional. Another widely used model has been proposed by Dell Hymes (1972), in which no less than thirteen separate variables determine the linguistic items selected by a speaker, apart from the variable of 'dialect'. It is very doubtful if even this number reflects all the complexities of register differences. Nevertheless, each of these models provides a framework within which any relevant dimensions of similarity and difference may be located. For example, the relations between speaker and addressee involve more than one such dimension (as we shall see in 4.4.2), including the dimension of 'power', on which the addressee is subordinate, equal or superior to the speaker, and the dimension called 'solidarity', which distinguishes relatively intimate relations from more distant ones. In English the speaker locates his relations with the addressee on these two dimensions largely by means of his choice of terms of address – *Mr Smith, sir, John, mate*, and so on.

We have so far presented the concept of 'register' in the way in which it is normally used, as the name of one kind of variety that is parallel to 'dialect'. However, we have already shown that dialects do not exist as discrete varieties, so we must ask whether registers do. The answer is, predictably, that they do not seem to have any more reality than dialects. For example, it is easy to see that the selection of items within a given sentence reflects different factors, depending on which items are involved. One item may, for instance, reflect the formality of the occasion, while another reflects the expertise of the speaker and addressee. This is the case in a sentence like *We obtained some sodium chloride*, where *obtained* is a formal word (in contrast with *got*) and *sodium chloride* is a technical expression (in contrast with *salt*). The dimension of formality is totally independent of the dimension of technicality, as reflected by the fact that the choice between *obtain* and *get* has no connection at all with that between *sodium chloride* and *salt*. Thus four combinations of formality with technicality can be represented by the following perfectly normal sentences:

formal, technical	*We obtained some sodium chloride.*
formal, non-technical	*We obtained some salt.*
informal, technical	*We got some sodium chloride.*
informal, non-technical	*We got some salt.*

Simple examples like these suggest that different linguistic items are sensitive to different aspects of the act of communication, in the same way that different items react to different properties of the speaker (5.4.2). We can only speak of registers as varieties in the rather weak sense of sets of linguistic items which all have the same social distribution, i.e. all occur under the same circumstances. This is a far cry from the notion of variety in which a speaker sticks to one variety throughout a stretch of speech, speaking 'one dialect' (perhaps the only one he can speak) and 'one register'. However, it is also probably fair to say that those who use the term 'register' (which is used only by sociolinguists as a technical term) have never really intended it to be taken in this sense, as witness the fact that all the models presented lay great stress on the need for multi-dimensional analysis of registers.

Another point of similarity between dialects and registers is that they overlap considerably – one man's dialect is another man's register. For example, the items which one person uses under all circumstances, however informal, may be used by someone else only on the most formal occasions, where he feels he needs to sound as much like the first person as he can. This is the relation between 'native' speakers of standard and non-standard dialects. Forms which are part of the standard speaker's 'dialect' are part of a special 'register' for the non-standard speaker. Again, we shall present massive evidence in support of this claim though evidence is scarcely necessary where the facts are so commonplace.

In conclusion, we have now developed a model of language which is radically different from the one based on the notion 'variety'. In the latter, any given text may reasonably be expected to represent just one variety (though it is recognised that 'code-switching' may take place; see 2.5), and for any given variety it is possible to write a grammar – a description covering all types of linguistic item found in texts which represent that variety.

We may call this the VARIETY-BASED MODEL, in contrast with the ITEM-BASED MODEL which we have developed so far in this book. In the latter model, each linguistic item is associated with a social description which says who uses it, and when. There is scope for similarities between items in their social descriptions, and to the extent that items are similar they may be grouped together as members of a weak version of 'variety', but there may be many such groups of items in a given person's language, and there will also be many items with unique social descriptions. The social descriptions of different items need not, and do not, all refer to the same factors, so within a single sentence some items (say, words) may reflect the speaker's region of origin, others his social class, others his relation to the addressee, others the formality of the occasion, and so on. According to this view the object of description, in descriptive linguistics, is not the 'variety' but the linguistic item, and the question to which we shall seek an answer is to what extent we can generalise about linguistic items, both within the language of one individual and across individuals – and, of course, what kinds of generalisation there are.

2.4.2 *Convention and necessity*

One particularly interesting question, which arises in connection with the 'social descriptions' referred to in the last paragraph, is whether they represent social norms, resulting simply from convention, or are necessary consequences of the ways in which language is learned and used. This problem arises with regard to both 'dialects' and 'registers', i.e. with regard to social descriptions whether they refer to the speaker or to circumstances. However, we shall restrict the discussion here to the latter, where the issues are clearer.

The English used in formal letters includes such expressions as *further to our letter of . . .*, *we note that . . .*, *we regret to inform you that . . .*, and so on. Why are these particular expressions found, whereas others with the same meaning (e.g. *we are sorry to tell you*) are not? One answer is that it is simply a matter of convention, and a historical accident that the forms which are now used were selected in preference to the alternatives, which would have done just as well. It may be that once conventions have been fixed they become necessities, in the sense that they must be used if a letter is to be accepted as 'normal', but there was no necessity for these forms to be have been preferred in the first place. The other answer is that there simply are no alternatives with the same meaning, so the use of the items concerned is unavoidable if the meanings concerned are to be expressed at all.

It is not hard to find a general solution to the conflict between convention and necessity as explanations for the facts. It is that one explanation is right in some cases, and the other in others. For example, the choice between *get* and *obtain* is a matter of convention, since there is no general requirement that the more specific of two terms should be the more formal (compare *car* and *vehicle*). In contrast, the choice between *salt* and *sodium chloride* as a technical term is (presumably) a matter of necessity since, on the one hand, it is important to avoid ambiguity in technical terms and *salt* is already used as a technical term in chemistry (meaning a compound formed by the combination of two ions) and, on the other hand, it is helpful to have a name for table-salt which reveals its chemical relationships to other substances, as the compound noun *sodium chloride* does. Similarly, it is hard to think of alternative 'ordinary language' ways of expressing the meanings of *further to our letter of . . .* and *we note that . . .*, so their use in formal letters, where such meanings need to be expressed, is a matter of necessity. In contrast, *we regret to inform you that . . .* expresses the same meaning as *we are sorry to tell you that* . . . and preference for the former is therefore simply a matter of convention.

This distinction has important practical consequences, since there is a tendency among lay people to present all 'register' differences as equally important, and as important for the same reason. Consequently a child may have to put as much time and effort into learning matters of linguistic convention (such as using the passive in writing up scientific experiments) as he does in matters of linguistic necessity, such as the technical terms of chemistry.

The distinction between conventional and necessary social restrictions is also interesting in view of the strength of feeling which the former arouse. This is particularly clear in the case of *linguistic taboo*, such as the so-called 'four letter words' of English (see Bloomfield 1933: 155, 400 and Bolinger 1975: 255). There is a very powerful convention which says that certain words, such as *shit*, ought never to be used, and many people know these words but observe the convention to the extent that from birth to death they never say them (not even to report that their children have said them) – a truly amazing fact, seen objectively. Moreover, the convention is even supported by law, so that publishers were until recently in danger of prosecution for printing certain words. For many more people, the effect of linguistic taboo is to give these words extra value as symbols of protest, for instance. It is particularly clear in these cases that the social value of a word is just a matter of convention, since other words with precisely the same meanings are not taboo (though they may be restricted for use as technical terms, like *faeces*, or with children, like *poo-poo*, etc.). The whole area of taboo and semi-taboo language (slang, swearing, insults, etc.) merits serious research by sociolinguists, which should tell us a lot about language in relation to society.

2.4.3 *Diglossia*

Having emphasised the theoretical possibility of each individual linguistic item having its own unique social distribution with respect to circumstances of use, it is now important to report that this possibility need not be exploited, and that in some societies there is a relatively simple arrangement called DIGLOSSIA in which at least one type of social restriction on items can be expressed in terms of large-scale 'varieties', rather than item by item. The term 'diglossia' was introduced into the English-language literature on sociolinguistics by Charles

Ferguson (1959) in order to describe the situation found in places like Greece, the Arabic-speaking world in general, German-speaking Switzerland and the island of Haiti. In all these societies there are two distinct varieties, sufficiently distinct for the layman to call them separate languages, and one is used only on formal and public occasions while the other is used by *everybody* under normal, everyday circumstances. Ferguson's definition of diglossia is as follows:

> Diglossia is a relatively stable language situation in which, in addition to the primary dialects of the language (which may include a standard or regional standards), there is a very divergent, highly codified (often grammatically more complex) superposed variety, the vehicle of a large and respected body of written literature, either of an earlier period or in another speech community, which is learned largely by formal education and is used for most written and formal spoken purposes but is not used by any sector of the community for ordinary conversation.

For example, in an Arabic-speaking diglossic community, the language used at home is a local version of Arabic (there may be very great differences between one 'dialect' of Arabic and another, to the point of mutual incomprehensibility), with little variation between the most educated and the least educated speakers. However, if someone needs to give a lecture at a university, or a sermon in a mosque, he is expected to use Standard Arabic, a variety different at all levels from the local vernacular, and felt to be so different from the vernacular that it is taught in schools in the way that foreign languages are taught in English-speaking societies. Likewise, when children learn to read and write, it is the standard language, and not the local vernacular, which they are taught.

The most obvious difference between diglossic and normal English-speaking societies is that no one in the former has the advantage of learning the High variety (as used on formal occasions and in education) as his first language, since everyone speaks the Low variety at home. Consequently, the way to acquire a High variety in such a society is not by being born into the right kind of family, but by going to school. Of course, there are still differences between families in their ability to afford education, so diglossia does not guarantee linguistic equality between poor and rich, but the differences emerge only in formal public situations requiring the High variety, rather than as soon as a speaker opens his mouth. We shall have more to say about the situation in non-diglossic societies in 6.2 and 6.4.

It will be noticed that the definition of 'diglossia' given by Ferguson is quite specific on several points. For example, he requires that the High and Low varieties should belong to the same language, e.g. Standard (or Classical) and Colloquial Arabic. However, some writers have extended the term to cover situations which do not strictly count as diglossic according to this definition. Joshua Fishman, for example, refers to Paraguay as an example of a diglossic community (1971: 75), although the High and Low varieties are respectively Spanish and Guaraní, an Indian language totally unrelated to Spanish. Since we have argued that there is no real distinction between varieties of one language and of different languages, this relaxation seems quite reasonable.

However, Fishman (following John Gumperz) also extends the term diglossia to include any society in which two or more varieties are used under distinct circumstances (1971: 74). This may be a regrettable development, as it would seem to make *every* society diglossic, including even English-speaking England (i.e. excluding immigrants with other languages as their mother tongues), where different so-called 'registers' and 'dialects' are used under different circumstances (compare a sermon with a sports report, for example). The value of the concept of diglossia is that it can be used in sociolinguistic *typology* – that is, in the classification of communities according to the type of sociolinguistic set-up that prevails in them – and 'diglossia' provides a revealing contrast with the kind of set-up found in countries such as Britain and the United States, which we might call 'social dialectia' to show that the 'varieties' concerned were social dialects, not registers.

Finally, how are we to reconcile the definition of diglossia with our claim that varieties do not exist except as informal ways of talking about collections of linguistic items which are roughly similar in their social distributions? If we are to maintain this position, we may see diglossic communities as those in which most linguistic items belong to one of two non-overlapping sets, each used under different circumstances. In contrast with this situation, the linguistic items in a non-diglossic community do not fall into a small number of non-overlapping sets, but are nearer to the opposite extreme where each item has its own unique social distribution. Seen in terms of this model, the difference between diglossic and non-diglossic communities is no less interesting or worth investigating, but may well turn out to be somewhat less clear-cut than Ferguson's definition would imply.

2.5 **Mixture of varieties**

2.5.1 *Code-switching*

To help the discussion in this section we shall use the term 'variety' to refer to the kind of thing which is traditionally referred to as a language, dialect or register. However, there are yet more reasons for not taking the notion seriously as a part of sociolinguistic theory, since so-called varieties may be hopelessly mixed up together even in the same stretch of speech. The most obvious and widespread example of this is what is called CODE-SWITCHING, in which a single speaker uses different varieties at different times. This of course is the automatic consequence of the existence of 'registers', since the same speaker necessarily uses different registers on different occasions (for clear accounts of code-switching in particular communities, see Denison 1971, Parkin 1977). If this was all that was involved in code-switching, the concept would not add anything to what we know already. However, there is more.

First, there is so-called METAPHORICAL CODE-SWITCHING (Blom & Gumperz 1971), where a variety normally used only in one kind of situation is used in a different kind because the topic is the sort which would normally arise in the first kind of situation. An example which is quoted by Jan-Petter Blom and John Gumperz arose out of their research in a town in northern Norway, Hemnesberget, where there is a diglossic situation, with one of the two standard Norwegian languages (Bokmål) as the High variety and a local dialect, Ranamal, as the Low one.

> In the course of a morning spent at the community administration office, we noticed that clerks used both standard and dialect phrases, depending on whether they were talking about official affairs or not. Likewise, when residents step up to a clerk's desk, greeting and inquiries about family affairs tend to be exchanged in the dialect, while the business part of the transaction is carried on in the standard. (Blom & Gumperz 1971: 425)

Examples like this show that speakers are able to manipulate the norms governing the use of varieties in just the same way as they can manipulate those governing the meanings of words by using them metaphorically. This is something everyone knows from his everyday experience, but it is worth explicit reference in a book on sociolinguistic theory, since it helps to avoid the trap of seeing speakers as kinds of sociolinguistic automata, able to talk only within the constraints laid down by the norms of their society.

Another thing which makes code-switching more interesting is that a speaker may switch codes (i.e. varieties) within a single sentence, and may even do so many times. John Gumperz (1976) suggests the term CONVERSATIONAL CODE-SWITCHING for this type, in order to distinguish it from SITUATIONAL CODE-SWITCHING (which he in fact calls 'diglossia' in the more general sense noted above), in which each point of switching corresponds to a change in the situation. There is no such change in the situation in conversational code-switching, nor is there any change in the topic which might lead to metaphorical code-switching. Instead, one gets the impression that the aim is simply to produce instances of the two varieties in some given, say roughly equal proportion. This balance may be achieved by expressing one sentence in one variety and the next one in the other, and so on, but it is equally possible for the two varieties to be used in different parts of a single sentence. It appears that conversational code-switching is permitted in some societies and not in others; it is not something which the bilingual individual does except when talking to a fellow-member of a community which permits it.

The clearest cases of conversational code-switching are of course those in which the varieties concerned are most clearly different, as they are when they are distinct languages. The following is an extract from the speech of a Puerto-Rican speaker living in New York, quoted by William Labov (1971). The stretches in Spanish are translated in brackets.

> Por eso cada [therefore each . . .], you know it's nothing to be proud of, porque yo no estoy [because I'm not] proud of it, as a matter of fact I hate it, pero viene Vierne y Sabado yo estoy, tu me ve hacia mi, sola [but come (?) Friday and Saturday I am, you see me, you look at me, alone] with a, aqui solita, a veces que Frankie me deja [here alone, sometimes Frankie leaves me], you know a stick or something . . .

Examples like these are interesting since they show that the syntactic categories used in classifying linguistic items may be independent of their social descriptions. For instance, in the above extract the Spanish verb *estoy* 'am' is followed by an adjective, but in this case an English adjective (*proud*). This supports the view that at least some syntactic (and other) categories used in analysing language are universal rather than tied to particular languages.

An even clearer example of conversational code-switching within a single sentence is quoted by Gillian Sankoff, from a speech by an entrepreneur in a village in New Guinea (Sankoff 1972: 45). Here the languages concerned are a language called Buang and Neo-Melanesian Pidgin, or Tok Pisin (to which we shall return in 2.5.3). In Buang, negation is marked by using *su* before the predicate (i.e. the verb and its objects), and *re* after it; but in one sentence (which is too long to quote here) the predicate was mostly in English, but was enclosed within the Buang *su . . . re* construction. Again we may conclude that items from languages even as different as Buang and Neo-Melanesian Pidgin are classified, by speakers as well as by linguists, in terms of a common set of syntactic categories (in this case something like the category 'predicate'). A worthwhile subject for research in a community which allows conversational code-switching is whether there are any constraints on where the switching may take place – for instance, may it happen in the middle of a noun phrase? Whether such constraints turned out to be due to conventions of the society or limitations of the human brain, the results would surely be interesting.

2.5.2 *Borrowing*

Another way in which different varieties may become mixed up with each other is through the process of *borrowing* (a good brief survey is Burling 1970: ch. 12, and a longer one is Bynon 1977: ch. 6). It is obvious what is meant by 'borrowing' when an item is taken over lock, stock and barrel from one variety into another, e.g. when the name of a French dish like *boeuf bourguignon* is borrowed for use as an English term, complete with its French pronunciation (with a uvular *r*, etc.). English speakers who know that the item is a part of the foreign language simply reclassify the item by changing its social description from 'French' to 'English' (or more probably 'used by Frenchmen' to 'used by me'). In contrast with code-switching, this does not in fact involve any change of variety when such an item is used in an English sentence like *Let's have some boeuf bourguignon*, since *boeuf bourguignon* is now part of the English language, as far as the speaker is concerned. If on the other hand the speaker had said *Let's have du boeuf bourguignon*, he would have been code-switching since the word *du* 'some' is French but *not* English, and would only occur with a French noun, so we might predict fairly safely that *Let's have du bread* would never occur, unless *bread* had been borrowed from English into French and therefore counted as a French word. Words like *du* are of course much less likely to be borrowed as individual items than words like *boeuf bourguignon*, simply because there is likely to be no need for them in the borrowing variety.

It is common for items to be *assimilated* in some degree to the items already in the borrowing variety, with foreign sounds being replaced by native sounds and so on. For instance, the word *restaurant* lost its uvular *r* when it was borrowed from French into English, so that it would occur with a uvular *r* in an English sentence only as an example of code-switching. On the other hand, assimilation need not be total, and in *restaurant* many English speakers still have a nasal vowel at the end, which would not have been there had the word not been borrowed from French. Words like this make it very hard to draw a neat line round 'English' and describe 'the English phoneme system', since the English system gets mixed up with systems from other languages. On the other hand, this is an extremely common phenomenon both in English and in other languages. (Consider, in British English, the velar fricative at the end of *loch* and the voiceless lateral fricatives in *Llangollen*, either of which could occur in an ordinary non-switching English sentence.)

The completely unassimilated loan-word is at one end of a scale which has at the other end items bearing no formal resemblance to the foreign words on which they are based. Such items are called LOAN TRANSLATIONS (or 'calques'). For example, the English *superman* is a loan translation of the German *Übermensch*, and the expression *I've told him I don't know how many times* is a direct translation of the French *Je le lui ai dit je ne sais pas combien de fois* (Bloomfield 1933: 457). What these examples illustrate is that borrowing may involve the levels of syntax and semantics without involving pronunciation at all, which brings us back to the question of areal features, discussed in 2.3.4, where we saw that it is particularly common for features of syntax to be borrowed from one language into neighbouring ones, via people who are bilingual in both. We now have three mechanisms which may help to explain how this happens. First, there is a tendency to eliminate alternatives in syntax (see 2.3.4). Then there is the existence of specific loan-translations like those just quoted, which may then act as models from which regular 'native' constructions can be developed. And third, there is conversational code-switching (2.5.1), which encourages the languages concerned to become more similar in their syntax so that items from each may be more easily substituted for one another within the same sentence. If both languages put the object on the same side of the verb, for example, code-switching is easier than if one puts it before and the other after.

The question is, whether there are any aspects of language which *cannot* be borrowed from one language into another. The answer appears to be that there are not (Bynon 1977: 255). Even the inflectional morphology of a language may be borrowed, as witness a Tanzanian language called Mbugu which appears to have borrowed a Bantu inflectional system from one or more Bantu neighbours, although other aspects of its grammar are non-Bantu. Its non-Bantu features now include the personal pronouns and the numbers from 1 to 6, which would normally be considered to be such 'basic' vocabulary as to be immune from borrowing (Bynon 1977: 253). In such cases there are of course problems for the family tree model, since it ought to be possible to fit the language into just one tree, whereas some features suggest that it ought to be in the Bantu tree, and others, like those mentioned above, indicate that it belongs in some other tree (possibly the tree for 'Cushitic' languages). How should one resolve the conflict? Can any general principles be applied in balancing the evidence of inflectional morphology against that of basic vocabulary? (It should be noted, incidentally, that the inflectional morphology is matched by Bantu-type rules of concord, which are presumably part of syntax.) One wonders whether there is *any* kind of external reality against which an answer to questions such as these might be measured.

Assuming that there are no areas of language which cannot be borrowed, it is still possible to ask questions about language which may distinguish one area from another. For example, are there any restrictions on the circumstances under which different aspects of language may be borrowed? We might suspect, for instance, that some kinds of item will be borrowed only under conditions of widespread bilingualism, while others may occur where only a few members of a society are bilingual in the relevant languages. Aspects of the first type would count as least, and the second type as most, subject to borrowing, so we could set up a scale of accessibility to borrowing, on which inflectional morphology, and 'basic vocabulary' such as small numbers, would presumably be at the 'least accessible' end, and vocabulary for artefacts (like *aeroplane* or *hamburger*) at the other. A word for the number 'one', for instance, will be borrowed only when almost everyone speaks both the 'borrowing' and the 'source' languages, whereas a word for 'aeroplane' could easily be borrowed when nobody is fully proficient in the two languages, but one or two people are familiar enough with the source language to know the word for 'aeroplane'. However, the truth may turn out to be much more complex than is suggested by this hypothesis, which is in any case by no means simple as far as the organisation of linguistic items into separate levels, such as syntax, vocabulary and phonology, is concerned, since different vocabulary items are put at opposite ends of the scale. Thus borrowing is a phenomenon which may throw light on the internal organisation of language, and certainly on the relations of language to society once the right research has been done.

2.5.3 *Pidgins*

There is another way, apart from code-switching and borrowing, in which varieties may get mixed up with each other, namely by the process of creating a new variety out of two (or more) existing ones. This process of 'variety-synthesis' may take a number of different forms, including for instance the creation of artificial auxiliary languages like Esperanto and Basic English (for which see Bolinger 1975: 580). However, by far the most important manifestation is the process of pidginisation, whereby PIDGIN LANGUAGES, or PIDGINS, are created. These are varieties created for very practical and immediate purposes of communication between people who otherwise would have no common language whatsoever, and learned by one person from another within the communities concerned as the accepted way of communicating with members of the other community. (An excellent survey of the issues discussed here and in 2.5.4 is DeCamp 1977.)

Since the reason for wanting to communicate with members of the other communities is often trade, a pidgin may be what is called a TRADE LANGUAGE, but not all pidgins are restricted to being used as trade languages, nor are all trade languages pidgins. Instead, the language of some community in the area may be used by all the other communities as a trade language. It will be recalled that in the north-west Amazon area, Tukano is the language of one of the twenty-odd tribes but is also used as a trade language by all the others. Similarly, English and French are widely used as trade languages in many parts of Africa. In contrast with languages like this, a pidgin is a variety specially created for the purpose of communicating with some *other* group, and not used by *any* community for communication among themselves.

The term 'pidgin' is thought by many (though not by all) to come from the English word *business*, as pronounced in the pidgin English which developed in China (i.e. the latter was called 'business English', pronounced 'pidgin English'; see DeCamp 1971a). There are a large number of pidgin languages, spread through all the continents including Europe, where migrant workers in countries like Germany have developed pidgin varieties based on the local national language. Each pidgin is of course specially constructed to suit the needs of its users, which means that it has to have the terminology and constructions needed in whatever kinds of contact normally arise between the communities, but need not go beyond these demands to anticipate the odd occasion on which other kinds of situation arise. If the contacts concerned are restricted to the buying and selling of cattle, then only linguistic items to do with this are needed, so there will be no way of talking about the quality of vegetables, or the emotions, or any of the many other things about which one can talk in any normal language.

Another requirement of a pidgin is that it be as simple to learn as possible, especially for those who benefit *least* from learning it, and the consequence of this is that the vocabulary is generally based on the vocabulary of the dominant group. For instance, a group of migrant workers from Turkey living in Germany will not benefit much from a pidgin whose vocabulary is based on Turkish, since few Germans would be willing to make the effort to learn it, consequently they take their vocabulary from German. Similarly, in a colonial situation where representatives of a foreign colonial power need to communicate with the local population in matters of trade or administration, and if it is in the interests of the local population to communicate, then the pidgin which develops will be based on the vocabulary of the colonial power – hence the very large number of pidgins spread round the globe based on English, French, Portuguese and Dutch.

However, although the vocabulary of a pidgin may be based mainly on that of one of the communities concerned, the 'dominant' variety, the pidgin is still a compromise between this and the subordinate varieties, in that its syntax and phonology may be similar to the latter, making the pidgin easier for the other communities to learn than the dominant language in its ordinary form. As for morphology, this is left out altogether, which again makes for ease of learning. To the extent that differences of tense, number, case and so on are indicated at all, they are marked by the addition of separate particles. Indeed, one of the most characteristic features of pidgins is the lack of morphology, and if some variety is found to contain morphology, especially inflectional morphology, most specialists in this field would be reluctant to treat it as a pidgin (which does not of course mean that every language without inflectional morphology must be a pidgin).

The lack of inflectional morphology in pidgins is interesting in itself, especially since it is just as much a feature of contact situations where the languages concerned all have rich inflectional morphologies as where the dominant language is short of inflectional morphology (e.g. English). This may point to a general characteristic of human language: that inflectional morphology is in some sense an unnatural mechanism for expressing semantic and syntactic distinctions. Thus, even when a language has an easy way of making distinctions by inflection (e.g. English regular plural -s ending), it is never used as the marker of the distinction concerned in a pidgin based on that language, but is always replaced by a separate word. If there is indeed something inherently difficult, or inefficient in communication, about inflectional morphology, it is strange that it is so widespread among languages, and even stranger that many languages tolerate so much complexity and irregularity in their inflections, given that this benefits nobody. In 1.3.1 I suggested that the driving force behind the maintenance and development of inflectional irregularity is pressure on the individual to conform. It could be that there is some similar pressure from society which explains the development and maintenance of inflectional morphology in general, whether regular or irregular, and which prevents it from being eliminated as it is when the sole criterion is efficiency and ease.

In other words, if a variety is your native language, then you will use it to identify yourself with the community which uses it by conforming to the latter's norms down to the finest detail of pronunciation, including matters of inflectional morphology. To simplify or regularise the morphology would be to mark oneself as an outsider. But if the variety concerned is a pidgin, nobody uses it as a means of group identification so there is no pressure to maintain inefficient aspects of pronunciation. This suggestion is of course quite speculative, but the lack of inflectional morphology in pidgins demands some explanation, and this is at least one possibility which deserves to be explored. It is easy to see from the above discussion why so much attention has been paid by linguists to pidgins, as evidence for what would happen to language if it was not used as a symbol of social identity.

Let us return to the more general question of the relation between pidgins and the societies which create them. As we have seen, pidgins are sometimes developed as trade languages, which we may take in a fairly broad sense as varieties used only for trade and administration. An example of a pidgin developed under these conditions is Neo-Melanesian Pidgin or Tok Pisin, i.e. 'pidgin talk' (see 2.5.1). This is an English-based pidgin used in New Guinea and various islands nearby, which has developed during the present century for communication between the English-speaking administrators and the local population, who themselves speak a large number of mutually incomprehensible languages (one of which is Buang). The following sentences from Tok Pisin (quoted from Bolinger 1975: 356) give an idea of its relationship to English. The words in brackets show the English source for the preceding Tok Pisin word.

> Bimeby [by and by] leg belong you he-all-right gain [again].
> 'Your leg will get well again'
> Sick he-down-im [him] me.
> 'I am sick'
> Me like-im saucepan belong cook-im bread.
> 'I want a pan for cooking bread'

Like a number of other pidgins, Tok Pisin has developed so effectively and become accepted as the medium of communication in so many situations that it has now been adopted as a *national language* in New Guinea (Hall 1972). (It has also recently turned into a creole language, as we shall see in 2.5.4.)

However, not all pidgins have arisen as trade languages, as Tok Pisin did. Another situation in which pidgins are needed is when people from different language backgrounds are thrown together and have to communicate with each other, and with a dominant group, in order to survive. This is the situation in which most Africans taken as slaves to the New World found themselves, since the slavers would break up tribal groups to minimise the risk of rebellion. Thus the only way in which the slaves could communicate either with each other or with their masters was through a pidgin which they generally learned from the slavers, based on the latter's language. Since most slaves had little opportunity to learn the ordinary language of their masters, this pidgin remained the only means of communication for most slaves for the rest of their lives. This had two consequences. One was that pidgins became very closely associated with slaves, and acquired a poor reputation as a result (and the slaves also got the reputation of being stupid since they could not speak a 'proper' language!). The other consequence was that pidgins were used in an increasingly wide range of situations, and so gradually acquired the status of creole languages (see 2.5.4).

It may be helpful to bring together some characteristics of pidgins which distinguish them from other types of variety and variety-mixture. (1) A pidgin based on variety X is not just an example of 'bad X', as one might describe the unsuccessful attempt of an individual foreigner to learn X. A pidgin is itself a variety, with a community of speakers who pass it on from one generation to the next, and consequently with its own history. Indeed, it has even been suggested that many pidgins have a common origin in the Portuguese-based pidgin which developed in the Far East and West Africa during the sixteenth century, under the influence of Portuguese sailors, and that this Portuguese-based pidgin might have its roots in the 'Lingua Franca' developed in the Mediterranean as early as the crusades. This suggestion represents one of a number of attempts to explain the existence of a fairly large number of similar features which have been found in pidgins from many different parts of the world. (For an excellent survey of these issues, see DeCamp 1971a, 1977.)

(2) A pidgin is not simply the result of heavy borrowing from one variety into another, since there is no pre-existing variety into which items may be borrowed. An 'X-based pidgin' is not a variety of X which has borrowed a lot of syntactic constructions and phonological features from other varieties, since there may well be no model in these other varieties for any of the changes in word-shapes, notably the loss of inflections to which we referred above. Nor is it a variety of some other language which has borrowed a lot of vocabulary from X, since the syntax, phonology and morphology need not be the same as those of any of the other varieties involved. In any case, it is not clear which community would be the borrowers, since the pidgin is developed jointly by both sides of the communication gap, each trying to help bridge the gap. Of course, there is an interesting problem in relation to borrowing, since we *can* talk of borrowing into a pre-established pidgin, just as we can in connection with any other kind of variety, whereas we cannot invoke borrowing as a process in the establishment of the pidgin in the first place. The problem is that this implies too clear a distinction between the periods before and after the establishment of the pidgin. The problem is probably the result of putting too much weight on the concept 'variety', which we have already seen reason to distrust.

(3) A pidgin, unlike ordinary languages, has no native speakers, which is

a consequence of the fact that it is used only for communication between members of *different* communities, where no ordinary variety is available as a link. On the other hand, this distinction too is not clear-cut, since there are situations, such as those of slavery, where a community can come into existence with a pidgin as its only common variety, although all the members of the community learned it as a second language. The lack of a clearly defined group of native speakers has the effect of putting most pidgins near the 'diffuse' end of the scale contrasting 'focussing' and 'diffusion' (1.3.1), in contrast with highly focussed standard languages such as French, and this is another reason why pidgins are of such considerable interest to sociolinguists. However, as we have already noted there are a few pidgins which are now used as standard languages, which presumably means that they have moved along the scale towards the 'focussing' end – another phenomenon worth investigating by those interested in the relations of language to society.

2.5.4 *Creoles*

A pidgin which has acquired native speakers is called a CREOLE LANGUAGE, or CREOLE, and the process whereby a pidgin turns into a creole is called 'creolisation'. It is easy to see how pidgins acquire native speakers, namely by being spoken by couples who have children and rear them together. This happened on a large scale among the African slaves taken to the New World, and is happening on a somewhat smaller scale in urban communities in places like New Guinea.

From a social point of view, creoles are of more interest than pidgins for three reasons. Firstly, there are more speakers of creoles than of pidgins, one estimate being between 10 and 17 million speakers of creoles compared with between 6 and 12 million regularly using pidgins (DeCamp 1977). Secondly, most creole languages are spoken by the descendants of African slaves and are of great interest, both to their speakers and to others, as one of the main sources of information on their origins, and as a symbol of their identity. A similar interest is shown by people who speak varieties whose origins are in a creole, but which have since been 'decreolised', i.e. moved towards the dominant variety at the expense of most distinctive characteristics of the creole. It seems likely that the English of blacks in the United States is such a variety, and because of this creoles are of particular interest to many American linguists (see 1.3.2, 5.4.2 and, a good survey, Wolfram 1971).

And thirdly, there are minority groups, such as West Indian immigrants in Britain, whose members speak some form of creole. If their creole is one based on the majority language of the country into which they have immigrated – for example, an English-based creole in the case of immigrants to Britain – then serious educational problems may arise if neither teachers nor taught can be sure if this creole is a different language from the majority one or a dialect of it. If the former, it may be appropriate to use foreign-language teaching methods to teach the majority language, but this is by no means an appropriate method if it is a dialect. Consequently research is needed in order to establish the extent of the difference between the creole and the majority language. Similar problems arise in countries where the majority language is itself a creole, if the language expected by the education system is the standard version of the language on which the creole is based, as in many Caribbean countries. The problem is not helped, of course, by the fact that the difference between 'same' and 'different' is rather meaningless when applied to language varieties, as we argued in 2.2, so it may be that a more realistic model of language might help to solve some of these problems. (For further discussion see e.g. Le Page 1968b.)

From the point of view of what they tell us about language, however, creoles are of less immediate interest, since they are just ordinary languages like any others, except in their origins (Sankoff 1977). There is perhaps one qualification to be made to this claim, namely that there may be a rather special relationship between a creole and the variety which is the present-day representative of the dominant language on which its parent pidgin was based, if the two coexist in the same country, as they often do. One country in which this is the case is Guyana, whose creole has been studied in particular by Derek Bickerton (1971, 1973, 1975). Following the terminology of William Stewart, one of the founders of creole studies in the United States, Bickerton called the pure creole the BASILECT (pronounced with short *a* as in *massive*) and the local version of Standard English the ACROLECT (Greek *akro-* 'highest', as in *Acropolis* and *acrobat*). He postulated a *continuum* linking the basilect to the acrolect via a succession of MESOLECTS as the only route available for speakers wanting to 'improve' their language by moving it nearer to the acrolect, and provided quite persuasive research evidence to show that at least the great majority of speakers in the large sample which he studied could be located in this continuum (see 5.5.2 for further discussion). He also showed that there are substantial differences in syntax and semantics between the acrolect and the basilect, notably in their treatment of time and tense relations. For instance, in the basilect the same form of the verb is used to refer to things happening at the moment of speaking as for those which happened at the same time as others previously mentioned, even in the past, whereas in the acrolect, Standard English, different forms of the verb would be used in these two cases (compare *I see my mistake* with *After looking for an hour I saw my mistake*) (Bickerton 1975: 46).

There are two peculiarities about a 'creole continuum' like this, compared with the situation one might expect where there is no creole. First, there are more profound differences between the varieties which coexist in the community than one might expect in a community fragmented by the normal processes of dialect formation; and in particular there is more variation in *syntax* than one would expect, for the reasons discussed in 2.3.4. The differences found are in fact more like those to be expected under conditions of diglossia, though of course a creole continuum is not a case of diglossia since the acrolect and basilect are both used domestically, by different groups. The reason for these big differences between acrolect and basilect is that they were not in fact separated in the first place by the usual processes of diffusion which are responsible for dialect differences, but rather by the process of pidginisation, which automatically leads to drastic differences between the pidgin and the dominant language.

The other peculiarity of a creole continuum is that only a single chain of varieties connects basilect and acrolect, allowing speakers only a single linguistic dimension on which to locate themselves with reference to the rest of society. The picture as described by Bickerton is in fact somewhat more complex, as individual speakers may be able to use a *range* of varieties on the continuum, rather than being restricted to a single one (Bickerton 1975: 203), but there is still only one linguistic dimension on which a speaker can locate himself on a given occasion. This situation contrasts sharply with the large number of independent dimensions that items in a variety normally provide for a speaker to use in locating himself. The reason for this must again presumably lie in the history of creoles, but it is hard to understand precisely what that reason is (for one suggestion, see Bickerton 1975: 17, 178).

Creoles are ordinary languages apart from this rather important qualification about their continua, and do not add anything specific to our understanding of language in general. This claim is certainly true and uncontroversial when applied to well-established creoles which have existed, as such, for generations. Most creoles already fall into this category, since they originated in the slave trade and already started to exist as creoles in those days. Many of them can even be traced through written records back through several centuries (for an example of this, with reference to the English-based creole of Nicaragua, see Holm 1978). However, the difference between pidgins and creoles is less clear than might be expected from their definitions, and the *early* stages of a creole may be of as much interest to linguistic theory as pidgins.

It will be recalled that the 'early stages' of a creole occur when it is acquiring native speakers, and therefore ceasing to be a pidgin, and when two hypothetical kinds of change might be expected. First, there are changes due to the variety being learned as a first language and not as a second one. To the extent that children are prepared genetically to learn only 'ordinary' languages, and in so far as pidgins do not have the properties of such languages, we might expect to see changes as children try to learn a pidgin, since they will need to adapt it where it is not like an ordinary language in order to make it learnable. (The idea that children are prepared genetically to learn only ordinary languages is associated in particular with Noam Chomsky; see for instance Chomsky 1965: 47, and 1968.) However, there is no evidence at present that such changes actually take place.

The other kind of hypothetical change is due to the fact that the language is now used in a wide range of domestic situations, for talking about things which a trade language as such would not need to deal with. However, it is clear that changes of this kind are simply a continuation of what was happening already in the pidgin, and so not unique to the process of creolisation. The parents must have developed some way of talking to each other in the pidgin about domestic matters before the child's birth, and we have seen that some pidgins are already sufficiently developed to be used as standard languages, as in the case of Tok Pisin. One particularly interesting piece of research has been done on Tok Pisin in this connection, by Gillian Sankoff and Penelope Brown (1976), who studied the recent history of relative clauses in Tok Pisin and showed how a consistent marker of relative clauses was gradually developed out of the word *ia* (based ultimately on the English *here*), which is now put both before and after many relative clauses.

Na pik *ia* ol ikilim bipo *ia* bai ikamap olsem draipela ston.
(Now pig here past kill people here future become huge stone)

'And this pig which they had killed before would turn into a huge stone.' (Sankoff & Brown 1976: 632)

This construction may illustrate the influence of the syntax of the local languages on that of the pidgin, since Buang, for instance, has a word which is used both as a demonstrative and as a marker of relative clauses in the same way as *ia*. What is particularly interesting about this research is that speakers of a pidgin continue to develop it, using whatever resources are available, in a process that does not depend on creolisation. Indeed, Sankoff & Brown have evidence that it had started at least ten years before there were any significant numbers of native speakers of Tok Pisin. Again, there is no research evidence of changes that have happened during creolisation which cannot be matched by changes to a pidgin without native speakers.

The conclusion to which this discussion seems to lead is that there is no clear difference between pidgins and creoles, apart from the fact that creoles have native speakers and pidgins do not. No other differences between pidgins and creoles seem necessarily to follow from this one. Since we have also claimed that creoles are just ordinary languages (with some reservations about creole continua) and that pidgins are rather peculiar, it follows that the distinction between the 'normal' and the 'peculiar' (as represented by early stages of pidginisation) is unclear, and is in fact a continuum rather than a qualitative difference. Moreover, it is clear that there is no moment in time at which a particular pidgin suddenly comes into existence, but rather a process of variety-creation called pidginisation, by which a pidgin is gradually built up out of nothing. We might well ask whether this process is essentially different from what happens in everyday interaction between people who think they speak the same language, but who are in fact constantly accommodating their speech and language to each other's needs. (Compare the suggestion by Robert Le Page (1977b) that 'every speech act is . . . the reflex of an "instant pidgin" related to the linguistic competence of more than one person'.) For instance a parallel may be drawn between the New Guinea natives learning an approximation to English vocabulary from each other and the local English speakers, on the one hand, and students of linguistics learning an approximation to the vocabulary of their teachers from each other and from their teachers, on the other. In both cases it is clear who has to do the bulk of the learning, though the dominant group may sometimes use the forms which they know the subordinate group use, in order to make things easier for them. In both cases what develops is a variety of language which is passed on from one person to another, developed out of countless encounters between teachers and students and between students themselves. The reader of this book may be amused at the idea of himself as a speaker of 'pidgin linguistics', but the suggestion is intended to be taken quite seriously.

2.6 Conclusions

This chapter has ranged over several types of language variety, including 'languages', 'dialects' (both regional and social), 'registers', 'standard languages', 'High' and 'Low' varieties in diglossia, 'pidgins' and 'creoles'. We have come to essentially negative conclusions about varieties. First, there are considerable problems in delimiting one variety from another of the same type (e.g. one language from another, or one dialect from another). Secondly, there are serious problems in delimiting one *type* of variety from another – languages from dialects, or dialects from registers, or 'ordinary languages' from creoles, or creoles from pidgins. (We could have shown similar uncertainties on the border between 'standard' and 'non-standard' varieties.) Thirdly, we have suggested that the only satisfactory way to solve these problems is to avoid the notion 'variety' altogether as an analytical or theoretical concept, and to focus instead on the individual linguistic item. For each item some kind of 'social description' is needed, saying roughly who uses it and when: in some cases an item's social description will be unique, whereas in others it may be possible to generalise across a more or less large number of items. The nearest this approach comes to the concept of 'variety' is in these sets of items with similar social descriptions, but their characteristics are rather different from those of varieties like languages and dialects. On the other hand, it is still possible to use terms like 'variety' and 'language' in an informal way, as they have been used in the last few sections, without intending them to be taken seriously as theoretical constructs.

We also came to rather similar conclusions regarding the concept 'speech community', which seems to exist only to the extent that a given person has identified it and can locate himself with reference to it. Since different individuals will identify different communities in this way, we have to give up any attempt to find objective and absolute criteria for defining speech communities. This leaves us, on the one hand, with the individual speaker and his range of linguistic items and, on the other, with communities defined without reference to language but to which we may find it helpful to relate language.

Having reduced the subject-matter of sociolinguistics to the study of individual linguistic items of particular speakers, we may ask what kinds of generalisation it is possible to make. We have seen that there are many general questions to which it would be interesting to have answers, such as whether different kinds of linguistic item are related to different aspects of society (i.e. of the individual's private model of his society). I have suggested some answers to this question, and to others raised in this chapter, but at this stage they can be little more than speculative. However, it should now be clear that such questions are worth asking, and that future research will provide answers supported by empirical evidence.

3
Language, culture and thought

3.1 Introduction
3.1.1 *Culture*

In the last chapter we saw that the phenomenon of language does not have natural divisions between 'varieties' of language, which we could call 'languages', 'dialects' or 'registers', though there may be natural internal divisions within it on the basis of 'levels' of language, such as vocabulary, syntax, morphology and phonology. We now turn to the external relations of language, to ask whether there are natural boundaries between the phenomena covered by the term 'language' and other kinds of phenomena, notably those called 'culture' and 'thought'. Once again we shall arrive at a somewhat complex answer, but it is one which emphasises the similarities between language and other phenomena rather than the differences (for a similar approach cf. Lakoff 1977), and which also stresses the close connections between the phenomena rather than their independence. For instance, I shall argue that many of the properties of language looked at in the last chapter are also properties of culture in general, and that meaning is best studied in relation to culture and thought. To the extent that these conclusions are correct, they present a challenge to the view which has dominated twentieth-century linguistics, that language is both unique and autonomous.

To avoid confusion we must start with some matters of terminology. First, the word CULTURE is taken in the sense in which it is used by cultural anthropologists, according to whom culture is something that everybody has, in contrast with the 'culture' which is found only in 'cultured' circles – in opera houses, universities and the like. The term is used differently by different anthropologists, but always refers to some 'property' of a community, especially those which might distinguish it from other communities. Some anthropologists are interested in what is called 'material culture' – the artefacts of the community, such as its pottery, its vehicles or its clothing. However, we shall follow Ward Goodenough in taking culture as socially acquired *knowledge*:

> As I see it, a society's culture consists of whatever it is one has to know or believe in order to operate in a manner acceptable to its members . . . Culture, being what people have to learn as distinct from their biological heritage, must consist of the end-product of learning: knowledge, in a most general . . . sense of the term. (Goodenough 1957)

As Goodenough points out, we must take 'knowledge' here in a broad sense, to include both 'know-how' and 'know-that' – for instance, to cover both the ability to tie knots and the knowledge that one pound note buys as much as ten ten-penny coins. One attraction of taking this view, widely accepted among anthropologists, is that it will allow us to compare culture with language (as in 3.2.1).

If culture is knowledge, it can exist only inside people's heads, so there is a problem in studying it: how can one know what the cultural knowledge of Mr X is? Worse still, how can one know what the culture of community X is? Does one need to examine the cultural knowledge of every member of the community? And what if there are differences between people? Problems like these are completely familiar to the student of linguistics, of course, and the solutions are much the same whether one is interested in culture or in language. Firstly, we can observe people's natural behaviour (i.e. outside artificial experimental situations) and draw our own conclusions about the knowledge that must underlie it. Secondly, we can arrange interviews and ask people more or less direct questions about their knowledge, taking their answers with a pinch of salt if need be. Thirdly, we can use ourselves as informants. And fourthly we can conduct psychological experiments of one kind or another, such as measuring the length of time it takes people to perform certain tasks in order to develop a measure of the relative complexity of the knowledge involved. (For more discussion of methodology, see 5.2.) All these methods can be used, and have been used in both cultural anthropology and linguistics.

Having discovered the relevant facts about a number of individuals, there is a problem of generalisation in both disciplines – to what extent may we assume that the people studied are representative of the community as a whole? And to what extent may we assume that if two people share one item of knowledge, they will also share some other item? In discussing linguistic items in chapter 2 we came to the conclusion that generalisations are very hard to make, across both people and linguistic items, and the same would certainly be true of items of cultural knowledge (Sankoff 1971). In short, problems of methodology that exist in the study of language are also found in the study of culture.

Before leaving the question of culture, we should note that the knowledge included in a culture need not be factually or objectively correct in order to count. For instance, some people think that strenuous exercise shortens life and others think the opposite, but so long as we can show that each view is learned socially (i.e. from other people), they both count as items of culture. Lay people's knowledge is often referred to as COMMON-SENSE KNOWLEDGE, and is the kind which is of most interest to anthropologists, just as linguists are more interested in day-to-day usage than in prescriptive grammars or dictionaries. On the other hand, the specialist knowledge of scientist or scholar is also a part of culture, and one of the most interesting questions in the study of culture is about the relations between common sense and specialist knowledge, since it is clear that influence goes in both directions. For example, one of the problems in writing this book is that there is a good deal of common-sense knowledge about language in any culture, some of which is right and some badly wrong, but it is hard to predict the particular beliefs of each reader. And a similar problem in socio-linguistics itself is that the sociolinguist knows in principle that some of his beliefs about language may be wrong and unhelpful, while others may be near enough to the truth for him to build them into his theory; but he does not know in advance which are which.

3.1.2 *Thought*

The term 'thought' covers a number of different types of mental activity, and lies in the province of cognitive psychologists. To help our discussion, I shall distinguish first between MEMORY and INFERENCE, and then between CONCEPTS and PROPOSITIONS, as the objects of memory or inference. The terms should be self-explanatory, if propositions are thought of as roughly equivalent to statements and concepts as general categories in terms of which propositions are formulated and experience is processed. For instance, the English words *oil*, *water*, *float* and *on* may be taken as the names of concepts (two substances, one state and one relation), and the sentence *Oil floats on water* can be seen as the 'name' of the proposition that 'oil floats on water', i.e.

that one of the substances maintains the state of floating in the 'on' relation to the other substance. This proposition may be either remembered (already stored in memory) or inferred (worked out), i.e. it may either be something one already knows, or something one discovers (and probably adds to one's memory, so that next time it will be there as knowledge). Similarly, a concept may either exist in one's memory, as a category used in thinking, or may be created as a new category which could then be stored away in memory. (It is normal in psychology to use the term 'concept formation' rather than 'inference' for the creation of new concepts, but the process seems rather similar to that of inferring propositions.) When we come to the relations of language to thought we shall find it important to distinguish these various kinds of 'thought'.

What then is the relation between thought and culture? Given the definition of culture as 'socially acquired knowledge', it is easy to see that culture is one part of memory, namely the part which is 'acquired socially', in contrast with that which does not involve other people. This distinction is anything but clear, so we must not put too much weight on it, but it might distinguish between propositions which are known to be true from one's own experience and those which have been learned from other people. An example of the first kind would be 'I had sausages for lunch today', which is excluded from the notion 'culture'; whereas a proposition like 'Columbus discovered America' clearly belongs to culture, as something one has learned from other people. Similarly, some concepts are cultural and others are not. We create the former because we see that others around us make use of them in their thinking, as may be illustrated by the concepts which a student of linguistics or sociolinguistics builds up because he finds that his teachers are using them. (In most cases there is a word for such concepts, so the main clue the student has about the existence of a concept such as 'diglossia' is the existence of the word.) A non-cultural concept, on the other hand, is one which we build without reference to other people, as a convenient way of interpreting our experience – 'me', or 'the way my wife talks', or 'the smell of paint'.

To the extent that a distinction can be made between cultural and non-cultural knowledge, it concerns the source of such knowledge. If it means an approximation to the concepts or propositions in other people's minds, it is cultural, but otherwise not. One of the most interesting things about cultural knowledge is the extent to which people can interpret each other's behaviour and arrive at more or less the same concepts or propositions. For instance, millions of people every year attend concerts of various kinds in Britain, but with very few exceptions they appear to share the same concepts for categorising concerts (pop, classical, jazz, and so on), and the same propositions about what constitutes appropriate behaviour during each type (for instance, during a classical concert audience participation is very closely restricted as to what may be done and when). If people did not share such detailed knowledge, their behaviour in concerts could not be as predictable as it in fact is, especially since the conventions are somewhat arbitrary.

On the other hand, it does not follow that non-cultural knowledge must differ from person to person, since different people can arrive at similar conclusions on the basis of similar experiences of the universe or similar genetic predispositions. For instance, if we find that all human beings have a concept 'vertical dimension', there is no need to assume that they have all learned it from other people in order to establish a chain of connections between them; it is much more likely that it is because they all live in a world dominated by gravity and full of human beings who walk upright. (See Clark & Clark 1977: ch. 14, especially p. 534, for an excellent discussion of similarities in non-cultural concepts.)

Thus we find that there are three kinds of knowledge:

(i) *cultural knowledge* – which is learned from other people;
(ii) *shared non-cultural knowledge* – which is shared by people within the same community or the world over, but is not learned from each other;
(iii) *non-shared non-cultural knowledge* – which is unique to the individual.

It is not difficult to find a place for language in this schema. Some parts of language are cultural knowledge, since they have to be learned from others, while other parts are shared non-cultural knowledge. We shall return to this point below, in 3.1.3.

The reader may be sceptical about the possibility of actually studying thought, as opposed to speculating about it, so it may be helpful to refer very briefly to the vast amount of such research that has been carried out, and the conclusions to which it has led. We might pick out for special mention one of the most recent developments in the study of concepts, since we shall be referring to this work later in discussing meaning (3.2.3). (Developments in the study of concepts are summarised and illustrated in Johnson-Laird & Wason 1977: Part 3, and also in Clark & Clark 1977: 464.)

One theory of concepts is that each one consists of a set of features which are necessary and sufficient for something to count as an instance of that concept. For example, the concept 'bird' would consist of a set of features referring to wings, feathers, eggs, being animate and so on. There are a number of problems with this theory, not least the fact that it is impossible to decide what is covered by 'and so on' – in other words, it is impossible, both in principle and in practice, to identify the necessary and sufficient conditions for something to count as a bird. To overcome these problems, a number of psychologists, notably Eleanor Rosch, developed an alternative theory according to which a concept is not a set of necessary and sufficient features, but rather a *prototype* – a description of a typical instance of that particular concept. Thus the concept 'bird' is seen as consisting of a description of a typical bird, such as a robin, in the form of a set of features or a visual image. According to this view, an object is not simply either a bird or not a bird, but it is a bird to a certain degree, according to how similar it is to the prototype (for further discussion, see 3.2.2 below).

There is a good deal of evidence in favour of the prototype theory of concepts as opposed to the 'criterial feature' theory. Some of the evidence comes from experimentation; for instance, it takes people less time to verify a sentence like *X is a bird* if the word *X* is the name of a typical bird than if it is a word like *ostrich* or *penguin*, names of very atypical birds (Rosch 1976). Evidence has also come from experiments in which people were asked to rate members of more general categories according to how typical they were of the category concerned. This exercise was significant because there was a large measure of agreement among people as to the relative ranking of the items. For instance, it was generally agreed that robins and swallows were the most typical birds from a list of eight, and chickens and penguins the least typical; among items of furniture, chairs and dressers were most typical, and radios and ashtrays the least; apples and plums were most typical instances of fruit, and coconuts and olives the least; trousers and coats were most typical items of clothing, and purses and bracelets least typical (Clark & Clark 1977: 464). If the concepts 'bird', 'furniture', 'fruit' and 'clothing' were each defined by a set of criterial features, there would be no way to explain why some things satisfied the features more than others. Instead one would expect a clear distinction between members and non-members of the categories concerned.

One of the attractions of the prototype theory for an anthropologist or sociolinguist is that it is not too hard to understand how people can *learn* such concepts from each other. Imagine a baby, without language, learning the concept 'place for sleeping in' – a clear example of a cultural concept, since it depends on what other people expect the baby to do, and not just on what it wants to do itself. The 'prototype' place for sleeping is of course the baby's own cot, and as long as the baby can identify this as the place, par excellence, for sleeping in, its main concept-formation task is over. Other places can then be subsumed under the concept as the need arises – other cots, or grown-up beds, or beds made up on the floor, or back seats of cars, and so on. In some cases the concept will be extended only temporarily, but if the same situation arises again the baby may store the new kind of sleeping place in his memory and might even replace the original prototype by the new one. The point of this example is to show that a prototype-based concept can be learned on the basis of a very small number of instances – perhaps a single one – and without any kind of formal definition, whereas a feature-based definition would be very much harder to learn since a much larger number of cases, plus a number of non-cases, would be needed before the learner could work out which features were necessary and which were not.

Another attraction of the prototype theory is that it allows for the kind of creative flexibility in the application of concepts which we find in real life – in other words, it predicts that the boundaries of concepts will be fuzzy, as they in fact are. For example, let us assume that we have two concepts 'fruit' and 'vegetable', built partly on the basis of other people's speech but also on the basis of our own non-linguistic experience – for instance, fruits are typically eaten as dessert or between meals, typically grow on trees or bushes, and are typically sweet, while vegetables are typically eaten with the meat course, typically grow on or under the ground, and are typically savoury. An apple has all the characteristics of a prototypical fruit, and a cabbage all those of a prototypical vegetable, but there are anomalous cases such as tomatoes and rhubarb which might count as either, according to which criterion seems most relevant to the occasion concerned. The task of the person applying the concept 'fruit', for example, is not simply to look for the defining characteristics of fruit in the tomato or rhubarb, but to show initiative and sensitivity to the needs of the occasion in deciding between the criteria he could apply. Compared with the feature-based model, the prototype model puts more burden on the user, but gives him virtually unlimited freedom to apply his concepts creatively.

A third attraction which the prototype theory specifically offers the sociolinguist is that he can make use of the theory in explaining how people categorise the social factors to which they relate language – factors such as the kind of person who is speaking and the circumstances in which he is doing so. As we saw in the last chapter, people learn that certain linguistic items are associated with certain types of people or circumstance, but we did not discuss how people categorise speakers and circumstances. If concepts are based on defining features, it should be equally easy to decide whether any speaker or set of circumstances is or is not an instance of any given category. On the other hand, if they are based on prototypes, all we need do when learning a new linguistic item is to work out what kind of speaker typically uses it, or what are the typical circumstances under which it is used, leaving the unclear, borderline cases to look after themselves as the need arises.

This is indeed the basis for a well-established system of analysis developed by Joshua Fishman, in terms of what are called DOMAINS – concepts such as 'home', 'school', 'work', 'religion' and so on (see Fishman 1965, 1972d). The assumption underlying this system is that the choice of language in a bilingual community varies from domain to domain, and that domains are *congruent* combinations of a particular kind of speaker and addressee, in a particular kind of place, talking about a particular kind of topic. If a teacher is talking about history to a pupil, and they are in school, the contributory factors are congruent and define a domain – that of 'school' – and there will be no difficulty in deciding which language to use. If, however, we make one of the factors incongruent – by moving the scenario into the pupil's home, for instance – the interaction is no longer covered unambiguously by any one domain, so the speaker has to use his intelligence and imagination in deciding which language to use.

It should have become very clear from this discussion of the prototype theory of concepts that the sociolinguist stands to learn a lot from cognitive psychology and psycholinguistics. Any attempt to erect boundaries between 'the psychological' and 'the sociological' approaches to language is likely to be to the detriment of ourselves and also of those who are more specifically interested in psychological questions.

3.1.3 *Language, culture and thought*

The main purpose of the two previous sections was to clarify the terminology relating to culture and thought, and the relations between them. We have said little about language as such, so we can now try to fit language into the picture described so far. Let us see first of all what that picture looks like.

As we have seen, culture may be defined as the kind of knowledge which we learn from other people, either by direct instruction or by watching their behaviour. However, we distinguished two other kinds of knowledge, 'shared non-cultural knowledge' and 'non-shared non-cultural knowledge'. Of these, the shared kind is relevant to language, although it is not learned, but the non-shared kind can now be ignored since language always relates to concepts which are shared (or believed to be shared).

All three kinds of knowledge (as the term is used here) fall under the heading of 'memory' rather than 'inference', though of course one could extend the term to include things worked out for oneself on a particular occasion. For instance, if we were talking about the effects of multiplying two numbers together, a person's knowledge in this sense would include the answers which he has memorised as a result of learning the multiplication tables (e.g. 'two threes make six') and also the general rules for multiplication. However, if we extended 'knowledge' to include the product of inference, we could say that a person's knowledge includes the fact that twenty-three nineteens make 437, once he has done the necessary calculations.

All three kinds of knowledge may also involve concepts on their own, or related to each other in propositions; and both concepts and propositions are involved in inference as well as in memory. We can disregard the question whether there is any real difference in principle between a concept and a proposition, though we have been assuming that there is. We can also leave the relation between 'knowledge that' and 'knowledge how' (know-how), but assume for the present that they can both be included in the notion of a proposition. (This is a particularly important matter for the linguist, since it is questionable whether the rules of a language are a matter of knowing *that* such-and-such sentences are well formed and mean such-and-such or are a matter of knowing *how* to produce and understand sentences.) We have, however, taken a particular position on the nature of concepts. I have argued that at least some concepts are best seen as prototypes which define the clear cases, leaving less clear ones to be handled by inference, as and when they arise.

We can now turn to language. There are four points at which language makes contact with knowledge, which will be introduced in this section, and discussed in more detail later in this chapter.

(1) *Linguistic items are concepts.* In whichever way we understand the notion 'linguistic items' (see 2.1.2), we can see them as the categories which we use to analyse our experience, i.e. as concepts. For instance, each lexical item represents a combination of phonological, syntactic and semantic properties in just the same way that the concept 'fruit' represents a combination of properties to do with when the object is eaten, where it grows and whether it is sweet or savoury; similarly, a syntactic construction is defined by a complex configuration of properties in much the same way as the concept 'table' is defined by a particular arrangement of vertical and horizontal pieces. Moreover, it is increasingly clear that many (if not all) linguistic items are defined in terms of prototypes, just like non-linguistic concepts, which is why it is often impossible to draw a hard and fast distinction between 'good' and 'bad' sentences. For instance, the typical subject of a verb like *cook* is the person who does the cooking (*Mary cooked the meat*), but it can also be the instrument (*The oven cooked the meat*) or even the thing cooked (*The meat cooked well*). The prototype subject of *cook* combines a number of different properties, including being the 'agent' and 'having primary responsibility', but it is possible to generalise from this combination to cases where the subject merely has primary responsibility for the cooking, such as *The oven cooked the meat*. If even this feature is absent, the sentence becomes much less acceptable, as in *?The saucepan cooked the meat*. (For detailed discussion of examples like this, and arguments for a prototypical approach to linguistic items, see Lakoff 1977.)

(2) *Meanings are concepts.* There is considerable controversy over the definition of 'meaning'. but there is widespread agreement that the meaning of a linguistic item is its *sense*, that is, what is permanent about its relation to the world, rather than its *referents*, the objects or events to which it refers on particular occasions (see e.g. Kempson 1977: 12; Lyons 1977: ch. 7). More controversially, however, we can go on to identify the sense of an item with the concept to which it is related in the speaker's memory – in other words, with the concept that the item expresses. For instance, the sense of the word *cat* is the concept 'cat', which may well have existed in the person's memory before he ever learned the word to express it (for this view see Clark & Clark 1977: 439, 449). Not all linguistic items correspond to concepts like 'cat', however. For instance, some seem more like clues to help the hearer,

such as *the* in contrast with *a*. Perhaps the proper generalisation about meaning is that it is a mental entity, which may either be a concept or a procedure.

(3) *Linguistically relevant social categories are concepts.* As was pointed out at the end of 3.1.2, we may assume that people categorise speakers and circumstances in terms of concepts based, as usual, on prototypes. In the previous chapter we argued that speakers locate themselves in a multi-dimensional space in relation to the rest of their society, and locate each act of speaking in a multi-dimensional space relative to the rest of their social lives. We can now suggest that each 'dimension' is defined by a particular concept of a typical speaker or typical situation. This view allows us to predict many phenomena which are in fact found in sociolinguistics, such as the 'metaphorical code-switching' discussed in 2.5.1 and the different degrees to which people's speech identifies them with particular groups (chapter 5, especially 5.4.3, below).

(4) *Sentence-meanings are propositions.* To the extent that there is a distinction between concepts and propositions, we may say that most linguistic items which are stored in memory have concepts as their meanings, but the sentences formed by combining them express propositions. Unlike the meanings of stored linguistic items, such as words and constructions, the meaning of a spoken sentence is arrived at by inference, though there is of course nothing to prevent a whole sentence from being stored in memory, together with its meaning, and this frequently happens (typical examples are *A good time was had by all* and *Two and two make four*). This means that we ought to qualify the claim in (2) about meanings being concepts because that is true only of stored items which are smaller than clauses.

To simplify somewhat, we may conclude that what is stored as a language system is a set of remembered concepts, which are the items of language, together with the concepts or propositions which constitute their meanings, and more concepts which define their social distribution. When we speak or listen we make use of the concepts we already know in order to infer propositions (the meanings of sentences), and also to infer social categories, defined in terms of concepts.

As for the relation between language and culture, most of language is contained within culture, so it would not be far from the truth to say that 'a society's language is an aspect of its culture . . . The relation of language to culture is that of part to whole' (Goodenough 1957). The area of overlap between language and culture consists of all those parts

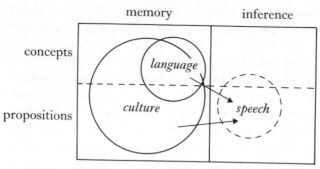

Figure 3.1. The relations between thought, culture, language and speech

of language which are learned from other people. However, we must allow some aspects not to be learned in this way, just as some concepts are clearly not learned from others. At least some of the concepts attached to words as their meanings are presumably of this kind (for instance a baby is likely to understand the concept 'vertical' before he learns the name for it), and there may be other aspects of language which a child does not need to *learn*, such as the inventory of phonetic features or the concepts 'noun' and 'verb'. To the extent that there are aspects of language which are not learnt from other people, language is not wholly contained within culture.

Figure 3.1 may help to clarify these relations between thought (the whole box), culture, language and speech (represented by the three circles within the box).

3.2 Linguistic and cultural relativity

3.2.1 *Word-meaning and semantic components*

Having clarified some of the connections between language, culture and thought, attention can now be paid to the two issues which have dominated the study of language in relation to culture and thought. Firstly, to what extent do languages and cultures differ from one another? Are they all in some sense cut to the same mould, reflecting a common underlying 'humanity', or do they differ arbitrarily and unrestrictedly from one another, reflecting the fact that different people live in very different intellectual and physical worlds? This is the question of RELATIVITY, which may be considered in relation either to language, or to non-linguistic aspects of culture, or to the area of contact between language and non-language in culture. The last of these relations is considered in this section, where we shall concentrate on how far meanings may differ from variety to variety, and whether there are any connections between differences in meaning and in culture. The second issue is DETERMINISM (to which we turn in 3.3), which is concerned with the influence of language on thought.

One aspect of relativity is very easily demonstrated since we can point to items in some languages which certainly express meanings not expressed in others. This can be seen in the difficulties of translating between languages that are associated with different cultures, and consequently have names for different ranges of customs (e.g. *birthday-party*), objects (*hovercraft, sausage*), institutions (*university*) and so on. When a need arises to express a concept for which there is no ready-made form in the language, two things can be done: the language can be changed, perhaps by introducing a new form to carry the desired meaning, or the existing resources of the language can be used to 'unpack' the meaning to be expressed. (Thus, 'university' might be expressed by the equivalent of *place where people go to learn difficult things when they are over eighteen.*) Either way, however, concepts which are expressed by remembered linguistic items in one language need not be expressed by such items in another language.

We can extend this claim in two directions. Firstly, we can take account of what we saw in chapter 2 and abandon the notion 'language' as an unhelpful and misleading concept, concentrating instead on the linguistic items known to an individual. This allows us to show that the kinds of difference referred to above with reference to whole communities are exactly paralleled by differences between individuals within a single community. Everyday experience tells us that some people know names for objects, institutions and so on which their family or friends do not know, and to that extent we may say that there are individual differences in the meanings expressed by people's collections of linguistic items. For instance, anyone who has read this far will already have a number of linguistic items in his or her memory (e.g. 'diglossia', 'linguistic item', 'isogloss') which are lacking in the language of someone who knows no sociolinguistics.

Secondly, we can remove any reference to non-linguistic culture, since there are meaning-differences in language which have nothing to do with other aspects of culture (at least so far as one can tell). For instance, in German there are two verbs meaning 'eat', one referring to eating by humans (*essen*) and the other to eating by animals (*fressen*), in contrast with English, where one verb *eat* covers both. German and English thus express different meanings by their linguistic items: German lacks the equivalent of English *eat*, and English lacks equivalents for the more specific German verbs (though both languages have a more general verb meaning 'consume', which covers the meaning of *drink* as well and is therefore irrelevant). Yet it would surely be hard to find any other aspect of the cultures of German and English speakers which relates in any way to this difference.

So far, then, we have seen that there are *some* differences between one person or community and another in the concepts that are expressed by their linguistic items, but this conclusion leaves a number of important questions unanswered. Is it possible that these differences would disappear if we looked at the COMPONENTS out of which meanings are made up rather than at the particular combinations in which these components appear in different language systems? If we did this, we should for instance find that German and English were less different than we thought in their verbs for eating, since all the individual components which contribute to the meaning of *essen* and *fressen* can be expressed in English by items such as *eat*, *human* and *animal*. More generally, it might seem that the possibility of 'unpacking' a meaning (as we did for the word *university*) shows that the components of meaning are shared by the language systems concerned. That is, even if someone has no single item for 'university', he will presumably have items for 'people', 'learn' and so on, which are arguably the components out of which meanings are built.

This possibility is widely accepted by linguists as the basis of their theory of semantics (for a useful discussion, see Kempson 1977: 96.) It poses problems, but before we consider them, let us look at a somewhat more extended example of semantic analysis in terms of components. (Generally called COMPONENTIAL ANALYSIS, this was first developed by anthropologists, notably William Goodenough (1956), for studying aspects of culture such as kinship.) The example deals with the pronouns of Palaung, a language spoken by a small tribe in Burma (Burling 1970: 14), where pronouns can be arranged in a neat system that distinguishes three separate components:

(i)   Does the pronoun refer to the speaker (among others)?
(ii) Does it refer to the addressee (among others)?
(iii) Does it refer to one, two or more than two entities?

Table 3.1. *Palaung pronouns (adapted from Burling 1970:17)*

(i) Speaker?	(ii) Hearer?	(iii) One	Two	More than two
yes	yes	–	ar	ɛ
yes	no	ɔ	yar	yɛ
no	yes	mi	par	pɛ
no	no	ʌn	gar	gɛ

Table 3.1 shows how these components intersect to determine the form of the pronoun.

Pronouns make more distinctions with respect to these components in Palaung than in English. In particular, English makes no distinction between 'two' and 'more than two' or between 'speaker and hearer' ('inclusive *we*') and 'speaker and someone other than hearer' ('exclusive *we*'). On the other hand, all three components are in fact used at some point in English. For the components 'speaker' and 'hearer', we need look no further than the pronoun system, where both are needed to distinguish *we* (speaker included), *you* (hearer included, but not speaker) and *they* (neither included). For the number component, English distinguishes between *all* and *both*, or *none* and *neither*, precisely according to whether there are just two or more than two referents. It can therefore be seen that Palaung and English do not differ in their semantic components but in the way the components are used.

The hypothesis we are considering, that languages differ only in the way in which semantic components combine and not in their actual components, seems to be supported by such data (which could of course be multiplied many times over). However, there is an immediate problem if we take seriously the claim (made in 3.1.3) that meanings themselves are (single) concepts. If this is so, it follows that the meaning of a word like the English *we* is a single concept, which includes 'speaker' and 'many' among its defining features, rather than as components of the meaning of *we* as such. In other words, the relation between words and concepts like 'speaker', 'hearer' and 'many' is only indirect, mediated by the concept that brings them together as a 'meaning'. If we take this point of view it could be objected that what we have been calling 'semantic components' are not really part of semantics at all, but rather belong to the general cognitive structure. The conclusion of this argument is that meanings in different languages are very different after all (most Palaung pronouns have meanings which are not expressed by any English pronoun, and vice versa). However, we may consider this primarily as a matter of terminological debate, which need not be pursued seriously here.

3.2.2 *Prototypes*

One consequence of studying the components that contribute to meaning is that the semantic systems of different languages begin to look very much less different than if meanings are seen as unanalysed wholes. In the same way, if meanings are examined in relation to proto-types (see 3.1.2), it can be shown that the prototypes around which the meanings of words are organised are far less different than the total areas of meaning covered by the words. This is true of two areas of vocabu-lary – colour and kinship – which have frequently been quoted as show-ing extreme *differences* between languages. As far as colour is concerned, linguists and ethnographers had for long been struck by the fact that different languages seemed to divide the colour spectrum along com-pletely different lines. For instance, in Zuni a single term corresponds to English *orange* plus *yellow* (Bolinger 1975: 245), and the Welsh word *glas* covers the same range as the English *green*, *blue* and *grey*. Similarly there are some quite startling differences between languages in the way they cover kinship concepts, as we shall see below. (For further dis-cussion of colour terminology, see Clark & Clark (1977: 524) and Rosch (1974), which is also a good survey of recent empirical studies on linguistic relativity.)

The main developments to which we shall refer in connection with kinship terminology are due to the anthropologist Floyd Lounsbury, who arrived at the notion of meanings centred on prototypes inde-pendently of the psychological work of Eleanor Rosch referred to in 3.1.2 (see especially Lounsbury 1969 and discussion in Burling 1970: 49). Let us start by looking at the kind of data which confront the linguist or anthropologist studying kinship terminology.

In various societies, including the Seminole Indians of Oklahoma and Florida and the inhabitants of the Trobriand Islands (to the east of New Guinea), the same term (X) may be used to refer to the following relations:

(i)   father
(ii) father's brother (English *uncle*)
(iii) father's sister's son (English *cousin*)

(iv) father's mother's sister's son (English ?)
(v) father's sister's daughter's son (English ?)
(vi) father's father's brother's son (English?)
(vii) father's father's sister's son's son (English ?)

The English terms in parentheses, where there are any, are not at all accurate translations, as they have wider senses than the meanings given. For instance, *uncle* refers either to one's father's brother or to one's mother's brother, whereas X cannot be used to refer to one's mother's brother. Moreover, for most of us there is simply no term in English to refer to senses (iv)–(vii), though no doubt those who are sufficiently expert in these matters (a small minority in Britain) could construct some compound like *second cousin twice removed*. It is hardly worth emphasising that there is no term in English corresponding in meaning to term X in these languages.

Not only is the meaning of X baffling for the ordinary English speaker, but it would also puzzle the analyst in search of common features defining the people that can be referred to as one's X. One common feature is that the person concerned must be male, but beyond that it is hard to see any set of defining characteristics of the set covered by X. (It should be noted that X does not mean 'male blood relative on one's father's side' since it does not include 'father's father', for example.) However, if one takes the 'prototype' approach instead of looking for defining features, things look very different. According to Lounsbury, all of these meanings may be predicted by assuming that the basic meaning (the prototype) is simply 'father', and that the other meanings are derived from this by applying any of the following three equivalence rules:

A. a man's sister is equivalent to his mother;
B. siblings (i.e. brothers or sisters) of the same sex are equivalent to each other;
C. half-siblings are equivalent to full-siblings.

These three rules are needed to predict the meanings of other kinship terms in the same languages, and only these rules are needed.

To start with an easy example, 'father's brother' (ii) is derived from 'father' by rule B, since the father and his brother are siblings of the same sex and are therefore equivalent. For 'father's sister's son' (iii), we first apply rule B, converting 'father' into 'father's brother', then rule C, replacing 'brother' by 'mother's son' (a way of referring to a half-brother), giving 'father's mother's son', and finally rule A, replacing

Table 3.2. *Derivation of kinship terms in certain languages*

Rule	Meaning
prototype	father
B sibling = sibling	father's brother
C half-sibling = full	father's father's son
B sibling = sibling	father's father's brother's son
C half-sibling = full	father's father's mother's son's son
A sister = mother	father's father's sister's son's son

'father's mother' by 'father's sister', giving the desired relationship 'father's sister's son'. Table 3.2 shows how meaning (vii), 'father's father's sister's son's son', can be derived from 'father'.

One striking thing about this analysis is that the basic meaning of term X is now exactly the same as that of English *father*, and the differences between them are due to the existence of rules of derivation which exist in other languages but not in English. (It should be noted that the English word *father* too has secondary, derived, meanings, such as 'priest' and 'adoptive father'.) This discovery opens the possibility that if we compare the prototype meanings of kinship terminology from different languages (assuming that we can identify such meanings for them all), we shall find that there are relatively few variations on a few very general patterns, though we may expect differences in the rules of derivation. The differences in those rules cannot be dismissed as unimportant, of course, because they can have dramatic and far-reaching consequences, but at least we seem to have restricted the kinds of differences between kinship terminologies in different languages, and no longer see them as evidence for extreme relativity.

It would be wrong, however, to leave the impression that the prototype approach makes all kinship systems look the same except for their derivation rules, since this is certainly not the case. Even prototype meanings may be closely related to the social organisation of the society concerned. For instance, there is an Australian aborigine tribe called the Njamal whose marriage customs refer to a unit which anthropologists call 'moiety', since it divides the tribe into two halves (cf. French *moitié* 'half'). (The following account is based on Burling 1970: 21.) One's moiety is always the same as one's father's, but different from one's mother's since the rules require husbands and wives to belong to different moieties. The importance of moiety differences is reflected not only in the derivation rules (which are formulated so as not to mix relatives from different moieties under the same term) but *also* in the prototype meanings. For instance, there are four words referring basically to members of one's parents' generation: one each, as one would expect, for 'father' and 'mother', but also one for 'mother's brother' and one for 'father's sister'. Why should these two relations be picked out for special treatment, to the exclusion, say, of 'father's brother'? The answer is presumably that they provide a basic sex contrast independent of the moiety contrast (for instance, one's father and one's father's sister are of one's own moiety but of opposite sexes, and one's mother and her brother are of the other moiety but of different sexes). In contrast, one's father's brother is both of the same moiety and of the same sex as one's father, and would therefore not be a usefully distinct prototype.

Even if we take the prototype approach to kinship terminology, there is still ample scope for reflecting differences in social organisation, either in the prototypes themselves or in the rules for deriving other meanings from them. (For example, the concept 'father' itself can be defined in terms of a number of different factors such as biological paternity and status as guardian, and such factors may be given different emphases in different societies.) Moreover, it seems likely that a concept like 'moiety' will need to be referred to in defining prototypes in languages like Njamal, but not in languages which are associated with other kinds of social system, so we cannot even be sure that the 'semantic components' referred to in prototypes are 'universal' in any very significant sense.

One final point about the notion 'prototype' itself. We have considered three different ways in which a word's prototypical meaning may be extended. Firstly, a speaker or hearer may use what we called 'creative flexibility' (3.1.2), which means that he is making an original extension to the meaning, which we might quite legitimately call 'metaphorical' (e.g. when applying an established prototype to a totally exotic object which fits it only poorly). Secondly, there may be accepted and clear rules for extending meanings, as in the case of Lounsbury's analysis of kinship terminology, and we may perhaps assume that at least some of the extended meanings are worked out afresh each time, rather than being stored away in the speaker's memory. And thirdly, there are words whose meanings centre on some prototype but whose extended meanings are presumably stored in memory as well. For instance, we must assume that the sense of *father* which allows it to be applied to a Catholic priest is stored in memory, although it is derived, at least historically, from the primary, biological, meaning of *father*. There are many interesting and important questions to be asked about the relations among these three types of extension, which we cannot pursue here, but any reader who is at all familiar with the study of *word-formation* will see that the ways in which prototype meanings are extended can be matched exactly by the ways in which, say, 'ordinal' numbers are formed. For instance, a speaker who says *twenty-seventh* is presumably creating a new form by applying a rule (case 2), one who says *first* or *second* must be extracting a form from his memory (case 3), and one who wants to refer to an example numbered *3a* and refers to it as *the 3a-th example* is acting creatively (case 1). (For discussion of word-formation, see e.g. Bolinger 1975: 108, Leech 1974: ch. 10, Matthews 1974: ch. 3.)

3.2.3 *Basic-level concepts*

We have seen that focussing on components and prototypes has the effect of reducing the differences between languages in the meanings they express. We now come to a theory also developed by the psychologist Eleanor Rosch (who, it will be recalled, developed the notion of prototype in psychology), which suggests that there may be less difference than might be expected in the *organisation* of word-meanings (see e.g. Clark & Clark 1977, Rosch 1976; the theory was anticipated in some respects by Brown 1958a, b). It starts from the natural assumption that the way in which a language structures the world, through the meanings which it distinguishes, depends partly on the way in which the world itself is structured and partly on the communicative needs of its speakers. The notion of the 'prototype' arises from the fact that in the world itself features do not combine randomly, but tend to occur in complex bundles. For instance a thing which has feathers is likely also to have two legs, to fly, to lay eggs and to have a beak. All we are doing when we create a concept of a prototype is to recognise this fact about the world, while allowing for the fact that there are exceptional cases. It can be argued that this is a more efficient approach than the alternative, of working out watertight categories with their respective sufficient and necessary defining features.

Another consequence which Rosch draws from her basic assumption is that there should be what she calls BASIC-LEVEL CONCEPTS, in contrast with other concepts which are either more general or more specific. Assuming that there is at least some hierarchical structure in our concepts, with more general ones like 'furniture' subsuming less general ones like 'chair', it should be possible to work out which level in the hierarchy gives the most information (i.e. involves the most components in each concept) in return for the least effort (i.e. using the smallest number of distinct concepts). For instance, it is much more informative to say 'I bought a chair' than 'I bought a piece of furniture', because *chair* implies several physical features (a horizontal surface, legs, a vertical back), whereas there are no such features shared by all pieces of furniture, and similarly *chair* carries information about function, in terms of a 'motor programme', telling one what to do with it, in contrast with *furniture*, which only carries the vaguest of functional information. On the other hand, *kitchen chair* conveys only one extra feature compared with *chair*, a feature which in any case would normally be of little relevance to the situation, and the effort needed in order to identify an object as a kitchen chair, rather than just a chair, is greater in that this particular feature has to be recognised. Accordingly, *chair* is a basic-level concept, in the sense that it is the category that comes to mind most naturally when we have to refer to an object which could equally truly be described as a piece of furniture, a chair or a kitchen chair. There is obvious support for this conclusion in the fact that *chair* is just one word, in contrast with both *kitchen chair* and *piece of furniture*, but the main evidence comes from the ways in which speakers use these terms, as studied by Rosch.

The relevance of basic-level concepts to the question of relativity is two-fold. First, if it is true that concepts tend to be organised hierarchically around basic ones, we should expect to see similarities between languages in the hierarchical organisation of their vocabulary. This prediction has been confirmed by studies of 'folk biology' carried out by the anthropologist Brent Berlin and colleagues (summarised in Clark & Clark 1977: 528), who found that the names for plants and animals are organised into five or six levels, in a wide variety of languages, of which the third from the top is the 'basic' one. For instance, English has a hierarchy represented by terms like *plant*, *tree*, *pine*, *Ponderosa pine* and *northern Ponderosa pine*, and in this hierarchy the third level, represented by *pine*, is the lowest at which a single word is used, suggesting that it is basic. Rather amazingly, Berlin and his colleagues found that all the languages they studied had about the same number of level-3 terms in the 'biology' hierarchy – about 500. Taken together, these findings represent a high degree of similarity between languages in their semantic structure, even though the particular concepts concerned might be quite different according to the kinds of plants and animals found where the particular language was spoken.

The second connection between basic-level concepts and relativity is that they offer an additional area with respect to which people may *differ* in their language, thus making the relativity of language look rather greater. People differ in the particular concepts which they treat as basic. For instance, research done by Rosch showed that people who live in towns treat 'tree' rather than, say, 'pine' as basic (Rosch 1976) – presumably because they are less familiar with the specific properties of pine trees than the country-dwellers with whom Berlin and his colleagues mainly worked. Conversely, we might expect that 'Ponderosa pine' might be the basic level for a forester, and that this would be reflected by an abbreviation of the name to a single word, *Ponderosa* (Clark & Clark 1977: 553). (An alternative name for 'pine' is *pine tree*, and it would be interesting to know whether those who treat 'tree' as the basic-level concept are more likely than country-dwellers to use this longer form for 'pine'.)

3.2.4 *Conclusions*

There are a number of important aspects of relativity which have not been discussed in the preceding sections, in particular the question of relativity in those areas of meaning that are reflected in syntax or morphology rather than vocabulary. We have concentrated on the latter, however, because our intuitive expectation is that we will find less variability in the propositions which can be expressed through syntax, than in the concepts defined in vocabulary. It is therefore of more significance if relativity is found to be limited even in vocabulary. Similarly, there are vast differences between languages in the concepts which morphology reflects, varying from those where there is no morphology at all to languages where it is incredibly rich and expressive. On the other hand, a number of concepts such as those dealing with time, number and 'mood' (the speaker's attitude to what he is saying, such as his certainty about a proposition) are among those which are expressed through morphology in many languages. There may thus be quite severe restrictions on relativity in the semantics corresponding to morphology, which, like syntax, would be a less promising area to search for relativity than vocabulary.

The following conclusions therefore refer only to meaning as reflected in the vocabulary, which means in effect that we are considering only the half of meaning that deals with concepts rather than propositions. We have found that the position called 'extreme relativism' is untenable, since there are clear restrictions on the nature and extent of differences between people in the concepts that their languages express. Some of these restrictions are because different people, from widely different societies, may use the same concepts in defining the meanings of words, i.e. their word-meanings may be defined in terms of 'semantic components' which may be common to many, or even all, humans. A semantic component can be universal because it is part of the normal human cognitive make-up, such as the human ability to perceive shapes and colours, or because it is part of the normal human environment, such as the contrast between 'vertical' and 'horizontal', or between different members of the biological family group.

Other restrictions on relativity can be explained in terms of the common communicative needs of humans, notably the need to convey the maximum amount of information with the minimum amount of effort. This leads to the apparently universal tendency to give priority to 'basic-level' concepts over both higher- and lower-level concepts, and the similarities in the hierarchical structures of the vocabulary irrespective of the actual content of the meanings expressed. Other restrictions are because of the tendency of the world to structure itself, by offering ready-made concepts to be used as prototypes, which seem to vary less from one society or person to another than the 'extended' concepts built onto the prototypes (see the discussion above of the word for 'father' in various languages).

It must be emphasised that all these conclusions are hypotheses which have only been tested against quite small bodies of data, but they are at least as convincing as the alternative hypotheses of extreme relativism and extreme universalism (which claims that there are *no* differences in the meanings expressed by different vocabulary systems). What is more, they have the attractions of being supported both by extremely simple explanations and by a certain amount of plausible data.

To balance the conclusions showing that differences are restricted, we must now summarise the conclusions which show that differences exist and are, in fact, extensive. We have seen that there are differences in the semantic components involved in even highly structured and universal areas such as kinship terminology (e.g. 'moiety' is relevant in some systems but not in others); and it is obvious that there are differences in the ways in which the components combine in word-meanings (cf. pronouns in Palaung and English). Similarly, there are differences in the prototypes which are recognised (e.g. 'university' or any prototype which refers to 'moiety'), and vast differences in the ways in which prototypes may be extended (e.g. the three rules for extending kinship prototypes in languages like Seminole, which are not found elsewhere). Finally, there are differences in the concepts which different people take as basic, varying from one large community to another, or varying within one community according to a speaker's expertise. In short, similarities and differences exist in sufficiently large numbers, and in sufficiently specific forms, to make the semantics of vocabulary worth a good deal more comparative study than it has so far received.

3.3 **Language, speech and thought**
3.3.1 *Language and the rest of culture*
We now turn to the question of *linguistic determinism*. To what extent, and in what ways, does language determine thought? This question is normally answered with reference to the SAPIR–WHORF HYPOTHESIS, according to which language determines thought to a very great extent and in many ways, and we shall discuss this hypothesis briefly in 3.3.5. However, there are several other points of contact between language or speech and thought.

The first connection to be established is between language and other aspects of culture. To the extent that linguistic items are learned from other people, they are one part of the culture as a whole and as such are likely to be closely associated with other aspects of the culture that are learned from the same people. We might therefore expect that if a particular person learns two different linguistic items from different groups of people, each might be associated with a different set of cultural beliefs and values. Furthermore, it would not be surprising if each item activates a different set of such beliefs and values as it is used, and to that extent we could say that language (in this case, the choice of one linguistic variety rather than another) was determining thought.

There is some evidence that this can indeed happen, as was shown by the behaviour of a number of women born in Japan who moved to the

United States as wives of American ex-servicemen and learned English there. These women took part in an experiment organised by Susan Ervin-Tripp, a pioneer in the psychological and sociological study of language (Ervin-Tripp 1954, 1964). Each woman was interviewed once in English and once in Japanese and asked to perform various tasks that involved the creative use of language. One was to complete, in the language appropriate to the interview, a number of sentence-fragments, e.g. *I like to read* ... (or its Japanese translation). In a typical Japanese interview this might be completed by ... *about sociology*, reflecting a Japanese set of values, whereas in her English interview the same woman might produce *I like to read comics once in a while because they sort of relax my mind*, reflecting, presumably, the values which she had learned in America. Similar differences emerged from another of the tasks, in which the women were asked to say what was happening in a picture showing a farm, with a farmer ploughing in the background, a woman leaning against a tree, and a girl in the foreground carrying books on her arm. In the Japanese interview, a typical description was as follows:

> A student feels in conflict about being sent to college. Her mother is sick and the father works hard without much financial reward. Nevertheless, he continues to work diligently, without saying anything, praying for the daughter's success. Also he is a husband who never complains to his wife.

When the interview was in English, on the other hand, the same woman might give the following description:

> A sociology student observing farmers at work is struck by the difficulty of farm life.

It would be unwise to base too many conclusions on this rather small and in some ways unsatisfactory piece of research. For instance, it is not clear how many of the women involved showed such considerable changes in attitude from one language to another, or how many tasks produced such changes; and in any case it is always dangerous to generalise from what people do in formal experimental interview situations. However, the findings are at least compatible with what we predicted on the basis of the connections between language and the rest of culture, so it is quite plausible to suggest that we make use of different value and belief systems according to which linguistic varieties we happen to be using at the time.

3.3.2   *Speech and inference*

The next connection to be established is between speech and what we are calling 'inference', which is meant to include all aspects of thought which are not covered by 'memory' (see 3.1.2). There is no doubt that in some cases speech influences inference by making it easier or more difficult, i.e. in some cases speech acts as a *tool*. For instance, most readers will probably agree that they use speech to help them if they have a relatively complicated calculation to do in their heads, such as adding up a column of figures or multiplying two numbers which go beyond their memorised tables. Similarly, many people mutter to themselves if they have to solve some complicated problem like putting a clock back together or organising an essay. Of course, the value of speech as a tool is even more obvious if the inference has to be done cooperatively, since speech allows two people, or more, to agree on a definition of the problem and then to discuss its solution.

These connections between speech and inference are sufficiently obvious to need no supporting evidence, but there is evidence that the influence of speech on inferential thought is even more pervasive. Speech used in defining a problem may have radical consequences for our ability to solve it. For instance, in an experiment reported in Clark & Clark (1977: 556), subjects were given a candle, a box of tacks and two or three matches, and asked to find a way of fixing the candle to the wall in an upright position so that the wax would not drip. Some subjects were simply given the objects and told what to do, but others were also told what the objects were – a box, some tacks, some matches and a candle. Naming the objects drew attention to the box as a separate object, rather than just a container for the tacks, and this led those concerned to see the solution to the problem – tack the box to the wall and stand the candle on top of it. Those who were simply given the objects took an average of nearly fifteen times longer to solve the problem than those who had the objects named. On the other hand, it seems likely that the help came not simply from being given names, but from having the *relevant* ones. If *a box of tacks* had been used instead of *a box* and *some tacks* we must assume that they would have been of no help – indeed, it is conceivable that they would have made the problem even harder to solve, since they would perhaps have reinforced the tendency to disregard the box. It is a pity that this possibility was not tested in the experiment.

The relevance of this to sociolinguistics may not at first be obvious, but it becomes clearer when we remember that one of the main social functions of speech is in the area of problem-solving, to enable us to 'talk through a problem' with other people. Often the solution comes simply from the act of talking about it, rather than from any particular suggestion made by someone else – talking about a matter helps us to see it more clearly. As we come to a better understanding of the influence of speech on inference, we shall see why this is so.

3.3.3 *Speech and socialisation*

Another point of contact between speech and thought is its use by an older generation to transmit its culture to a younger one. In other words, speech is an instrument of SOCIALISATION – the process whereby children are turned into fully competent members of their society. Obviously not all of culture is transmitted via speech – for instance there are many aspects of observable behaviour which are learned simply by watching, such as how to walk, how to laugh and how to beckon (all things which vary from society to society). Indeed, one could say that most of language itself is learned in this way, since speech is not normally used as an instrument for imparting knowledge of language, but rather as a model to be emulated. However, a good deal of culture is transmitted verbally, and it is often said that the development of the faculty of language by the human species made it possible for 'biological evolution', working on genes, to be replaced as the dominant factor in our development by 'cultural evolution', working on our minds. There is no need to labour the point that speech is a crucial component in the process of socialisation.

Interestingly, however, people appear to differ in the ways in which they use speech in socialisation. Different university or college lecturers, whose main task is in fact to socialise students into their own particular areas of culture, provide a good illustration of this. Some lecturers use speech to communicate specific facts rather than general principles; others put the emphasis the other way round; others put as much emphasis on entertainment or arousing interest; and still others try hard to involve the students emotionally and intellectually by getting *them* to use speech in developing issues. Similar differences exist between politicians, preachers, advertisers and journalists. Differences that are of interest in the present context are not those of register (see 2.4), which have to do with *how* something is said, but rather with *what* is said, and which aspects of the socialisation process are most emphasised.

Turning to the most obvious subjects of socialisation, young children, there is some evidence that parents – specifically, mothers – make different uses of speech in socialising their children. This evidence comes mainly from the work of the sociologists Basil Bernstein, of London, and Robert Hess, of Chicago (Bernstein & Henderson 1969, Hess & Shipman 1965; for a useful summary see Robinson 1972: ch. 9). The hypothesis under investigation was that mothers from different social classes used speech differently in socialisation. If true, this hypothesis was expected to offer a partial explanation for differences between children from different social classes in the ways in which they in turn used speech. We shall discuss the claimed differences in the children's speech in 6.3.2 and 6.4.2, and shall restrict ourselves here to the question of the mothers' speech.

Most of the evidence comes from interviews in which mothers were asked about hypothetical situations – for instance, 'How much harder would it be for parents to do X with young children if parents could not speak?' (where X might be 'playing games with them' or 'showing them what is right and wrong', or a variety of other specially selected types of activity, covering different aspects of socialisation), or 'What would you say if your child brought home some object picked up on a building site?' There are obvious problems in interpreting the answers to questions like the latter if one is primarily interested in what the mothers actually *do* say in real-life situations rather than in what they say they would say; in particular, there is a danger that some mothers would idealise their behaviour. However, there was such consistency among the answers, and they accorded so well with the results of a few experiments which tested mothers' actual behaviour (in an experimental situation), that we can take them as reflecting more or less directly what the mothers really would do and say.

The conclusion of this research is that there are indeed differences between 'average' mothers from the middle class and the lower working class (the two classes compared in Bernstein's work). 'Average' middle-class mothers use speech more than lower-working-class mothers in personal matters involving emotions, whereas the latter are more likely than the former to use speech for teaching skills. Middle-class mothers are also more likely than lower-working-class mothers to use speech in explanation of commands ('You mustn't do that because . . .'), and to give factual information about things and people, with the consequence (presumably) that they are more likely to stimulate and satisfy curiosity in the children.

If these findings are correct, it is clear that they have far-reaching implications, both theoretical and practical, and we shall discuss some of these in 6.4. Unfortunately, the evidence for differences in 'maternal style' is part of a general theory which also contained, at one time, a sub-theory about specifically linguistic differences between middle-class and working-class children which is now largely discredited (see 6.3.2), and has distracted critics from taking the question of maternal style seriously.

As we might expect, gross differences can be found in the role that speech is allowed to play in socialisation between cultures. For example, the Gonja of West Africa regard questioning as a way of asserting authority over another person, so it is considered inappropriate for a pupil to ask his teacher questions. Consequently apprentice weavers, for instance, are expected to pick up the art of weaving without ever asking direct questions about it (Goody 1978). Examples like this show how the demands of one aspect of socialisation (not using questions to one's superiors) may conflict with those of other aspects (learning to weave), and the same may be said too of the social class differences in maternal styles mentioned above.

3.3.4 *Language and socialisation*

Speech is an important factor in socialisation, not only through the information that it is used to impart, but also through the concepts which it requires the child to identify as meanings for the linguistic items he learns from other people's speech. In other words, the language which a child learns is closely related to the concepts he learns as part of his socialisation. The question is whether language can be said to influence these concepts, or whether it simply reflects concepts which would be there in any case. The answer seems to be 'A bit of each'.

We can be sure that some concepts are independent of language, including those we learned as babies before the acquisition of language towards the end of the first year of life, and others which are formed later, but without recourse to language since we have no words for them in our adult vocabulary. For instance, we have a concept for the kinds of things we buy at a newsagent (or a tobacconist, or a 'do-it-yourself' shop), but no name for any of these concepts, in contrast with concepts for things bought in other kinds of shop, e.g. *groceries*. Whether or not there is a name for these concepts seems to have little to do with our ability to learn them. Similarly, we can see the similarities among nails, screws, rivets, and nuts and bolts – they have similar functions and we might expect people to store them together – but there is no name for this concept. Examples like this are easy to multiply, and warn us against the danger of assuming that concepts only exist when there is specific linguistic evidence for them. Interestingly, it seems that such 'lexical gaps' tend to occur at the levels above the 'basic' one (see 3.2.3). (Gaps below this level are harder to identify, since they can easily be filled by a compound form like *Ponderosa pine*.)

On the other hand, we can be equally sure that there are other concepts which we should not have if it were not for language. The most obvious cases are those which relate to language as a phenomenon – the concepts 'language', 'meaning', 'word' and so on. However, there are other concepts which we learn *after* we have learned their names, and for which the name is our main evidence. For instance, Clark & Clark (1977: 486) quote an incident where a mother said to her 5-year-old child, 'We have to keep the screen door closed, honey, so the flies won't come in. Flies bring germs into the house with them.' When the child was asked afterwards what germs were, the answer was 'Something the flies play with'! This example illustrates nicely the way in which a new word may act as evidence that an unknown concept exists, leaving the learner with the problem of somehow working out what that concept is, making use of any evidence that may be available. Many students of linguistics must find themselves doing just this on occasions, when they come across terms like *complementiser* or even *empirical*.

Moreover, we learn many concepts by being told about them, especially during our formal education, so we do in fact learn them through language, whether or not we could have learned them without it. If it were not for language we should probably not have concepts to which we could attach words like *peninsula*, *feudal*, *metabolism*, *classical* or *factor*. One of the main functions of education is to teach concepts, and technical terminology is the teacher's most important teaching aid in this task. (It should be noted, however, that there is a tendency for teachers to confuse knowledge of the concept with knowledge of the correct technical term for it.)

In conclusion, we can say that language is more important in learning some concepts than others, and the general principle may be that language becomes more important as the concepts concerned get further from one's immediate sensory experience – in other words, more abstract.

3.3.5 *The Sapir–Whorf hypothesis*

Finally we come to the celebrated 'Sapir–Whorf hypothesis', so named after the American linguists Edward Sapir (1884–1939) and Benjamin Lee Whorf (one of Sapir's pupils 1897–1941). Both Sapir and Whorf worked extensively on American Indian languages and made important contributions to our knowledge of those languages and also to linguistic theory (to say nothing of Sapir's contributions to anthropology and psychology). The work most clearly relevant to the hypothesis was done in the 1930s, towards the end of their respective careers, so their ideas represent the results of two distinguished lifetimes devoted to the serious study of language and culture, and cannot be dismissed lightly. On the other hand, it is not at all clear exactly what formulation of the hypothesis Sapir and Whorf would themselves have accepted, since neither tried to define any such hypothesis, and both changed their views radically on relevant matters from time to time. Accordingly, it is best to start with an extreme version of what later scholars have understood by the 'Sapir–Whorf hypothesis', stated in terms of the categories we have already introduced. (For discussions of the Sapir–Whorf hypothesis, see e.g. Brown 1958b: 229–63, Carroll 1956: 'Introduction', 1964: ch. 7, Slobin 1971; Sapir's collected works are available in Mandelbaum 1949, and Whorf's in Carroll 1956.)

Our extreme version of the hypothesis is a combination of extreme relativism with extreme determinism. It claims that there are no restrictions on the amount and type of variation to be expected between languages, including their semantic structures, and that the determining effect of language on thought is total – there is no thought without language. If we put these two claims together, we arrive at the conclusion that there are no constraints on the variation to be found between people in the way they think, especially in the concepts they form. It also follows that if one can find a way to control the language that people learn, one would thereby be able to control their thoughts, as in George Orwell's novel *1984*.

It is clear that the extreme hypothesis is wrong. We have cited reasons for rejecting both of its constituents in the last two sections so we need not repeat the arguments, but at the same time there is *some* truth in both relativism and determinism, so we may expect language to be responsible for *some* differences in people's concepts. An extract from Whorf (1940) can be quoted, which gives one of the most extreme formulations of his and Sapir's theory, in order to see how it compares with our extreme hypothesis:

> ... the background linguistic system (in other words the grammar) of each language is not merely a reproducing instrument for voicing ideas but rather is itself the shaper of ideas, the program and guide for the individual's mental activity, for his analysis of impressions, for his synthesis of his mental stock in trade. Formulation of ideas is not an independent process, strictly rational in the old sense, but is part of a particular grammar, and differs, from slightly to greatly, between different grammars. We dissect nature along lines laid down by our native language. The categories and types that we isolate from the world of phenomena we do not find there because they stare every observer in the face; on the contrary, the world is presented in a kaleidoscopic flux of impressions which has to be organized by our minds – and this means *largely* by the linguistic systems in our minds. We cut nature up and organize it into concepts, and ascribe significances as we do, *largely* because we are parties to an agreement to organize it in this way – an agreement that holds throughout our speech community and is codified in the patterns of our language. The agreement is, of course an implicit and unstated one, BUT ITS TERMS ARE ABSOLUTELY OBLIGATORY; we cannot talk at all except by subscribing to the organization and classification of data which the agreement decrees ... We are thus introduced to a new principle of relativity, which holds that all observers are not led by the same physical evidence to the same picture of the universe, unless their linguistic backgrounds are similar, or can in some way be calibrated.

In this quotation we see something of the problem of interpreting Whorf and Sapir. Some passages represent extreme relativity and extreme determinism – e.g. 'We dissect nature along lines laid down by our native language' – yet others are qualified by the word *largely* (italicised by me, not Whorf), which leaves open the possibility of some thought independent of language. So can this passage really be said to represent the extreme version of the hypothesis?

It should be clear, however, that virtually everything that this passage says, so eloquently, runs counter to the points we have made in this chapter. It is ideas that shape language, rather than vice versa, except in relatively abstract areas of thought. Formulation of ideas *is* on the whole an independent process, relative to language. We dissect the universe along lines laid down by nature and by our communicative and cognitive needs, rather than by our language. The meanings of linguistic items *can* be adjusted by the individual to fit his needs, by metaphorical extensions; and to the extent that meanings are learned from others there is no need for a 'speech community' as a whole to agree on them, since there are many specialist sub-communities with their own semantic systems. On the other hand, the fact that two linguists as outstandingly competent and experienced as Sapir and Whorf could believe otherwise offers sobering food for thought, suggesting that any claims about language and thought (including those made in this chapter) should not be accepted lightly.

4
Speech as social interaction

4.1 The social nature of speech

4.1.1 *Introduction*

In this chapter we shall focus on what we have been referring to as 'speech' – that is, shorter or longer strings of linguistic items used on particular occasions for particular purposes. We have been using the term to include both written and spoken texts though we have had little to say about the former as such. We shall say nothing about written texts in this chapter, and indeed we shall also ignore various kinds of spoken texts, in order to concentrate on what is called FACE-TO-FACE INTERACTION – in other words, what happens when one person talks to another whom he can see and who is near enough to hear him. Although we shall, therefore, exclude all kinds of impersonal communication such as the mass media, despite their importance in modern life (and also the speech of a person talking to himself), this still leaves a wide range of activities: conversations, quarrels, jokes, committee meetings, interviews, seductions, introductions, lessons, teasing, chit-chat and a host of others.

One of the main questions we must again ask concerns the balance between the social and the individual. For *language*, in the sense of knowledge of linguistic items and their meanings, the balance is in favour of the social, since people learn their language by listening to others. At the same time, each individual's language is unique, since no two people have the same experience of language. What about the balance in the case of speech? Ferdinand de Saussure claimed that speech was totally individual, in that it depended only on the 'will of the speaker' (1916/1959: 19), and conversely that language was entirely social, being identical from one member of a speech community to another. He was clearly wrong about language, but was he any nearer to the truth about speech? We shall see that he was not.

106

We have seen that speech is crucial in a number of social activities, including socialisation (see 3.3.3), and it is hardly necessary to stress the general importance of speech in social life. Speech allows us to communicate with each other at a much more sophisticated level than would otherwise be possible, and since communication is a social activity it could be said that speech is also social. Although this is true, it is not directly relevant to de Saussure's claim about speech being individual, since he was referring to the knowledge involved in speech, rather than the uses to which that activity is put, holding that speech involved no social constraints, in contrast with language, which was entirely so constrained. So long as a speaker knew the relevant language – which for de Saussure meant knowing which sound-sequences were allowed to be used for which meanings – he would be able to speak it properly simply by applying it as he chose. What we need to show, therefore, is that there are social constraints on speech over and above those which are reflected in the linguistic items which people know.

It is clear that there are many such contraints, which may differ from society to society. For example, in Britain we are required to respond when someone else greets us; when we refer to someone, we are required to take account of what the addressee already knows about him; when we address a person, we must choose our words carefully, to show our social relation to him; when someone else is talking we are required to keep more or less silent (but not totally so). However, the same is not necessarily true in all societies, as we shall see. Our task in the present chapter is to consider the types of constraint that are imposed upon us by the society in which we live, and to relate them to what we do as individuals – either obeying or flouting the social constraints, and, in situations where custom offers no guidelines, using our own initiative. By the end of the chapter, it should be clear that the balance between society and individual is in favour of the latter as far as speech is concerned – so to that extent de Saussure was right – but that there are far more social constraints on our speech than we may at first realise.

Another thing which will become apparent is that the distinction between 'language' and 'social constraints on speech' is anything but clear, since many of the constraints discussed below refer to specific linguistic items, or more or less large classes of items, and could therefore be treated as part of language, along with what we know about meanings. This is not surprising, since many items have meanings which refer specifically to aspects of the speech-events in which they are used –

notably all the items with DEICTIC meanings, referring to the speaker (*I*, *we*), the addressee (*you*), the time of speaking (present/past tense, *today*, etc.) and the place of speaking (*here*, etc.) (for a thorough discussion of such items, see Lyons 1977: ch. 15). Moreover, we have seen (2.4) that many items are often restricted in their use to certain social circumstances (e.g. *get* versus *obtain*), and took for granted that such information was part of our language. Consequently, it would be natural to make the same assumption about the information that the French word *tu* 'you' is to be used only to intimates (and small children and animals). And having made that decision, it is only a small step to including in 'language' similar information about whole classes of items, such as the class of first names in English, which are also to be used only to intimates (in contrast with names like *Mr Brown*). (For further discussion of the restrictions on French pronouns and English proper nouns, see 4.2.2 below.)

It is easy to see how 'language' and 'social constraints on speech' merge, and it will also be clear from several points in the discussion below that social constraints on speech can apply not just to speech but to social behaviour in general. (This conclusion supports the view put forward in chapter 3 that there is no clear distinction between 'language' and other aspects of thought, especially in matters of meaning.) The accepted term for aspects of behaviour through which people influence and react to each other is SOCIAL INTERACTION, and speech is only one aspect of such behaviour, closely meshed with other aspects. One of the leading investigators in this field, Michael Argyle (a social psychologist), has described the field as follows (Argyle 1973: 9):

> One achievement of recent research has been to establish the basic elements of which social interaction consists; current research is concerned with finding out precisely how these elements function. It is now agreed that the list consists of various signals: verbal and non-verbal, tactile, visible and audible – various kinds of bodily contact, proximity, orientation, bodily posture, physical appearance, facial expression, movement of head and hands, direction of gaze, timing of speech, emotional tone of speech, speech errors, type of utterance and linguistic structure of utterance. Each of these elements can be further analysed and divided into categories or dimensions; each plays a distinctive role in social interaction, though they are closely interconnected.

In 4.4 below we shall look in more detail at some of the non-verbal aspects of social interaction and see how they relate to speech.

The study of speech as part of social interaction has involved many different disciplines, including social psychology, sociology, anthropology, ethology (the study of behaviour in animals), philosophy, artificial intelligence (the study of human intelligence via computer simulation), sociolinguistics and linguistics. Each discipline brings a different range of questions and methods to bear on the study, and all can learn a lot from the others. The main methods used in the study are introspection and participant observation, with a certain amount of experimentation (by social psychologists and ethologists) and computer simulation (by artificial intelligence workers). One of the most important contributions has been made by anthropologists who engage in what is called THE ETHNOGRAPHY OF SPEAKING or THE ETHNOGRAPHY OF COMMUNICATION, a field dominated by the work of Dell Hymes (see e.g. Hymes 1962, 1964, 1974, and the following anthologies: Bauman & Sherzer 1974, Gumperz & Hymes 1964, 1972). The importance of this work has been to feed into the discussion data on societies other than the advanced western ones in which most linguists live, and to make it clear how much variety there is in the social constraints on speech. Most readers may expect some surprises in the next few pages, but relativity is not unlimited in this field any more than it was in the field of meaning (see 3.2), as we shall see below.

4.1.2 *The functions of speech*

What part does speech play in social interaction? There is no simple answer, nor even a single complicated one, as speech plays many different roles on different occasions. The anthropologist Bronislav Malinowski claimed that 'in its primitive uses, language functions as a link in concerted human activity, as a piece of human behaviour. It is a mode of action and not an instrument of reflection' (Malinowski 1923). An example of this would be the kind of speech one hears from people shifting furniture: *To you . . . now up a bit . . .* and so on, where the speech acts as a control on people's physical activity, in contrast to its function in a lecture where it is intended to influence the thoughts rather than the actions of the listeners. Another use of speech is simply to establish or reinforce social relations – what Malinowski called PHATIC COMMUNION, the kind of chit-chat that people engage in simply in order to show that they recognise each other's presence. We might add many other uses of speech to this list – speech to obtain information (e.g. *Where's the tea-cosy?*), for expressing emotions (e.g.

What a lovely hat!), for its own sake (e.g. *She sells sea-shells by the sea-shore*) and so on. We shall not try to develop a proper classification of speech functions at this level, but just restrict ourselves to noting that speech in social interaction does not have just one function, such as communicating propositions which the hearer does not already know. (For a good survey of attempts to classify the functions of speech, see Robinson 1972: ch. 2.)

One particular approach to the functional classification of speech certainly ought to be mentioned, however, as it has been extremely influential. This is the approach based on SPEECH-ACTS, which has been developed in the main by philosophers and linguists following the British philosopher J.L. Austin (see Austin 1962, and excellent reviews in Lyons 1977: ch. 16, Kempson 1977: chs. 4, 5). Austin argued that the study of meaning should not concentrate on bald statements such as *Snow is white*, taken out of context, since language is typically used, in speech, for many other functions – when we speak we make suggestions, promises, invitations, requests, prohibitions and so on. Indeed, in some cases we use speech to perform an action (as Malinowski had argued), in the extreme sense that the speech is itself the action which it reports – for instance, *I name this ship 'Saucy Sue'* has to be said if the naming is to be accomplished. Such bits of speech are called PERFORMATIVE UTTERANCES. It can be seen that an account of all these different functions of speech must be formulated in terms of a general theory of social activity, and this is what Austin and his followers have tried to provide.

A speech-act is a bit of speech produced as part of a bit of social interaction – as opposed to the linguist's and philosopher's decontextualised examples. Our culture includes a rich set of concepts for classifying bits of social interaction, reflecting the importance of social interaction in society. For instance, we distinguish between 'work' and 'play' or 'leisure', between 'playing' and 'fighting', and between 'visiting', 'living with' and 'dropping in on' people. Similarly, as we might expect, there are many cultural concepts, with linguistic labels, for types of speech-acts, and the study of such acts seems to be largely concerned with the meanings of these terms – for instance, what precisely is meant by the term *promise*? (For an answer, see Searle 1965.)

One of the important distinctions which Austin introduced was between what he called the ILLOCUTIONARY FORCE of a speech-act and its PERLOCUTIONARY FORCE. The former is not easy to define precisely, but it is in some sense the 'inherent' function of the speech-act, which might be established by simply looking at the act itself in relation to existing beliefs. For instance, one could classify *He'll soon be leaving* as a promise if one believed that the addressee would be pleased at the news, that 'he' actually would be leaving soon, and so on. Perlocutionary force concerns the *effects* of the act, whether intended or actual – for instance, the intended perlocutionary force of *He'll soon be leaving* might be to please the addressee.

The distinction is especially interesting since it would seem to reflect a general tendency to categorise bits of social interaction in two different ways, according to (i) their inherent properties and (ii) their effects. For instance, we distinguish between 'fighting' and 'winning', and between 'playing' and 'enjoying oneself' or 'passing the time'. This parallel between the functional classification of speech and of other types of social behaviour is exactly what we might expect, given the view that speech is just one kind of social behaviour. We might also expect that concepts used in classifying speech-acts will be typical of cultural concepts, in being defined in terms of prototypes (see 3.1.2); indeed, in defining the conditions for something to count, say, as a promise, this is just what we do find. A prototypical promise is sincere, but it is quite normal to report that someone promised insincerely to do something.

If speech-act categories are cultural concepts, we might expect them to vary from one society to another, and that is again what we find. One of the standard examples of a type of speech-act which has a distinctive illocutionary force is the baptising of a person into the Christian faith, for which there is a specific verb (*baptise*) which can be used in performative utterances (*I baptise you* . . .). This particular illocutionary force is clearly restricted to societies in which baptism takes place, and there are many other similar examples of culture-specific illocutionary forces (for others see Lyons 1977: 737). It is interesting to compare the concepts reflected by English with those of an exotic community, such as those of the Tzeltal Indians (a branch of the Maya, of Mexico) reported by Brian Stross (1974). The Tzeltal have an extremely rich terminology for classifying speech-acts, such as 'talk in which things are offered for sale' or 'talk in which the speaker has spread the blame for something, so that he alone is not blamed'. These concepts seem to be instances of illocutionary force categories, but the terminology goes well beyond such categories, to include concepts such as 'inhaled talk, talk produced while breathing inwards' or 'speech occurring at night or late evening' or 'speech by someone who comes to another's house and spends time talking even though the other is quite ill'. All these concepts are expressed in Tzeltal by the same kind of linguistic item, consisting of a single word followed by the word *k'op*, meaning 'speech'. It seems fair to assume that a Tzeltal has the concepts concerned stored in his memory (whereas the reader will have had to construct them as new, internally complex, concepts), just as we have the complex concepts 'promise', 'baptise' and 'suggest' stored in ours, but there is little overlap between the two systems of concepts, even if we concentrate on the Tzeltal terms which seem to refer to illocutionary forces.

How does the classification of speech-acts fit into that of speech-functions, discussed at the start of this section in terms of 'phatic communion', 'speech for obtaining information', etc.? One possible answer is that the two sets of concepts are appropriate for classifying bits of speech of different lengths, with speech-acts as the smallest bits, classified by illocutionary and perlocutionary force, and longer stretches classified as 'phatic communion' and so on. This answer presupposes the existence of some kind of hierarchical organisation to speech, a possibility considered in 4.3.2 below, but we cannot take it for granted that speech is organised hierarchically. An alternative is to think of speakers as having a variety of intentions at any given moment in speech, varying in scope from relatively long-term intentions like maintaining good relations with the addressee, through shorter-term intentions such as pleasing the addressee, to other types of intentions such as producing a promise. This view differs from the hierarchical model in that it allows for changes in the speaker's intentions. However, the functional analysis of any given bits of speech cannot be satisfactorily made in terms of a single set of mutually exclusive categories, since different purposes can coexist. Once again we find the speaker locating his speech in a multi-dimensional space, just as he did with reference to other people (see 1.3.1 and 2.1.4) and other kinds of situation (see 2.4.1).

4.1.3 *Speech as skilled work*

We have just seen that speech is sufficiently important to society for it to be given special treatment in the culture – in any culture, we may assume – as an object to be classified and talked about. This still does not in itself show that speech is social, in de Saussure's sense, since it is likely that the socially recognised categories reflect rather than determine the ways in which speech is used in the community. In other words, if someone wanted to say something which would not fit into any recognised category, this would presumably not deter him from saying it (though this is of course debatable).

We now move to a somewhat more constraining aspect of speech, which we may call 'skilled work'. It is *work*, since it requires effort, and its degree of success depends on the effort that is made. It is *skilled* in that it requires the 'know-how' type of knowledge, which is applied more or less successfully according to how much practice one has had (and according to other factors such as intelligence). Putting these two characteristics together, we can predict that speech may be more successful at some times than at others, and some people may be better at it than others. There is no doubt that this is the case: we all know that sometimes we get 'tongue-tied' or 'drop a brick', and that some people are more likely than others to be stuck for 'the right thing to say'. (In this chapter we shall *not* be concerned with differences due to dialect, where what is 'good' is simply a matter of social convention and prejudice (see 6.2).)

If speech is skilled work, the same is true of other aspects of social interaction in face-to-face communication (or 'focused interaction'): 'it is fruitful to look upon the behaviour of people engaged in focused interaction as an organised, skilled performance, analogous to skills such as car driving' (Argyle & Kendon 1967). Just as some people are better drivers than others (to the extent that some pass the driving test and others fail), so some people are better at social interaction than others. However, there are two major caveats. Firstly, success in speech varies considerably according to its function and other aspects of the situation. Thus, some people are good at intellectual debate and poor at phatic communion, and vice versa; and we shall see (6.4) that children who are highly skilled in verbal games may flounder in the classroom or in a formal interview. Secondly, it is not obvious how success should be measured, except against the intentions of the speaker. For instance, if a chatterbox (C), is with a person (S) who habitually stays silent while others do the talking, C may think S is very unsuccessful at speaking, because he does not do his fair share towards filling any awkward gaps; but S may feel that his own speech is totally successful (since he has nothing of special importance to say), and that C's is an unimpressive empty chatter. The same two caveats apply equally, of course, to other aspects of social interaction.

This is not the place to try to specify the particular kinds of skill needed for successful speech, since they presumably include all the general skills needed for social interaction plus all the specifically linguistic skills concerned with the use of linguistic items. They vary from very specific skills, dealing with particular linguistic items (e.g. when to say *sir*) or with particular situations (e.g. how to conduct a business transaction on an expensive transatlantic telephone call), to much more general skills, such as how to pick the right kind of noun phrase for referring to an entity. We may perhaps think of these skills arranged hierarchically, with the most specific ones at the bottom and the most general at the top, and assume that in dealing with a particular situation the speaker will look for a specific skill which is appropriate in preference to a more general one, since the latter will always involve more cognitive effort and may be less successful. For instance, in asking for a ticket on a bus, it is easier and safer to use what you know about asking bus-conductors for tickets than to use a more general rule for requesting anything from anybody (e.g. by saying *Excuse me, would you mind selling me a ticket to . . .*). (This notion of the hierarchy of knowledge has been developed in artificial intelligence, where it has proved very fruitful – see e.g. Winograd 1975.) We may guess that one of the reasons why some people perform particularly well in some situations is that they have learned very specific skills for use in those situations, but at present this has to remain a guess without supporting evidence. It also raises the question to what extent skills are tied to particular situations – for instance, Karen Watson-Gegeo and Stephen Boggs (1977) have shown that children in Hawaii can transfer skills normally used in insulting each other to the telling of stories, which clearly constitutes a different situation.

We can now see in what respect speech is *social*: the rules or skills for using it are for the most part learned from others, in just the same way that linguistic items are learned. For example, one learns how to get a ticket from a bus-conductor by watching and listening to other people doing it, just as one learns how to arrange nouns and verbs into sentences by hearing it done by others.

There is another social aspect to speech, however, which has to do with 'work' rather than 'skill', namely that the effort one puts into speaking depends on motivation, which in turn derives in part from one's relations to the other people involved. Social psychology offers a number of theories to explain why people are willing to put effort into social interaction (and are also willing to be bound by the kinds of social constraint discussed in 4.1.4). The main recurrent theme in these theories, however, is that people accept the demands of others because they want their approval and liking.

One particular theory, developed by the sociologist Erving Goffman, is of particular interest in a discussion of speech, and is concerned with what Goffman (1955) has called FACE-WORK, i.e. the way in which a person maintains his 'face' (in the same sense as in the expression *to lose face*). This is done by presenting a consistent image to other people, but one can gain or lose face by improving or spoiling this image. The better one's image, the more others will approve, but it is dangerous to aim too high, because of the increased risk of losing face by a mistake. Accordingly, there is a strong tendency to aim at the average of one's group, rather than above it, and for everyone in a group to apply the same criteria in judging people, since each member knows that these are the criteria by which they are themselves being judged. For example, it would be difficult to belong to a group where everyone thought it important to keep the house tidy, or to be good at roller-skating, or to do well at examinations, without coming to accept the same criteria as important oneself.

Speech is one of the most important ways in which one presents a personal image for others to evaluate, both through what one says and the way one says it (Brown & Levinson 1978). Moreover, most people want to present to the world an image of considerateness, because this is most likely to make them popular, and this turns speech into a highly *cooperative* activity, where everyone tries hard to help everybody else maintain their personal images. We usually try to avoid exposing other people's weaknesses, or raising heated controversy, unless we are sure that it will not affect the attitude of others towards us or we are indifferent to their opinion. As hearers, we try hard to make sense of what other people say, even when this means reading far more between the lines than is in them (see the large literature on the 'cooperative principle' of Paul Grice, and how it is used for reading between the lines – e.g. Kempson 1977: 69, Lyons 1977: 592). But as speakers we try to anticipate problems which the addressee may have in making sense of what we say, by saying only what we may reasonably expect him to understand. Of course, people differ in their capacity either to anticipate how the addressee will take what they say, or to avoid possible mis-understandings, but the theory of face-work maintains that all adults at least are aware of the need for speakers to make concessions to those whom they address.

The consequences of failure to cooperate successfully have been dramatically described by Goffman (1957):

> A person who chronically makes himself and others uneasy in conversation and perpetually kills encounters is a faulty inter-actant; he is likely to have such a baleful effect upon the social life around him that he may just as well be called a faulty person.

If we see speech, and social interaction in general, as skilled work, we may say that failure such as Goffman describes here is due to lack of either skill or motivation (or both). As we now see, both skill and motivation to work are due to the society in which a person lives, and (to the extent that they influence speech) we may conclude that de Saussure was wrong in thinking of speech simply as an individual activity, owing nothing to society.

4.1.4 *The norms governing speech*

Skill in speaking depends on a variety of factors, including a knowledge of the relevant rules governing speech. Such rules are of various types, dealing with different aspects of speech, but all we can do here is to mention a few examples. The rules chosen vary from one society to another, which makes it easier to see that there *are* rules, but this should not be taken to imply that all rules are similarly variable. (It is possible that there are widespread, if not universal rules, though the emphasis in the literature is on differences rather than similarities between cultures.) We shall call such rules NORMS because they define normal behaviour for the society concerned, without being associated with any specific sanctions against those who do not follow them. (Brown & Levinson (1978) contains an excellent discussion of the complex interaction between norms and rationality as determinants of speech.)

First, there are norms governing the sheer quantity of speech that people produce, varying from very little to very much. Dell Hymes describes a society where very little speech is the norm (Hymes 1971b):

> Peter Gardener (1966) did some fieldwork . . . in southern India, among a tribal people called the Puliya, describing their socialization patterns. There is no agriculture and no industry, and the society is neither particularly cooperative nor particularly competitive; so children are led neither to be particularly inter-dependent nor to be aggressively competitive with each other, but simply to busy themselves with their own concerns in reasonable

spatial proximity. He observed that, by the time a man was forty, he practically stopped speaking altogether. He had no reason to speak. People there, in fact, just didn't talk much and seldom seemed to find anything much to talk about, and he saw this as a consequence of the particular kind of socialization pattern.

We may contrast this society with one in Roti, a small island in eastern Indonesia, described by James Fox (1974):

> For a Rotinese the pleasure of life is talk – not simply an idle chatter that passes time, but the more formal taking of sides in endless dispute, argument and repartee or the rivalling of one another in eloquent and balanced phrases on ceremonial occasions ... Lack of talk is an indication of distress. Rotinese repeatedly explain that if their 'hearts' are confused or dejected, they keep silent. Contrarily, to be involved with someone requires active verbal encounter.

There may be problems when people from societies with different norms meet, as shown by the following anecdote quoted by Coulthard (1977: 49, where other instances of different norms relating to quantity of speech may also be found):

> An ... ethnographer describes staying with in-laws in Denmark and being joined by an American friend who, despite warnings, insisted on talking with American intensity until 'at 9 o'clock my in-laws retired to bed; they just couldn't stand it any more'.

Another kind of norm controls the number of people who talk at once in a conversation. Most readers would probably accept the principle that only one person should speak (otherwise there must be more than one conversation taking place, as at a party), but apparently this norm is not universal. The practices in a village in Antigua, in the West Indies, are described by Karl Reisman (1974):

> Antiguan conventions appear, on the surface, almost anarchic. Fundamentally, there is no regular requirement for two or more voices not to be going at the same time. The start of a new voice is not in itself a signal for the voice speaking either to stop or to institute a process which will decide who is to have the floor. When someone enters a casual group, for example, no opening is necessarily made for him; nor is there any pause or other formal signal that he is being included. No one appears to pay any attention. When he feels ready he will simply begin speaking. He may be heard, he may not. That is, the other voices may eventually stop and listen, or some of them may; eyes may or may not turn to him. If he is not heard the first time he will try again, and yet

> again (often with the same remark). Eventually he will be heard or give up.

Similarly, most readers would accept that there must be a limit on the number of interruptions permissible in a conversation; not so in Antigua:

> In a brief conversation with me, about three minutes, a girl called to someone on the street, made a remark to a small boy, sang a little, told a child to go to school, sang some more, told a child to go buy bread, etc., all the while continuing the thread of her conversation about her sister.

Other norms refer to the content of what is said. For instance, the 'cooperative principle' of Paul Grice (referred to briefly above) covers several norms including the requirement that one should 'be informative' when speaking (Grice 1975). One effect of this norm is that one should specify a referent as informatively, that is as precisely, as one can. Thus if I am talking to you, and I want to say that your sister is outside, I should say *your sister* (or use her name if I know it), rather than simply *somebody* or *a girl* or *either your sister or your brother*. If I use any of these less precise expressions, you will be entitled to 'read between the lines' that I don't know any more precisely who the person is, because you know that we are subject to the norm 'be informative' and I would have used a more precise expression if I had been able to.

This norm is not as universal as one might expect. According to Elinor Keenan (1977), in at least one part of Madagascar the norm is waived under many circumstances. For instance, it would be quite normal to refer to one's own sister as 'a girl' (Keenan quotes a specific occasion when a boy said to her – in Malagasy – 'There is a girl who is coming', referring to his own sister). Similarly,

> if A asks B 'Where is your mother?' and B responds 'She is either in the house or at the market', B's utterance is not usually taken to imply that B is unable to provide more specific information needed by the hearer. The implicature is not made, because the expectation that speakers will satisfy informational needs is not a basic norm.

There are a number of reasons why speakers are so uninformative in this community. One is that they are afraid that identifying an individual may bring him to the attention of evil forces, or get him into trouble in other ways. Another reason is that news is in short supply in small isolated villages, and people like to keep it to themselves as a precious commodity! Consequently, there is no reluctance to give information when it is easily available to anyone – for instance, if there is a pot of rice cooking over a fire, people will refer to it as 'the rice' since anyone can see that there is rice there. Clearly, different norms for speech in different societies can often be explained by reference to other aspects of their cultures and cannot, therefore, be satisfactorily studied in isolation.

Finally, there are very specific norms which may vary from society to society, such as the way one asks bus-conductors for tickets. To take another example, in Germany the hostess at a formal dinner party would probably say to her guests *Ich darf jetzt bitten, Platz zu nehmen* ('I may now ask (you) to take (your) places'), using a declarative construction, in contrast with the interrogative that would be used by an English hostess: *May I ask you to come and sit down now?* Other examples of quite specific constraints will be mentioned in the following sections.

4.1.5 *Conclusion*

This discussion has shown that de Saussure was wrong in seeing speech as the product of the individual's will, unconstrained by society. This might be nearer the truth for certain aspects of speech in Antigua, but it is far from true in the societies familiar to most readers (and to de Saussure himself).

Society controls our speech in two ways. Firstly, by providing a set of *norms*, which we learn to follow (or occasionally to flout) more or less skilfully, but which vary from society to society, though some may be more universal than others. For instance, even in Madagascar the norm of informativeness seems to apply *unless* it conflicts with other principles (of safeguarding individuals or keeping news to oneself), and this norm may be recognised by all societies. Secondly, society provides the *motivation* for adhering to these norms, and for putting effort into speech (as into social interaction in general). The theory of face-work explains this motivation, and could explain why it is that speech can run as smoothly as it usually does, given the possibilities for misunderstanding and other difficulties that exist.

In addition to controlling it in these two ways, society takes a great interest in speech, and in particular provides a set of concepts for thinking and talking about it. One such set of concepts has to do with the functions of speech, and the theory of speech-acts reflects this social categorisation of speech according to its functions. To some extent these functional categories are referred to by the norms of speech, e.g. if you are to name a ship, you find out what the norms for this specific functional category of speech are; and the norm for making a promise is to say *I promise that/to* . . . (though this is of course not the only way of making a promise). Consequently, the functional categorisation of speech is at least partly an instrument by which society *controls* it.

We have referred in very general terms to 'society', but it would be wrong to give the impression that societies are any more homogeneous with respect to the ways in which they control speech than they are with respect to the linguistic items which their members use. There is no reason to believe that this is so, and we may expect just as much individual variation in norms of speech as in linguistic items. Similarly, it is clear that people use speech just as much as linguistic items in order to locate themselves in relation to the social groups that they can identify in the world around them. The only difference is that norms of speech are relatively hard to study compared with linguistic items, especially in quantitative terms, so it is more difficult to cite empirical evidence in support of this contention.

4.2 Speech as a signal of social identity

4.2.1 *Non-relational social categories*

There are, perhaps, linguistic items in every language that reflect social characteristics of the speaker, of the addressee, or of the relation between them. Consequently speech which contains such items tells a hearer how the speaker sees these characteristics, and he will be considered to have infringed a norm that governs speech if he uses items which indicate the wrong characteristics. The norms reviewed below are possibly the best known and the most widely studied of those that govern speech.

The simplest cases are linguistic items which reflect the social characteristics of just one person, either speaker or addressee. One of the oddest cases described in the ethnographic literature is that of the Abipon of Argentina, who according to Hymes (1972) add *-in* to the end of *every* word if either the speaker or addressee is a member of the warrior class. Similarly, the Yana language of California contained special forms for use in speech either by or to women (Sapir 1929). However, in most cases the norm refers specifically only to the speaker or to the hearer.

As far as speakers are concerned, the commonest characteristic to be reflected by specific linguistic items is sex. There are many known instances of this from the Americas and Asia (see the survey in Trudgill 1974b: 84, Haas 1944). For instance, in the Koasati language spoken in Louisiana there are quite regular morphological differences between the verb forms used by males and females, with males typically adding -*s* to the end of the female forms (e.g. males say *lakáws* where females say *lakáw*, both meaning 'he is lifting it'). A rather different kind of sex-marker is found in the Island Carib language of Central America, whose history is specially likely to show sex differences since the Island Caribs are descended from Carib-speaking males and Arawak-speaking females whose males were slaughtered by the Caribs. (Arawak is unrelated to Carib.) In modern Island Carib, males and females differ in various aspects of their common language, including the genders given to abstract nouns, which are treated as grammatically masculine by female speakers and feminine by male ones (Taylor 1951: 103).

Although it may seem unusual to have linguistic items specifically reserved for use by male or female speakers, or to have different genders according to the sex of the speaker, we shall see (5.4.3) that there may be quantitative differences between male and female speakers even in English, where female speakers tend to use more prestigious forms than males with the same social background. However, it is probably misleading to treat these quantitative differences as instances of the same phenomenon as the qualitative differences found in languages like Koasati, because their function seems rather different. Whereas the sex-based differences in Koasati act as clear markers of the sex differences between speakers, reinforcing whatever other observable differences there may be, the quantitative differences in English are probably the consequence of women having a more positive orientation towards the standard dialect (or accent). (For a somewhat more sophisticated explanation see Elyan et al. 1978.) The differences in English do not seem to function as distinctive markers of sex as such, since they would not distinguish a typical female member of one class from a typical male member of a somewhat higher class.

Turning to hearers, there are many more ways in which people's speech varies according to who they are addressing. It seems likely, in particular, that in *every* language there are special linguistic items for use when speaking to a child, like the English *gee-gee* for 'horse'. (It is interesting to note that such differences in English are not restricted to vocabulary; for instance, sentences like *Mummy pick up baby* are commonly used, and differ from adult sentences both in their syntax, being 'third-person imperatives', and in their pragmatics, since the pronouns *I* and *you* are avoided.) Similar 'baby-talk' has been reported for other languages – for instance, in the American Indian language Comanche (Casagrande 1948). It has even been suggested by Charles Ferguson (1971) that some features of baby-talk, compared with normal speech, may be universal, such as the absence of inflections and of a copula verb (meaning 'be') in clauses which would contain one in normal speech (e.g. *Mummy tired*).

The most extraordinary of all the distinctions that have been reported is probably found among the Nootka Indians of Vancouver Island (Sapir 1915). Nootka apparently provides special word-forms for use when speaking either to or about people with various kinds of deformity or abnormality, namely 'children, unusually fat or heavy people, unusually short adults, those suffering from some defect of the eye, hunchbacks, those that are lame, left-handed persons and circumcised males'. For example, in talking either to or about a person with a squint a suffix is added to verbs, and all sibilant sounds ([s] and [c]) are changed into voiceless laterals (like the Welsh sound written '*ll*').

4.2.2 *Power and solidarity*

Speech may also reflect the social relations between the speaker and addressee, most particularly the POWER and SOLIDARITY manifested in that relationship. (These terms and the related concepts were introduced into sociolinguistics by the social psychologist Roger Brown – see Brown & Ford 1961 and Brown & Gilman 1960, the 'classic' papers on linguistic markers of social relations.) 'Power' is self-explanatory, but 'solidarity' is harder to define. It concerns the social distance between people – how much experience they have shared, how many social characteristics they share (religion, sex, age, region of origin, race, occupation, interests, etc.), how far they are prepared to share intimacies, and other factors.

For the English speaker, the clearest linguistic markers of social relations are personal names, such as *John* and *Mr Brown*. Each person has a number of different names by which he may be addressed, including first and family names, and possibly a title (such as *Mr* or *Professor*). Let us consider just two possible combinations: the first name on its own (e.g. *John*), and the title followed by the family name (e.g. *Mr Brown*). How does one decide whether to address John Brown as *John* or as *Mr Brown*? The answer must refer to both power and solidarity, as Brown & Ford found in their study of American middle-class usage. Once again the notion of prototypes is useful, since we can define two prototypical situations, in which *John* and *Mr Brown* respectively would be used, and then relate other situations to them. *John* is used if there is high solidarity between the speaker and John Brown, and John Brown has less power than the speaker – in other words, if John Brown is a *close subordinate*. A clear example is when John Brown is the speaker's son. On the other hand, *Mr Brown* is used if there is low solidarity and John Brown has more power than the speaker – if he is a *distant superior*, such as a company boss or a headmaster whom the speaker knows only from a distance. It seems unlikely that there would be any disagreement among English speakers as to the names appropriate to these two situations.

There is less agreement, and less certainty, over the names to be used in intermediate situations. What does one call a close superior, for instance? Students joining a department in a British university, for example, generally start by calling the head of the department (i.e. departmental chairman) *Professor X*, since he is a distant superior, but they may gradually get to know him better through classes and perhaps less formal contacts, until they feel they know him quite well. The question then arises whether, and when, they should start to call him by his first name. In some departments the problem is resolved immediately by the head of department announcing on the first day that everyone is to call him by his first name, but elsewhere it is left to each student to judge when solidarity between him and the head has increased to a point where he feels entitled to use the latter's first name, and different students can have very different 'thresholds' indeed – for some it takes three years, for others only two or three days. Clearly, the explanations for these individual differences are complex, involving matters of personality as well as knowledge of the norms, but such differences should not obscure the fact that everyone agrees there is a point on the solidarity scale where it will become right to use a first name.

One of the advantages of showing power and solidarity in this way is that such problems may be avoided simply by not using *any* name to address the person concerned. However, other languages have other devices for signalling power and solidarity which in this respect are less accommodating (as we shall see in 4.2.3), such as the use in French of the pronouns *tu* and *vous*, both meaning 'you' and both singular, although *vous* is also plural. The norms for choosing between *tu* and *vous* in the singular are precisely the same as those for choosing between first name only and title plus family name in English, *tu* being used prototypically to a close subordinate, and *vous* to a distant superior, with other situations resolved in relation to these. In contrast with the English system, however, it is much harder to avoid the problems of choice in French, since to do so it would be necessary to avoid making any reference to the addressee at all.

The studies by Brown & Gilman show that there have been considerable changes through time in the norms for using the French pronouns, which derived from Latin pronouns where the distinction was one of number only (*tu* 'you, singular', *vos* 'you, plural'). For a number of complex historical reasons *vos* and its historical derivatives came to be used to refer to someone with greater power (especially the emperor), without regard to solidarity, but later solidarity became increasingly important until nowadays it overrides power in determining which form to use. For instance, it was normal until quite recently for French children to call their fathers *vous*, in recognition of his greater power, but now it is usual for them to call him *tu* because of high solidarity. Similar changes have taken place in many Western European languages such as German and Italian (Brown & Gilman 1960), and also in Russian (Friedrich 1972). (It will be noticed that the use of two different forms for the second-person singular pronoun, reflecting power and/or solidarity, is an 'areal feature' of Europe, like those we mentioned in 2.3.4, since it is not found in Latin and other Western European languages of two thousand years ago, and is found in non-Indo-European languages such as Hungarian (Hollos 1977). It can be traced at least as far east as Persian (Jahangiri 1980, Brown & Levinson 1978).) These historical changes are interesting for the light they shed on prototypes, showing that changes may affect both the prototypes themselves (solidarity gradually becoming a defining feature) and also their extensions (as the exact balance between power and solidarity changes in resolving intermediate cases).

Needless to say, it is not hard to relate changes in relative importance of power and solidarity in choosing pronouns to concurrent changes in social structure, and such connections are in fact made by the writers mentioned above. The Italian pronouns (*tu* for close subordinates and *Lei* for distant superiors) are one particularly fascinating and recent example. A survey of the use of *tu* and *Lei* by members of both middle and lower classes in Rome (Bates & Benigni 1975) showed that, surprisingly, those who used *Lei* most often were lower-class male youths, who might have been expected to be in the lead in extending the use of the 'democratic' form *tu*. The survey included older and younger speakers from both classes, and showed that lower-class youths used *Lei* more than their elders, in contrast with middle-class youths who used it less than middle-class older people. In interpreting these findings, Bates & Benigni suggest that middle-class youths are moving nearer to what they think is the more democratic usage of the lower class, while lower-class youths are moving towards what they consider a prestigious middle-class usage. If the process continues, we might expect middle and lower classes simply to exchange norms, to the bewilderment of many Romans!

Linguistic signalling of power and solidarity is sufficiently well studied for at least two possible linguistic universals to be suggested. Every language might be expected to have some way of signalling differences in either power or solidarity or both, which could be explained by reference to the extreme importance of both power and solidarity in face-to-face relations between individuals, and the need for each individual to make it clear how he sees those relations. It also seems that wherever power and solidarity are reflected in the same range of forms (as is the case in all the languages considered so far), the form which expresses high solidarity also expresses greater power on the part of the speaker and vice versa. The prototypes set up for English above may, once again, prove to be universal. This connection between power and solidarity was suggested as a universal by Brown & Ford (1961), who point out that it is always the superior who ultimately decides when solidarity is sufficient for the 'high solidarity' form to be used (as we saw in the case of a student and his relations with his head of department), so it is likely to be the superior who uses the high solidarity form first – hence the link between high solidarity and its use to a subordinate.

4.2.3 *Linguistic signals of power and solidarity*

In English the main markers of power and solidarity might fairly be described as peripheral to the system of English as a whole, in the sense that proper names used as vocatives (i.e. to address someone) could be handled in a separate section of the grammar with little or no consequence for any other parts of it. (In fact, we shall see below that things are not quite as simple as that, even in English.) English-speaking readers might think, therefore, that the same is true of all languages, but this is by no means the case. It is common for the power–solidarity contrast to be quite crucial, and for the grammar of such a language to refer to it at many points. What follows is a brief survey of some of the better known types of linguistic signal of power–solidarity (as we shall call the contrast for convenience, without wishing to imply that both power and solidarity are involved necessarily and equally in all cases). A fuller discussion may be found in Brown & Levinson (1978).

We start the survey with the general type of signal familiar in English and French, where the sensitive items (i.e. those whose form varies with power–solidarity) refer to the addressee. In English the only sensitive items are personal names, whereas in French they also include the pronoun 'you'. In other languages the sensitive items include ordinary noun phrases, built round common nouns, when used as vocatives. For instance, according to Mitchell (1975: 159) there is a widespread practice, possibly typical of Muslim communities, whereby 'the older generation affectionately address the younger with the term that is properly reciprocated to them by the younger'. Thus in Berber (spoken in North Africa) a mother might call her child *yəmma* which in other contexts means 'my mother'. (We may perhaps assume that affection is a special case of solidarity.) A similar situation is found in other languages where noun phrases which might be translated literally as 'your servant' or 'your slave', etc. can be used to refer to the *speaker*. One such language is Persian (Jahangiri, 1980) which also has a similar range of noun phrases with complimentary meanings for referring to the addressee, so that power relations between speaker and addressee may be defined by the noun phrases referring to both of them. We might guess that languages which have other ways of signalling power and solidarity will also have sensitive forms for referring to the addressee and perhaps the speaker.

In other languages, for example Japanese and Korean, there is a fairly direct relation between power–solidarity and *verb-forms* used. Since little can be said without using verbs, it is almost inevitable that speech will reflect those relations. In Korean there are no less than six distinct suffixes which reflect different power–solidarity relations between speaker and addressee, and a verb must have one of these suffixes attached to it (Martin 1964). Interestingly, the six suffixes fall into two groups, three reflecting different degrees of positive solidarity ('plain', 'intimate' and 'familiar') and three reflecting different power relations between people with low solidarity ('polite', 'authoritative' and 'deferential'). In other words, as in English and French, solidarity takes precedence in Korean over power among the linguistic markers of power–solidarity. (This is not always so, however, as witness the situation reported by Hill & Hill (1978) among the Nahuatl of Mexico, where even extreme intimacy is overridden by the power relation of an addressee who belongs to an older generation.)

Verbs are also signals of power–solidarity in Persian, but instead of varying the verb-form by inflections, differences are indicated by choosing between different lexical items with the same meaning (cf. English *try* and *attempt*). However, this choice is made according to the power–solidarity relations between the speaker and the verb's subject, so the verb will not reflect the relations between speaker and addressee unless the latter is the subject. (Moreover, if the verb has an object, its form reflects the power–solidarity between subject and object rather than between subject and speaker.)

A third type of linguistic marker of power–solidarity is *vocabulary level*. A good example of this is found in Javanese (Geertz 1960), which offers a range of alternative forms, listed in the lexicon, for each of a large number of meanings, but these alternatives are not restricted to verbs (and noun phrases referring to speaker and addressee) as in Persian but affect virtually every part of speech. For instance, Geertz gives the alternative forms for the Javanese sentence meaning 'Are you going to eat rice and cassava now?' (which apparently may be translated word-for-word from English), and shows that there are two or three different words in Javanese for each word in the English except *to* and *cassava*. Geertz claims that there are clear restrictions on the words which are compatible with each other in the same sentence, and identifies just six 'style levels', each marked by a definable range of vocabulary items so that any given sentence can belong to just one of the levels. The function of style levels is to signal the power–solidarity relations between speaker and addressee, and specifically to build a 'wall of behavioural formality' to protect the addressee's inner life (as Geertz puts it). The higher the style level, the more walls there are to protect the addressee against the encroachment that any communication inevitably makes on privacy.

There is one final, but important, point about the linguistic signals of power–solidarity, namely that the signals concerned are often not restricted to marking the power–solidarity relations between speaker and addressee, but may also mark the relations of the speaker to an entity other than the addressee. An easy example of this is the English use of personal names, which we have already discussed in relation to their use as vocatives (as in *Excuse me, John/Mr Brown . . .*). The same range of forms is available for use in referring to John Brown when he is not the addressee, and much the same rules govern the choice of form. Thus, if the speaker sees him as a close subordinate, he will refer to him as *John* (e.g. *I saw John yesterday*), whereas he will refer to him as *Mr Brown* if he sees him as a distant superior, and there may be uncertainty about how to refer to him if he is in an intermediate category. Clearly the problems of choosing between the alternative forms are less critical if the person concerned is not present, and it is interesting that in Nahuatl a somewhat less respectful form is used to refer to a person than would be used in addressing him (Hill & Hill 1978). It seems highly unlikely that the reverse would ever be the case.

This point is important in showing that power–solidarity relations between speaker and addressee may be considered as a special case of a more general phenomenon, concerning the speaker's relations of power and solidarity with the world at large. It seems that language often encourages, or even forces, us to define our relations with what we talk about. If we are referring to a person we locate ourselves relative to him in terms of solidarity and power, and if we are referring to an object we may even select our words to show our relations to its owner (as is said to happen in Javanese and Nahuatl). Thus the linguistic signalling of power and solidarity can be seen as another instance of the way in which a speaker locates himself in his social world when he speaks (cf. 2.6).

4.3 The structure of speech

4.3.1 *Entries and exits*

Whenever regularly recurring patterns are identified in some kind of behaviour, we say that behaviour is structured by those patterns. There is no difficulty in establishing that speech is structured, since grammars and dictionaries are full of recurrent patterns of words, constructions and so on. These relatively short patterns, contained within the sentence, are obviously only a part of the total structure of speech since all sorts of longer patterns can be identified, such as the one consisting of a question followed by its answer, and even longer ones such as some piece of interaction between two people, with a clearly recognisable greeting at the beginning and farewell at the end. What is controversial is the extent to which a hierarchical structure can be identified above the sentence, and we shall return to this question in the next section, after first looking at greetings and farewells, which offer the clearest examples of structure in speech.

It is reasonable to assume that every language includes a range of forms for use as greetings and another for farewells, in view of the importance of 'entries' (into pieces of interaction) and 'exits'. (The terms 'entry' and 'exit', borrowed from the stage, reflect the fact that discussions of speech norms often compare them with the 'lines' that an actor recites on stage.) Erving Goffman, the originator of 'face-work' (see 4.1.4), suggests that a greeting is needed to show that the relation which existed at the end of the last encounter is still unchanged, in spite of the separation, and that a farewell is needed in order to 'sum up the effect of the encounter upon the relationship and show what the participants may expect of one another when they next meet' (Goffman 1955). Everything we have seen so far shows that relations between the participants in some piece of interaction are of the greatest interest to the participants themselves, and it is easy to see why it is important for them to begin and end each piece of interaction by indicating their relations to one another. Having established mutual relations by the greetings, the participants can then get down to any 'business' they may have to transact – which might be no more than a five-minute chat across the garden fence – without paying more attention than they wish to maintaining those relations. Farewells occur at the end of the business as a mutual reassurance that relations are unchanged. Thus we may see the structure of a piece of interaction, very crudely, as consisting of three parts:

Greetings – Business – Farewell.

Of course, greetings and farewells, as defined functionally in this way, may vary enormously in their sincerity and creativity. Taking sincerity first, there is an interesting distinction to be drawn between greetings which express a proposition (e.g. *How nice to see you!*) and those which do not (e.g. *Hello*). Only propositional greetings can be said to be insincere, though the non-propositional kind may imply feelings (through intonation, in particular) which the speaker does not really have. (The same distinction can be made with regard to farewells.) Non-propositional greetings thus tend to be fairly neutral and short, simply recognising that an encounter (i.e. a piece of interaction) has started. Given the existence of such neutral greetings, one might wonder why anyone ever uses the propositional kind without meaning them, but the explanation is easy. People base their social behaviour on a compromise between what they really feel and what they know is expected of them, in order to maintain their face at a reasonable level. Accordingly, if A is really displeased to see B, he is not likely to tell B so in his greeting, since it is in A's interest for B to like him, and B is more likely to do so if he thinks A likes him. It is relatively easy to be insincere at the greeting or farewell stage in an encounter because those are the points where one comes nearest to 'reciting lines', like an actor on a stage.

Greetings also vary in the degree of personal creativity they reflect, with the non-propositional the least creative. It is important, however, to remember that the function of a greeting or farewell may be fulfilled by a wide range of forms outside the list of a few dozen fixed greetings. For instance, *Well, if it isn't my friend X!* and *Haven't we met somewhere before?* are perfectly acceptable greetings, although they are relatively far from the fixed type. What matters is that a greeting should be recognised as such by the addressee, to acknowledge that a new en-counter has begun. In some societies this means sticking to a list of formulae, including propositional greetings like the two just quoted, but in other societies it means using certain *types* of utterance, such as asking where the addressee has been or how his family are, member by member.

What then decides the form of a greeting or farewell? The answer clearly varies very much from language to language, and from society to society, but certain general patterns have emerged (see Ferguson 1976). For instance, the sheer length of a greeting is generally propor-tional to the length of time since the last meeting (i.e. a greeting to a friend last seen ten years ago will be longer than one to a friend seen yesterday) and to the importance of the relationship (i.e. a friend will receive a longer greeting than a mere acquaintance). Goffman's explana-tion for the role of greetings might lead us to expect that there will only be the briefest of greeting, or none at all, where no previous relation has existed, and this seems to be the case: witness the lack of greetings when people approach strangers to ask for information. Similarly we might predict (correctly) that longer greetings will be used when people are less certain of their relations, and therefore need more reassurance.

Goffman's predictions may be based on a rather American style of social behaviour, since there is at least one society to which they appear not to apply, namely the Apache Indians, studied by K.H. Basso (1970). Instead of using speech, in the form of greetings, to assure each other that relations are just as they were before the separation, they wait until they are sure that relations really *are* the same before they speak to each other at all, at least in situations where there is reason to think that relations may have changed, as when children return after a year in boarding-school. Many British or American parents might chatter hard with their children as soon as they come off the bus, but Apache parents apparently wait and say nothing for up to fifteen minutes, while they assess the effect of the year's schooling on their children's behaviour. Thus the Apache do not use greetings in the way that Goffman predicts, but do confirm his more general claim that it is important for people to know how they stand in relation to others before they start to talk.

4.3.2 *Other kinds of structure in speech*

There has been a great deal of research in the last decade on other aspects of what is called DISCOURSE STRUCTURE – the structure of speech above the sentence level (for good reviews see Coulthard 1975, 1977). It is clear that there is no lack of different kinds of structure linking sentences together in coherent wholes, but theoretical frameworks for the analysis of these coherent patterns are currently lacking. The most obvious fact about discourse structure is that many different kinds of structure run through discourse, and any attempt to reduce them to a single type is bound to fail.

One kind of structure is based on the fact that people take *turns* at speaking in most kinds of interaction, so that speech is divided up into separate stretches spoken by different speakers. In studying this aspect of discourse one can ask questions such as whether 'turns' are taken strictly in sequence or overlap one another, how speakers show that they are about to finish speaking, how listeners show that they would like to start, who decides who should speak next, who does most of the talking, who speaks to whom, and so on. Much of the work on this aspect of discourse has been done by social psychologists interested in 'group dynamics' (for a representative selection of papers, see Argyle 1973), and research has shown that turn-taking is a very highly skilled activity indeed. As we shall see, it involves many kinds of behaviour as well as speech (e.g. eye-movements), all of which are coordinated with split-second timing and reacted to with great accuracy by other participants.

A particular type of turn-taking structure is characterised by ADJACENCY PAIRS – a type of utterance by one speaker which requires a particular type of utterance by another. The most obvious adjacency pair is a sequence of question followed by answer, but there are many others, such as greeting + greeting, complaint + apology, summons + answer, invitation + acceptance and so on. It is not at all clear whether there is a distinction between adjacency pairs and other kinds of change of speaker, however. Some utterances obviously require a reaction from the addressee, and a failure to react as expected will itself be taken as a kind of meaningful reaction; for instance, if A says *Hello* to B but the latter does not return any kind of greeting, A will take it that B has a specific reason for not replying. However, other kinds of utterance are less clear in this respect. A warning is often followed by some kind of acknowledgment from the addressee, even if only a raised eyebrow or nod, but such acknowledgment is not necessary if it is clear that the other person has heard the warning. At the other extreme are the kinds of utterances which make up university lectures, where reaction from the addressees is minimal. The literature on adjacency pairs has not yet considered theoretical questions such as the delimitation of adjacency pairs, but has concentrated on discussing the use of certain types of pair, such as summons +answer (Schegloff 1968).

A second type of structure in discourse is based on *topic*, which clearly bears little relation to the type based on turn-taking, since speakers frequently change topics in the middle of their turn. It is tempting to think that topic-based structure is hierarchical, in the sense that a given text should be analysable into successively smaller units on the basis of topic. This temptation is reinforced by the writing practices to which highly literate people (such as any reader of this book) are accustomed. For instance, this book has a very clear hierarchical structure based on topic, with chapters as the largest units, sections as the next largest, then subsections (e.g. the present one, which is 4.3.2), then paragraphs, and finally sentences, all neatly delimited by one kind of typographic convention or another. In imposing this structure on the book, I have tried to make it reflect the topics discussed, so that the present sentence is an illustration of one kind of structure, dealt with in the present paragraph, which is part of the subsection on types of discourse structure other than entries and exits, which is one part of the section dealing with discourse structure, and that in turn is part of the chapter dealing with speech as social interaction.

Various researchers have claimed to be able to find a similar hierarchical structure in other kinds of discourse, both spoken and written. For instance, John Sinclair & Malcolm Coulthard (1975) analysed tape-recordings of a number of lessons from secondary schools, and identified a hierarchical discourse structure with 'lesson' as the largest unit, then 'transaction', then 'exchange', then 'move' and finally 'act', corresponding very roughly with the syntactic unit 'clause' (see Coulthard 1975 for a survey of other proposals for hierarchical analyses of discourse). However convincing we may find these proposals, it seems clear that there is no such hierarchical structure in certain kinds of interaction, but rather the topic 'drifts' gradually from one subject to another – perhaps starting off with a film about sheep-farming in Wales, leading to a sheep-dog trial somebody saw on holiday, and from there into further details of the holiday and a comparison with a holiday spent in Yugoslavia, and so on. Moreover it seems unlikely that participants in such a conversation have any clear plan at the start about the shape it will take, as would seem to be implied by the notion of a hierarchical structure.

On the other hand, speakers tend to stick to the same topic and may feel obliged to give a special signal if they are changing it (e.g. *Oh, by the way, on a completely different matter, . . .*). The reason for sticking to a given topic, or only drifting gradually away from it, is partly that this increases the chances of other participants being interested in what is said, and partly because it increases their chances of understanding the discourse, because for any given topic we all have a large amount of information about how the world works, which we can exploit both as speakers and hearers. Speakers who keep to the same topic can take most of this information for granted. For example, if we all know we are talking about the holiday someone had last year, the speaker can say simply *The food was disappointing* and we all know which food he means (what he had in the hotel where he stayed during that holiday) and we can also guess the kind of standard by which he was judging it (different, say, from the standard one would apply in a university refectory). If the topic for each sentence were different from that of the previous one, none of this information could be taken for granted. In short, sticking to one topic makes speech much easier, both for speaker and for addressee. (For perceptive discussion of this kind of shared knowledge, the reader is referred to the rapidly growing literature on artificial intelligence, notably Schank & Abelson 1977.)

The conclusion to which we seem to be led on the topic-based structure of discourse is that some kinds of discourse may have a hierarchical structure, especially if entirely under the control of one person who has the opportunity to plan the entire discourse before starting (e.g. a book or a lecture), but that most discourse probably has a much looser kind of structure. This is characterised by the change of topic through time, and consists only of the *current* topic at any given moment. An analyst can therefore trace the ways in which the topic has varied in the discourse from time to time, either by gradual drift or abrupt change.

A third type of discourse structure is based on what we know about the structure of the world – what we might call *encyclopedic* structure, which gives form to what we have been referring to as 'the current topic'. If the current topic is a holiday, we know there are various 'sub-topics' which are generally considered relevant, such as accommodation, weather, activities and travel, each of which can be further subdivided – for example, 'activities' might include sight-seeing, swimming, other sports, night-life and shopping. Alternatively, other sub-topics might cut across these, spoiling the neat hierarchical organisation implied so far – for instance, 'food' might cut across 'accommodation' and 'activities', since one can eat either in one's hotel or in a restaurant. To take a different kind of example, if we were describing a flat we could make use of one of two kinds of encyclopedic knowledge. We could either take the architect's view-point, and describe it statically: *There are four rooms, forming a square, . . .,* or we could take the point of view of someone visiting the flat and being shown around it: *First you come into a hall, then you go down a corridor on your left, . . .* Interestingly, according to the research of Linde & Labov (1975), most people take the visitor's view-point.

No doubt other types of structure could be identified in discourse in addition to those we have discussed – based on turn-taking, topic and encyclopedic knowledge. It should be clear from the discussion that there is no chance of reducing all these structures to a single type, and that the structures of discourse are complex mixtures of norms specific to speech and general knowledge of the world. It is hard to see how the study of discourse structure can be anything but interdisciplinary.

4.4 Verbal and non-verbal behaviour

4.4.1 *Relation-markers*

This section considers the relations between verbal and non-verbal behaviour in social interaction. The linguist David Abercrombie has claimed that 'we speak with our vocal organs, but we converse with our entire bodies' (Abercrombie 1968), and we shall see in what sense this is true. Non-verbal behaviour is involved in the two aspects of speech considered in this chapter – marking relations between speaker and addressee (4.2) and the structure of discourse (4.3); and it is also involved in the communication of 'content', that is, propositions and referents.

One very obvious aspect of non-verbal behaviour which helps to reflect power–solidarity is the distance one person stands from the other, the study of which has developed to such an extent that it has its own name – PROXEMICS. It would be a safe hypothesis that physical distance is proportional to social distance in all cultures, so that people who feel close in spirit will put themselves relatively near to each other when interacting. At one end of the scale are courting couples, and at the other end impersonal and formal occasions where speakers may be long distances from their addressees, as in theatres, or unable to see them at all, as on radio and television. What varies from culture to culture is the distance which is thought appropriate for a particular degree of solidarity. For instance, Arabs generally set the distance lower than Americans. This claim is supported by research (Watson & Graves 1966) in which comparisons were made between Arab and American students in an American university. The students were asked to converse in pairs in a room where they could be observed without their knowledge, and records were kept of their movements – how close to each other they sat, how they oriented themselves towards each other, how much they touched each other, how much they looked at each other, and how loudly they talked. Sixteen Arabs and sixteen Americans were studied in this way, with Arabs talking to Arabs and Americans to Americans. When the results were compared it was found that 'Arabs confronted each other more directly than Americans when conversing . . ., they sat closer to each other . . ., they were more likely to touch each other . . ., they looked each other more squarely in the eye . . ., and they conversed more loudly than Americans.'

This experiment introduced a number of variables other than distance, all of which are involved in some way in establishing power–solidarity relations between individuals. Cultural differences such as those between Arabs and Americans can of course lead to considerable misunderstanding on both sides. The interested reader will find many more similar examples discussed in a book aptly called *The Silent Language* by Edward T. Hall, founder of proxemics (Hall 1959).

4.4.2 *Structure-markers*

Non-verbal behaviour also helps to mark the structure of the interaction. One of the main kinds of structure considered above (4.3.1) was the pattern of behaviour associated with 'entries' and 'exits', where non-verbal behaviour is just as clearly patterned as verbal behaviour. Some aspects of the former are relatively conventionalised, such as hand-shaking, which in some cultures is replaced by nose-rubbing or supplemented by kissing or embracing, according to the relation between the participants. In Britain hand-shaking seems to be used to show that a relation is being given a fresh start, rather than as a sign of intimacy. Thus it is used to patch up quarrels between friends, or when one is introduced to a stranger, or to anyone not seen for a long time. In other cultures the rules for shaking hands are clearly different, so once again we find scope for relativity in the norms governing behaviour. An interesting example is the difference between British and Wolof (Senegal) practice when greeting a *group* of people. In Britain non-verbal behaviour is generally restricted to an occasional nod to some individuals in the group and the verbal greeting is directed to the group as a whole, whereas the Wolof use the appropriate non-verbal and verbal greeting behaviour separately towards each individual in the group (Irvine 1974).

Apart from entries and exits, non-verbal cues are important for structuring discourse as far as turn-taking is concerned. As we saw (4.3.2), one of the questions to be asked about turn-taking is how speakers signal that they are ready to stop and let the other person start. Eye-movements are one such cue. Research has shown that we normally look at the other person's eyes for much longer periods when we are listening than when speaking, so when we are about to stop speaking (and start listening) we look up at the other person's eyes, in anticipation of our next role as listener. Conversely, the other person looks down when he is about to start speaking, in anticipation of his change of role (Argyle & Dean 1965, Kendon 1967). Eye-movement is not the only signal of an approaching change of speaker. In some institutions (notably schools, conferences and parliaments), there are other, formalised, signals, such as a would-be speaker raising his hand. Less formalised signals include moving forward in one's chair or clearing one's throat. Equally, there are ways of countering such moves if the speaker does not want to yield the floor – such as deliberately looking away so that the would-be speaker cannot catch his eye.

4.4.3 *Content-markers*

Finally we come to the use of non-verbal behaviour for marking content. Again there is one very obvious instance of this in most cultures – the use of head movements to indicate 'yes' or 'no'. There are cultural differences in the particular head-movements used for each meaning – for 'yes', some cultures (e.g. Western Europe and the United States) use a top-to-bottom movement, others (e.g. the Eastern Mediterranean) use a bottom-to-top movement, and still others (e.g. the Indian subcontinent) use a diagonal movement. However, the use of a head-movement to mean 'yes' or 'no' seems sufficiently widespread to risk the hypothesis that it is universal, though it is hard to see why it should be.

Many other gestures also help to mark content. People may count on their fingers, and in some societies this is a recognised way of displaying numbers. Indeed, in East Africa there are differences between tribes in the rules for doing this, depending, for instance, on whether 'one' is indicated by the thumb or the little finger (Omondi 1976). There are also differences between the same tribes in the gestures used to show the height of a child, according to whether or not a hand is put, palm downwards, at the height of the top of the child's head. (Some tribes believe this could stunt the child's growth.) Every culture presumably has its own repertoire of gestures for commenting on people and objects, such as the various gestures in British culture for suggesting that someone else is crazy, or for saying that food is just right. Finally, one should not forget the gesture of pointing (done with different fingers in different societies), which is often associated with the use of demonstratives like *this* or *that* and *here* or *there*. It must be rather rare for *this* to be contrasted with *that* (e.g. *This is bigger than that*) without some kind of gesture as an accompaniment, even if it is only a nod of the head in the direction of the thing in question.

It would not be inappropriate to compare a speaker with the conductor of a large orchestra consisting of the various speech-organs and other visible organs of his body over which he has control. A successful performance requires the conductor to keep all these various organs moving in exact coordination with one another, whatever the speed of the performance and whatever the number of separate organs involved at one moment. To make his job even more taxing, he has to coordinate his performance with that of other conductors who are each conducting their own orchestras (that is, with other participants). It is no wonder that people sometimes find it easier to slip into fixed routines, nearer to music played from a score than to extemporised music like jazz. Nor is it surprising that the study of speech is still so rudimentary.

5

The quantitative study of speech

5.1 Introduction

5.1.1 *The scope of quantitative studies of speech*

For some sociolinguists the work we shall be describing in this chapter *is* sociolinguistics (see e.g. Trudgill 1978: 11), though the value of the work covered in the preceding chapters is generally acknowledged. The development of quantitative studies of speech has coincided with that of sociolinguistics and, for many linguists whose main interest is the structure of language, this part of sociolinguistics apparently makes the most relevant contribution, providing new data which need to be reconciled with current linguistic theories.

Quantitative studies of speech seem particularly relevant to theoretical linguistics because they involve precisely those aspects of language – sounds, word-forms and constructions – which theoretical linguists consider central. In chapter 2 we discussed the notion 'speech variety', covering the notions 'language', 'dialect' and 'register', but for many theoretical linguists these concepts are not problematic, and therefore not particularly important. In chapter 3 we explored the relations of language to culture and thought, an area that theoretical linguists have traditionally left to anthropologists and psychologists. Chapter 4 was about discourse, and showed (among other things) that the speaker selects his speech very carefully to fit the needs of the occasion. However, the aspects of speech referred to were mainly on the fringe of what many linguists would call language structure – vocatives, greetings, alternative pronoun-forms and so on, not to mention non-verbal behaviour. This is to some extent due to the historical accident that linguistics has recently been focussed on languages like English and French, in which discourse-markers happen to be rather peripheral to the rest of the system, in contrast with many of the other less familiar languages to which we have referred. Even so, many linguists see their main task as writing appropriate grammars for languages like English and French and believe that discourse-markers are the concern only of specialists in discourse.

In the present chapter we shall review work based largely on English (albeit often non-standard English) data and concerned with variations in the form of words and constructions. For instance, there are some speakers who never give words like *house* and *hit* an [h], in contrast with other speakers who do, so presumably these two groups of speakers have different language systems, one with an element (which for theoretical reasons we may or may not want to call a 'phoneme') [h], and the other without it. But for many speakers, the [h] comes and goes in such words – sometimes *house* has [h], at other times it does not. What are we to make of their language system? And what do we make of the fact that [h] sometimes appears in words like *apple*, where the people who regularly pronounce [h] in *house* and *hit* never have it? Similarly, there have been studies of the rules for making sentences negative. For some people, indefinite noun phrases after a negative *not* contain *any* (*I didn't eat any apples*), for others they contain *no* (*I didn't eat no apples*), and many speakers sometimes apply one rule and sometimes the other. What is the relation between these people's grammars? Exactly what kinds of differences are there between them – for instance, do they differ in morphology, in syntax or in semantics? And how should we allow for the people who alternate between the two systems? Questions such as these clearly lie at the heart of theoretical linguistics.

The work which we shall be reviewing below is all based on the study of spoken rather than written language (though in some cases the speaker is reading from a written text, such as a list of words), and its aim has been to find out about the everyday speech of ordinary people, in reaction to the high degree of idealisation that is typical of transformational-generative grammar (for a general critique, see Labov 1972a: ch. 8). As we shall see, this aim is harder to realise in practice than might be expected, and in some ways the work is just a continuation of a long line of careful studies by dialectologists (surveyed in Sankoff 1973a) and phoneticians. As in this earlier work, the investigator focusses his attention on a predetermined list of LINGUISTIC VARIABLES – elements which are known in advance to have different realisations, such as words which have more than one pronunciation (*house* with or without [h], *either* starting with [iː] or with [ai], and so on). For each variable, there is a list of its VARIANTS – the alternative forms known to be used – and the investigator goes through his texts noting which variants were used for each variable in his predetermined list.

The aim of this branch of sociolinguistics, like that of the 'dialect geography' branch of dialectology, is explicitly *comparative* – to compare texts with one another, rather than to make some kind of 'total' analysis of each text without reference to others. Each predetermined variable provides a separate dimension on which texts may be compared. For instance, we might have a hundred tape-recordings of different people talking in similar circumstances, and a list of ten linguistic variables which we know will show different variants from one text to another. When we have gone through the texts identifying the variants for each variable, we can group the texts on the basis of their use of variants – distinguishing for instance between texts where [h] occurs in words like *house* and those where it does not, between those where *any* and *no* are used after a negative, and so on. (Section 5.3 will show that the distinctions are not in fact so straightforward, but this complication can be ignored for the time being.) These groupings are similar in function to the dialect geographer's isoglosses (2.3.1) and (like isoglosses) typically *do not coincide with one another*. That is, it is unlikely that a hundred texts will fall into precisely the same groupings on the basis of any two of the different variables, just as it is unlikely that two different isoglosses will follow precisely the same route. (Of course, in both cases we can *make* different groupings coincide by choosing the texts, say from two different languages like English and French, and selecting variables which distinguish precisely between those two languages; but the methods under discussion here are neither used nor needed in order to make such gross distinctions.)

It should be clear that this way of studying linguistic variables in texts is precisely what is demanded by the view of language which has emerged from the previous chapters of this book, which have shown that individual speakers choose linguistic forms in order to locate themselves in a highly complex multi-dimensional social space. We have seen many examples of different linguistic variables, reflecting different social contrasts. For instance, in the sentence *John'll be extremely narked*, each word except *be* relates to a different dimension in this social space: *John* (rather than, say, *Mr Brown*) locates the speaker relative to John, *'ll* (rather than *will*) locates the occasion on the casual–formal dimension, *extremely* locates the speaker (I assume) on the educated–uneducated dimension, and *narked* (a regionalism meaning 'angry') locates him regionally. In some cases it may be fairly safe to use speakers' intro-spective judgments as evidence for distinguishing these different variables, but ultimately it should be possible to test any hypothesis formed in this way against what is found in texts, and this is the purpose of studying texts – to test hypotheses about relations among linguistic and social variables. The fact that the investigator starts with a pre-determined list of linguistic variables and their variants shows that he expects the variants in his list actually to occur in the sort of texts he has collected, and he also generally starts with a range of hypotheses about the social variables to which those in his list are related, such as region, social class or sex. All the work reported here is based on such hypotheses, but it is fair to acknowledge that some researchers feel there is a danger of prejudging the issue by starting with the wrong hypotheses about relations between linguistic and social variables (see e.g. Pellowe et al. 1972).

On the other hand, the study of texts is very time-consuming, and for purely practical reasons the studies carried out so far have concen-trated on linguistic variables which occur relatively frequently and which are relatively easy to identify. The frequency requirement tends to rule out the study of individual words, except for those like pronouns which occur very frequently; and instead of studying, say, how the word *house* is pronounced one asks how words spelt with *h* are pronounced, i.e. each of the linguistic variables tends to include a whole class of words (though we shall note a number of studies which have treated individual words, with interesting results). The frequency requirement also rules out many syntactic constructions, since those which are known to vary may only occur a few times each day (or week!) in the speech of a given person. The other criterion, that variables should be easy to identify, favours cases where it is clear that two forms are just different ways of saying the same thing – such as pronunciations of the same word. The two criteria may conflict – for example, individual words are good variables in that they are easy to identify, but poor from the point of view of frequency – and most instances of this type of work represent a com-promise which has weaknesses of one kind or another. However, there is no doubt (as I hope to show in this chapter) that the method has given rise to interesting and important results.

It is necessary, at this point, to mention the notation that is commonly used in the literature. Linguistic variables are given within parentheses: (h) would therefore represent the variable presence or absence of [h] in words like *house*, and (*no*/*any*) might be used as the name of the variable involved in *I didn't eat any*/*no apples*. We shall extend this convention by writing the name of a particular variant after the name of the variable concerned, separated by a colon. Thus, cases of the (h) variable where [h] was pronounced would be written (h):[h], in contrast with cases where it was absent, written (h):ø ('ø' is the symbol normally used in linguistics to represent 'zero' – i.e. the absence of some element).

5.1.2 *Why study speech quantitatively?*

If each text contained instances of only one variant for each variable, then it could be located in the relevant multi-dimensional linguistic space without using quantitative methods. For instance, if we were investigating (h) and (*no*/*any*) in a number of texts, we might (conceivably) find that some of the texts contained instances of (h):[h], but no instances of (h):ø, and that the other texts contained (h):ø, but no instances of (h):[h]; and similarly for the two variants of (*no*/*any*). In this case, each variable would define just two clearly distinct groups of texts, and the only complexity would be in the interaction between the two variables – on the basis of what we know about most English-speaking communities, we might expect (h):[h] to tend to occur in the same texts as (*no*/*any*):*any* and (h):ø to occur with (*no*/*any*):*no*, i.e. we might expect to find sentences like *We didn't see no 'ouses* and *We didn't see any houses*, but we might be less sure about *We didn't see no houses* and *We didn't see any 'ouses*. The study of a large number of texts would give us some indication of the extent to which these two linguistic variables are sensitive to the same social variables. If we found that (h):[h] was always found in the same texts as (*no*/*any*):*any*, and (h):ø and (*no*/*any*):*no* always occurred in the same texts, then we should be justified in concluding that both the linguistic variables were in fact sensitive to precisely the same social variable. Having come to this con-clusion, we might then look at the social background to the texts, so far as we knew it, and try to decide what this social variable was. Let us imagine that we found that all the texts with (h):[h] and (*no*/*any*):*any* were produced by people who were paid by their employers once a month, and all the others by weekly wage earners. It would then be reasonable to conclude that the relevant social variable was the kind of job the speaker held, and in particular whether it carried a monthly salary or a weekly wage, a conclusion that could be reached without any use of quantitative mathematical techniques.

Of course, the sociolinguistic world is not like this at all. Different variants of the same variable occur together in the same text, and texts can be arranged on a continuous scale according to how *often* the variants occur. For instance, in a study of the use of negatives by various groups of adolescents in the United States William Labov found that (*no/any*):*no* and (*no/any*):*any* occurred together in many of the texts he collected, with (*no/any*):*no* accounting for between about 80 and 100 per cent of the cases, according to the text (Labov 1972b: 181). Similarly, Peter Trudgill studied (h) in Norwich (England), and found that (h):[h] made up between 40 and 100 per cent of the occurrences of (h), according to the text concerned (Trudgill 1974a: 131). The *relations* between different linguistic variables are also a matter of degree, some being more closely related than others; and the same is true of relations between linguistic and social variables. It is rare indeed to find any linguistic variable whose variations *exactly* match those of any other linguistic or social variable, though it is common to find variables which match each other sufficiently closely to convince one that there is some kind of causal connection between them. Furthermore, social variables themselves are typically continuous rather than discrete – people are more or less wealthy, or manly, or educated, or intense, rather than falling into clearly discrete (and internally homogeneous) social groups.

All these facts call for a quantitative treatment of the data, using appropriate statistical techniques. The person mainly responsible for the use of quantitative methods in the study of texts is the linguist, William Labov, whose work will dominate the discussion in this chapter. (As we shall see, he has also made an important contribution to the methodology of data-collection and the theoretical interpretation of results.) However, Labov's work has stimulated many other very able researchers to study texts quantitatively, so there is now a large body of data on which we can draw for examples (see in particular the list in Labov 1972a: 205, and the following more recent anthologies: Bailey & Shuy 1973, Ervin-Tripp & Mitchell-Kernan 1977, Fasold & Shuy 1975, 1977, Sankoff 1978, Trudgill 1978). I will first outline what might be called the 'classical Labovian' approach to such work, and then illustrate some ways in which the method could be improved.

5.2 **Methodology**
5.2.1 *Problems of methodology*
Unlike most theoretical linguists, sociolinguists studying

texts quantitatively have paid a good deal of attention to methodology – how to collect reliable data, analyse it well, and interpret the results successfully (the standard discussion is Labov 1972a: ch. 8, especially 207–16). The methods used are unlike those which are applied in trans-formational-generative linguistics, where the input is usually the linguist's own judgments about isolated hypothetical sentences, and the main question is how to accommodate such data in a grammar with the least loss of generality or economy. Such questions usually play but a small part in the quantitative study of texts.

Methodology is both important and problematic at all stages in a sociolinguistic text study. The stages in such a study are:

A. selecting speakers, circumstances and linguistic variables;
B. collecting the texts;
C. identifying the linguistic variables and their variants in the texts;
D. processing the figures;
E. interpreting the results.

The stages inevitably follow in the order stated, but there is usually some cyclicity involving one or two small-scale pilot studies before the main study. Moreover, all the texts need not be collected before proces-sing starts, nor need all the variables be identified before the figures for some of them are processed. The order in which operations are carried out is less important than the methodology applied at each stage.

A. The *selection* of speakers, circumstances and linguistic variables involves some extremely important decisions, which are to a certain extent dictated by hypotheses about the expected results. For instance, we might start with the hypothesis that men and women in a particular community differ in their use of a particular set of linguistic variables, and that older and younger members of the same community differ with respect to some other set. In order to test these hypotheses, we clearly need to have speakers who represent all four possible combinations of age and sex, but we also need to make sure that other factors do not interfere with the results. For instance, if all the men selected were manual workers and all the women were 'white-collar' professionals, linguistic differences between them might result either from their occupation or from their sex, and no firm conclusion could be reached. Similarly, it is important that all the speech should be collected under the same circumstances, so far as this is possible.

There is a major problem of definition here, both for social variables relating to speaker and circumstances, and for the linguistic variables themselves. How do we define 'manual worker'? How do we distinguish 'old' from 'young'? How do we define circumstances precisely enough to keep them constant? How do we define the (h) variable? (If we define it with reference to orthography, then we should expect (h):[h] in words like *hour*; if we define it with reference to 'standard' speech, this presupposes that we can define 'standard' speech and can decide, for instance, whether *horizon* and *hotel* contain [h] in standard speech; and so on.) For that matter, how do we define [h] and ø, the variants of (h)? (That is, how much of a puff of breath does there have to be before we recognise an [h]?) Worse still, there are major problems in defining the community to be studied, since 'speech communities' are not self-defining, as we saw in 2.1.4. There are no easy answers to any of these questions, but somehow the would-be researcher has to provide solutions which are at least reasonably satisfactory, to avoid the real danger that his results will be valueless because of ambiguities in defining the variables.

B. After a decision has been reached as to what speakers will be appropriate under what circumstances, the *collection* of texts necessitates finding appropriate speakers who are willing to participate. Typically, this means finding people willing to be interviewed and recorded for about an hour in their homes, but many alternatives are described in the literature. This may mean gaining the confidence of a group of people and then obtaining their permission to tape-record them talking under otherwise ordinary circumstances (or the particularly ingenious alternative described on page 148). One practical problem is how to obtain tape-recordings which are sufficiently clear to be used later for identifying phonetic variants, without allowing the recorder to dominate the scene so much that it converts the conversation into the equivalent of a radio interview, thereby losing any chance of tapping the speaker's most natural kind of speech. There are no simple solutions, but with ingenuity (one of Labov's most noticeable characteristics) a satisfactory compromise can usually be found.

C. The *identification* of variants of the selected variables is the stage where one might expect the least difficulty, since we already know what the variants to be distinguished are, and all we need do is listen for them. However, there is a considerable degree of subjectivity in recognising phonetic variants (as opposed to 'higher-level' variants like (*no/any*)), and different researchers can produce different analyses of the same text, even when they are all highly trained phoneticians (Knowles 1978,

Le Page et al. 1974). One may also need to record information about the linguistic environment in which each instance of a variable is used, since this often influences the choice of one variant rather than another (see 5.4.1), but this is only possible if there is already a clear hypothesis as to which aspects of that environment are relevant. There may also be problems in identifying the linguistic environments – for instance, we may want to distinguish between cases where (h) occurs after a word-boundary (e.g. *house*) and where it occurs within a word (e.g. *behind*), but then have difficulty in deciding whether or not there is a word-boundary before the (h) in *greenhouse* and *summer-house*. Yet another problem at this stage is that it can be hard to decide which words or constructions should count as instances of some variable – we alluded to this problem briefly in connection with (h) (should *hour* be treated as an instance?), but it arises with virtually every variable, and leads to problems in interpreting the results as we shall see in 5.5.1.

D. The *processing* of the figures involves counting the number of identified occurrences of each variant in each text, and comparing the figures for different texts. The obvious first step is to reduce all the figures to percentages, since this makes comparison much easier. For instance, it is much easier to compare '80 per cent (h):[h]' and '65 per cent (h):[h]' with one another than to compare '73 out of 91 (h):[h]' and '97 out of 150 (h):[h]'. The next step is to discover which differences between texts are significant, i.e. which would form a reasonable basis for generalising to other texts of the same types. For instance, let us assume that we have analysed texts A and B and found that of the instances of (h), 20 per cent are (h):[h] in A and 40 per cent are (h):[h] in B. Have we here the basis for a generalisation about texts like A in contrast with those like B, to the effect that the former will contain a smaller proportion of (h):[h] than the latter? The answer depends on a number of factors, such as the number of instances of (h) in A and B on which the percentages are based, and the percentages found in any other A-like and B-like texts we may have available. In some cases the answer is obvious. For instance, if there were 1,000 instances of (h) in each of A and B, no one would hesitate in saying that the difference between 20 per cent and 40 per cent was significant; and if there were only five instances in each, the difference is clearly not significant (since it would take only one more instance of (h):[h] in A to bring it up to the same level as B). However, the answer is often not so obvious, and the investigator has to use statistical tests in order to decide how significant the figures are. This in itself raises problems, since there are many different statistical tests, each appropriate for a different type of data, and the investigator has to make sure that he uses the right one for his particular purposes. Since the start of quantitative studies of texts in the early 1960s the statistical techniques used have become steadily more sophisticated (for a recent survey see Sankoff 1978), but most would-be sociolinguists have little experience of even the most elementary aspects of statistics, so parts of the literature can seem somewhat daunting. It is certainly worthwhile for any serious student to learn about some of the commoner statistical terms and tests, such as standard deviations and chi-squared tests (a good and cheap introductory textbook is Miller 1975).

It is also important to understand that statistical techniques allow one to calculate the likelihood of some pattern of results occurring by chance – i.e. without any causal connection between the figures concerned – but never provide *proof* either for or against the existence of a causal connection. For instance, they can tell us that a particular pattern is likely to occur by chance only once in any thousand or more samples, but even such a remote possibility can never be ruled out entirely. However, the sociolinguist would feel fully justified in postulating a causal connection of some kind to explain the pattern. Even where a causal connection between two factors is reflected by the statistics, it does not follow that one factor is the cause of the other. It is possible that they are both results of some other factor. For instance, it would be easy to find a statistically significant connection between height and the ability to do mathematical operations, but this does not mean that either causes the other, but rather that both are part of the general process of growing up.

E. The *interpretation* of the results is in some ways the most difficult stage, since this is where the findings have to be fitted into a general theoretical framework dealing with the structure of language and its relations to society and individuals. Success at this stage depends not only on correct methodology at all the previous stages, but also on having an adequate general theoretical framework; and the most one can claim at present is that such a theory is only just beginning to appear. We shall outline some suggestions that have already been made in the sociolinguistics literature in 5.5, and need say no more about the interpretation of results at this point.

In view of all these problems, it should not be surprising that sociolinguists have paid a good deal of attention to methodology.

5.2.2 *An example: New York*

To give an idea of the range of methodology, we shall consider three separate pieces of work based on different methods. They do not represent all the types of work that have been done; for instance, they are all studies of urban communities, whereas a large amount of work has been done (especially on creole languages) in rural communities (see e.g. Bickerton 1975, Le Page 1972, Le Page et al. 1974), where the problems and methods are somewhat different. The first example is not so much an example of a widely used method, but of the personal ingenuity of William Labov (1972a: ch. 2).

Labov's first empirical work, carried out in 1961 on a small island off the New England coast (called Martha's Vineyard), demonstrated the existence of systematic differences between speakers in their use of certain linguistic variables (1972a: chs. 1 and 7), after which he worked in a very different kind of community in New York. The latter work mainly consisted of individual interviews with selected speakers, of the kind described in 5.2.3, but it was preceded by a preliminary study in which the data were collected in just a few hours and which is a classic example of the method of *rapid anonymous observation.*

Labov wanted to try out some hypotheses which he had already formulated about the use of a single linguistic variable, (r), in New York. This variable represents the presence or absence ((r):[r] versus (r):ø) of a consonantal constriction corresponding to the letter *r* in words like *farm* and *fair*, where the next sound is not a vowel in the same word (as in *very*). He was aware that New Yorkers sometimes use one variant and sometimes the other, which was of particular interest because the choice seemed to represent a change currently taking place, as New Yorkers moved from the previous norm of consistent (r):ø (as in British RP) towards a new and relatively consistent (r):[r] (as in many other United States accents). (The study of linguistic changes currently taking place has been one of Labov's recurrent interests, ever since his Martha's Vineyard work; see Bynon 1977: ch. 5.) Labov predicted that the proportion of (r):ø would be highest in the speech of older people (since (r):[r] is an innovation), and of lower-status people (since the new standard, (r):[r], is the result of influence from the high-status community outside New York). He further predicted that (r):ø would be most frequent when speakers were paying least attention to their speech, since they would then be worrying less about how their hearers were assessing their social status; and finally that the linguistic context of (r) would influence the variant used, (r):ø being favoured more by a following consonant than by a following word-boundary as could be predicted on general phonetic grounds from the widespread tendency to simplify consonant clusters.

The method used to collect data was very simple, but exactly suited the hypotheses to be tested. Labov walked round three New York department stores asking shop-assistants where some goods were that he in fact knew to be on the fourth floor. Predictably, each assistant would answer 'Fourth floor' or 'On the fourth floor'. He would then lean forward and pretend not to have heard the first answer, thus making the assistant say it again. By selecting the words *fourth* and *floor* he was able to test the hypothesis about the influence of linguistic context, because the (r) is followed by a consonant in *fourth* but not in *floor*. By asking for the answer to be repeated, he could test the hypothesis that the amount of attention to speech was relevant, since the assistant would clearly be more careful about the second utterance. The hypothesis about the influence of age could easily be tested by making a rough guess at the age of each assistant. Finally, Labov could test the hypothesis about social status by comparing the stores with each other, since they clearly served different ranges of clientele, and could be ranked from high status (Saks, Fifth Avenue), through middle status (Macy's) to low status (S. Klein). This ranking could be made on the basis of a number of easy criteria, such as the prices of their goods and the newspapers in which they advertised. Within each store further distinctions could be made among the assistants according to their jobs – between floorwalkers, sales-staff and stockboys – and even between different floors within each store, since higher-status goods are generally stocked on higher floors.

The method of recording was to note the relevant details about each assistant secretly, so that none of them realised that they were taking part in linguistic research, which might have influenced their speech. One of the difficulties of the method is that it requires an investigator who is not only a good phonetician but also an actor, although, as will be seen, it does effectively combine stages B (collecting the texts) and c (identifying the linguistic variables and their variants).

When the figures were processed they confirmed most of Labov's hypotheses. Figure 5.1, for instance, shows the percentage of (r) realised as (r):[r] for each word, taking 'first' and 'second' utterances separately in each of the stores. As predicted, the use of (r):[r] decreased

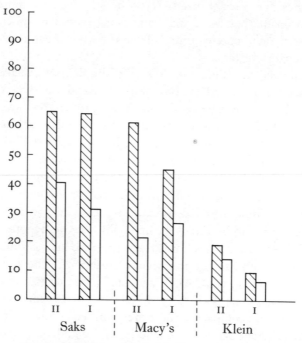

Figure 5.1. New York (r). Percentage of (r):[r] in first (I) and second (II) utterances of *fourth* (white) and *floor* (hatched) by assistants in three department stores (based on Labov 1972a: 52)

from high-status to low-status store, as witness the general decrease in height of the columns from left to right. Similarly, the hypothesis about the influence of attention to speech is confirmed by the tendency for the column labelled 'II' to be longer than that labelled 'I' for each store, except that there was virtually no change between first and second utterance of *floor* in Saks, and a decrease of (r):[r] between first and second utterance of *fourth* in Macy's. Before seeking an explanation for such deviations, however, it is important to find out whether or not they are statistically significant. No statistical tests have in fact been applied to these figures, so we cannot know whether it is more likely that the deviations are due simply to random fluctuation or that there actually is some reason for them. There is clear support for the hypothesis that *fourth* and *floor* are different, since the white columns are consistently shorter than the hatched ones. The percentage of (r):[r] in *floor* is consistently higher than in *fourth*, as Labov predicted.

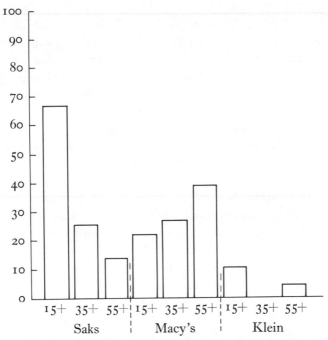

Figure 5.2. New York (r). Percentage of assistants in three age-groups and three stores using (r):[r] consistently (based on Labov 1972a: 59)

The hypothesis which was not confirmed in a direct and simple way was the one about age. It will be recalled that the original hypothesis was simply that older people would use the older variant, (r):ø, more than the younger, who would favour the innovating form, (r):[r]. The relevant figures (see figure 5.2) show that the hypothesis is confirmed for the high-status store, Saks, and data for Klein are at least not too hard to reconcile with the hypothesis, since the slight rise between the middle-aged and the elderly may be insignificant. (Incidentally, it should be pointed out that the percentages shown in figure 5.2 are not quite comparable with those in figure 5.1, since they show the proportion of *assistants* in each group who used (r):[r] in both occurrences of both words, whereas figure 5.1 shows the percentage of *utterances* of each word which contained (r):[r]; however, this difference is irrelevant for present purposes.) The problem is that the trend is in the wrong direction for Macy's, showing that older people used (r):[r] considerably more than younger ones at that store. This finding goes counter to

Labov's hypothesis, and led him to revise the hypothesis in an interesting way, by restricting it to people in the highest- and lowest-status groups. According to the revised hypothesis, these groups would be least likely to change their accents after adolescence, in contrast with the intermediate ones whose social aspirations might lead them to change accents in middle age to be more similar to the latest prestige accent. This is a clear example of the 'interpretation' stage of research, where the researcher goes beyond his processed figures and relates them to a general theory. The revised hypothesis was later tested and confirmed in Labov's main study of New York (Labov 1972a: ch. 5).

5.2.3 An example: Norwich

Another investigation, carried out in England by Peter Trudgill of Reading University, provides an example of the 'classical Labovian method', using *structured interviews* (Trudgill 1974a). The town selected was Norwich, of which Trudgill is a native – a fact which is highly relevant, since he not only had a good deal of 'inside' knowledge about the social structure of Norwich and its accent, but could use a Norwich accent himself when conducting the interviews, thereby encouraging speakers to speak more naturally than they might have done had he used RP. It is important to emphasise this kind of fact, since the influence of the interviewer's own speech on the interviewee is one of the main problems when using formal interviews for collecting data.

The selection of speakers was carefully planned, taking account of what was already known about the social structure of Norwich. Four areas were first selected as representing different types of housing and a range of social status, then individuals were randomly selected from the electoral registers of these four areas and contacted at their homes to see if they would agree to be interviewed. Most were willing (only 15 out of 95 people approached refused), but some had to be rejected for various reasons, such as that they had only moved into Norwich within the previous ten years. People who refused or were rejected were replaced at random by others, until a total of fifty adults who were willing and eligible had been identified. To these Trudgill added ten school children to broaden the age range, making sixty interviews in all. This may seem a small number on which to base general conclusions about the overall patterns of the 160,000 inhabitants of Norwich, but such a sample is statistically adequate to give a broad picture of patterns of variation, provided one does not want to take account of too many different social factors, or to make too fine a set of discriminations. (As a rule of thumb, one should aim at a minimum of five people in each social category, so twenty people would be adequate for a comparison of two social classes and two sexes, but forty would be needed if one were to add in a two-way age contrast as well; and so on.)

The circumstances under which speakers were to perform also needed to be selected. The preselection of speakers itself served to choose the circumstances, since a formal interview was the only feasible way to obtain the extensive data that was wanted. However, Trudgill followed Labov in structuring the interview so that it included a number of different types of circumstances. Most of the interview followed the usual pattern of an interview with a stranger, and could be expected to elicit a relatively formal style of speech. At one point the interviewee was asked to read a passage of continuous prose and a list of words, on the assumption that reading would produce a more formal style still, in which more attention would be paid to speech. At other points, however, the interviewee's speech moved towards a less formal style – such as when he was interrupted by another member of his family, or asked to talk about a time when he had had a good laugh. Trudgill, following Labov, claims that there are a number of 'channel cues', such as a change in tempo or pitch-range, which can be used to identify this less formal type of speech, so that each interview could be divided (unequally) into four styles: 'casual' (identified by the channel cues), 'formal' (the bulk of the interview), 'reading-passage', and 'word-list'. These categories may be taken to represent part of the repertoire of accents available to the speaker for use under different circumstances.

The linguistic variables were selected in advance from what was already known about variation found in Norwich. A total of 16 variables was selected for study (3 consonants and 13 vowels), so it is hard to give an overall picture of the results in the space available, and just one, (ng), will be cited to show how clearly it relates to the social variables studied. This shows alternative pronunciations of the *-ing* suffix, which is sometimes pronounced with [n] (represented conventionally by *n'*, as in *huntin', shootin' and fishin'*) as its consonant, and sometimes with [ŋ] (rhyming with *sing*). Thus there are two variants, (ng):[n] and (ng):[ŋ]. Of these (ng):[ŋ] is the one generally considered to represent standard English and RP, so we might predict in advance that (ng):[ŋ] will be used more often by high-status than low-status speakers, and more often under circumstances which draw attention to speech.

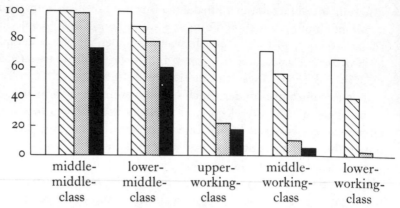

Figure 5.3. Norwich (ng). Proportion of (ng):[ŋ] in speech of five socio-economic classes in four styles: word-list (white), reading-passage (hatched), formal (dotted), casual (solid) (based on Trudgill 1974a: 92)

Trudgill's findings (figure 5.3) clearly confirm these two hypotheses. Each of the five histograms (i.e. groups of columns) represents the average scores for one group of speakers, reflecting a variety of factors: occupation, income, education, housing, locality and father's occupation (Trudgill 1974a: 36). Taken together, these factors are used to define a hierarchy of socio-economic classes. We shall have more to say later (5.4.2) about this kind of categorisation of speakers, but for the present they may be accepted as representing a hierarchy based on status. The findings confirm the hypothesis that (ng):[ŋ] is used more often by high-status than low-status people. Indeed, we can go further and make the hypothesis rather more precise: the use of (ng):[ŋ] in casual speech is very low (0–20 per cent) for members of the 'working-class' groups of speakers, and relatively high (60–80 per cent) for members of the 'middle-class' groups.

The hypothesis about the effect of differences in the amount of attention paid to speech is also confirmed by the general rise in the proportion of (ng):[ŋ] from the 'casual' to 'word-list' styles. However, the main difference for middle-class speakers is between casual and formal styles, whilst for working-class speakers it is between formal and reading-passage style. This raises interesting problems of interpretation, since it suggests that (at least with respect to this particular variable) middle-class speakers are sensitive to differences in the formality of what might be called unscripted conversation (using this term to cover both casual and formal styles), whereas working-class speakers are not, but are very sensitive indeed to differences between unscripted conversation and reading. If this hypothesis is true, could it be generalised to cover all variables, and not just (ng)? Some of the other variables show a somewhat similar pattern so the hypothesis looks reasonably promising, but it can be refined. There is no way in which the middle-class speakers could have increased their use of (ng):[ŋ] in reading compared with unscripted conversation, as they already used it nearly all the time, so it is possible that they are in principle just as sensitive as working-class speakers to differences between unscripted conversation and reading, and that their use of standard variants will be higher in the latter than in the former on variables where there is room for an increase. Just such a pattern is found in one of the other variables, the pronunciation of /t/ (which varies between standard [t] or [tʰ] and non-standard [ʔ] or [tʔ]): middle-class speakers increased their use of standard (t):[t] when reading just as sharply as working-class speakers (Trudgill 1974a: 96). On the other hand, there was very little change for the (t) variable between casual and formal styles, even for middle-class speakers, which seems to refute the first part of the hypothesis. Moreover, other variables seem to show very little change at all between styles within any group of speakers, although different groups of speakers differ clearly in their use of those variables.

So far as Norwich is concerned, one must conclude (with Trudgill) that the influence of style differs according to (i) the linguistic variable in question, (ii) the socio-economic class of the speaker, and (iii) the particular style-differences in question, with differences within unscripted conversation not necessarily in step with those between unscripted conversation and reading. The problem remains how to fit such findings into a general explanatory theory, but there is little doubt that we should not even have been aware that a problem existed without such quantitative studies of carefully collected data.

5.2.4 *An example: Belfast*
The final investigation we shall describe here is that by James and Lesley Milroy in Belfast, Northern Ireland, reported in a number of papers (J. Milroy 1978, L. Milroy 1976, Milroy & Margrain 1978, J. & L. Milroy 1978, L. & J. Milroy 1977). The methods used are quite different from those of the classical Labovian approach, as exemplified by Trudgill's Norwich study, but rather similar to those

used in the late 1960s by Labov himself in studies of the speech of black American adolescents (see especially Labov 1972b: ch. 7). We shall speak of the Milroys' work in the past tense, but they live in Belfast and were still developing their approach in 1978.

The main difference between the Milroys' work and that of Trudgill reported above is that Lesley Milroy, who did most of the field-work, was accepted as a friend by the groups whose speech she studied, which made it unnecessary to use the formal interview technique. This had the great attraction that it was possible to study genuinely casual speech, as used between friends, because the researcher's presence did not increase the formality of the situation. However 'casual' a stranger may try to be, an interview remains an interview, and there is no guarantee that what Labov and Trudgill referred to as 'casual' speech is at all close to the most relaxed speech of the speakers concerned. Another advantage of the method is that it opens new and exciting possibilities for the theoretical interpretation of sociolinguistic data. By becoming a friend of the people one is investigating one becomes part of a *network* of relations among them, and can use the structure of this network as social data to which speech may be related. We shall return to this point below (5.4.3).

Before starting their research, the Milroys decided not to try to cover a complete spectrum of the socio-economic classes, but to exclude this dimension and concentrate on the speech of working-class people in Belfast. Three specific working-class areas were selected, all typical 'decayed core working-class areas with a high incidence of unemployment and other kinds of social malaise' (J. & L. Milroy 1978). Behind these similarities, however, there were important differences between the areas. Two were unambiguously Protestant and one Catholic, and in one of the Protestant areas (Ballymacarrett) the traditional local industry, the ship-yard, was still employing local men, whereas the traditional employer of men in the other Protestant area (The Hammer) and the Catholic area was the linen industry, which has declined, leaving men either unemployed or travelling outside the area to work. We shall see later that this difference in employment patterns is highly relevant to speech differences.

Within each area Lesley Milroy gradually built up a relationship with a particular group of people, by being passed on from one to another as a 'friend of a friend' – a well-recognised status in this community, which confers a status almost equivalent to that of a member of the family. Of course, building and maintaining a large number of friendships makes heavy demands on a researcher's time and energy (not to mention courage and tact in a strife-ridden city like Belfast), and such research is not for the armchair sociolinguist. As a result of these efforts Lesley Milroy became accepted as a friend who could 'drop in' at certain houses at any time, to sit in the kitchen listening or taking part in the conversation for as long as she wanted and even to use her tape-recorder, after explaining that she was interested in Belfast speech. Under such circumstances it seems unlikely that her presence, or even that of the tape-recorder, affected the way in which people spoke.

The Milroys processed these recordings in much the same way as Trudgill, identifying variants of a predetermined list of variables and comparing their frequencies across texts. The main interest of their findings is the light which they throw on the effect of the social network structure on speech, which will be discussed later in relation to the various social correlates of variations in speech (see 5.4.3).

5.3 Linguistic variables
5.3.1 *Types of variable*
The linguistic variables which sociolinguists have studied are those where the meaning remains constant but the form varies, though in theory one could study such aspects as the different ways in which past-tense forms are used as a linguistic variable. There are, however, serious problems if we try to use this as a *definition* of 'linguistic variable' since it is hard to be clear about what counts as 'the same meaning'. For instance, it could be argued that *cat* and *pussy* have the same meaning, and therefore might be considered as a linguistic variable, in much the same way as, for example, alternative pronunciations of *house* with and without [h]. Against this it could be argued that 'meaning' ought to be defined more liberally, to include what is often called 'social meaning', in which case *cat* and *pussy* would have different meanings and could not be treated as variants of a linguistic variable. Fortunately, the notion 'linguistic variable' itself is not meant to be taken as part of a general theory of language, but rather as an analytical tool in the sociolinguist's tool chest, so we need not worry unduly about such problems of definition. Sociolinguists who use linguistic variables have made no attempt to define them rigorously, and there seems to be no point in trying to do so here.

Apart from saying that a linguistic variable should not involve a change

157

of meaning, there is little to be said about which aspects of language may have variables. They may be found in the pronunciation of individual words or of whole classes of words (say, all those beginning in one accent with [h], or all those ending in *-ing*), and in the patterns of syntax. In the studies just described the variables all concerned pronunciation, but there is now no shortage of studies of syntactic variables, as illustrated in the following list:

(*no/any*) in black and white adolescent American English (Labov 1972b: ch. 4)
    e.g. I didn't eat no/any apples.
presence/absence of *is/are* in black American English (Labov 1972b: ch. 3 is just one of many such studies)
    e.g. John (is) tired.
presence/absence of *that* as subordinating conjunction in standard American English (Kroch & Small 1978)
    e.g. They think (that) it's difficult.
presence/absence of *ne* in Montreal French (Sankoff & Vincent 1977)
    e.g. Pierre (ne) dort pas. 'Peter is not sleeping.'
avoir/être as auxiliary with certain verbs in Montreal French (Sankoff & Thibault 1977)
    e.g. Pierre a/est parti. 'Peter has left.'
fu/tu as preverbal particle ('to') in Guyanese creole (Bickerton 1971)
    e.g. You want fu/tu go.

The last item is just one of many syntactic variables which have been studied in creoles, where they seem to be particularly common. However, not many of these studies have been quantitative (two exceptions being Le Page 1977a, Le Page et al. 1974). There are general surveys of syntactic variables which either have been studied, or ought to be, in Sankoff (1973b) and Trudgill (1978: 13).

There are major problems which make pronunciation variables harder to study than might be expected. The current state of disarray in phonological theory, where, for instance, the status of phonemes and the nature of underlying forms of words is still in doubt, gives rise to one such problem. Is one justified, for example, in treating the [r] sound in *cart* as an instance of the same 'phoneme' as that in *car*? Could one use the differences which Labov found in his New York study as evidence that they are different phonemes (assuming that 'phoneme' is a meaningful term)? Is it justifiable to postulate a phoneme such as /h/ in the underlying forms of words like *house* when speakers nearly always leave the sound out in ordinary speech? If not, by what right do we assume that such speakers are illustrating the same variable in choosing between *house* with and without [h] as other speakers who normally have the [h], but sometimes 'drop' it? These problems seem less important if we treat linguistic variables simply as analytical tools, but the question remains how to interpret figures for linguistic variables which have been applied indiscriminately to all the speech in a sample, without paying attention to the details of each speaker's language system. (For an interesting suggestion for a solution to such problems which by-passes the linguistic questions entirely, see Sankoff & Thibault 1978.)

Apart from problems of defining the variables themselves, there are others in listing the variants for any given variable, including the question of *discreteness*. It is hard to think of any variables which do not raise this problem to some degree, but it looms particularly large in the case of vowels. For instance, one of Trudgill's variables in the Norwich study was (a:), the vowel in words like *after*, *cart* and *path* (Trudgill 1974a: 87). This vowel varies in Norwich from a back [ɑ:] to a very front low vowel [a:]. Trudgill recognises one intermediate value between these two extremes, which he transcribes [ä: ~ ä:], but this is presumably a matter of convenience rather than a division determined in some way by the facts of Norwich pronunciation. We can assume that there is a continuum between [ɑ:] and [a:], any division of which is at best arbitrary, and at worst misleading if it distorts the results. For instance, if a simple two-way distinction had been made, without any intermediate stage, it would have given the impression that Norwich speakers always locate their pronunciations of this variable at one extreme or the other, without providing any way of investigating the possibility that they also use the intermediate forms. The same problem arises even with variables like (h), which appears at first to refer simply to the presence or absence of some sound-segment, whereas [h] may be present to different degrees, just as the (a:) vowel may be pronounced with different degrees of 'backness' in the mouth.

Another problem concerns *dimensions* (see especially Knowles 1978). The last paragraph gave the impression that the (a:) variable involved only a single phonetic dimension, namely frontness/backness, but Trudgill's transcription involves a second dimension of nasal/oral, since the front variant (though not the back and central ones) may or may not be nasalised [ã:]. Trudgill groups [a:] and [ã:] together as instances of the same variant, so there is no way of finding from his analysis whether they were used by different kinds of people or under different circumstances, and we must assume that Trudgill was sure in advance that they were not. One could fairly object that this was something of which he could not have been sure until he had made the full analysis, but the Labovian system of analysis forces one to reduce all the phonetic dimensions on which variants may differ to a single dimension, represented by a single ordered list of variants. (We shall see why this is so in 5.3.2.)

The problems become even more acute where a larger number of phonetic variables are involved, as in the Belfast (a) variable (see J. & L. Milroy 1978), which is the vowel in words like *bag, back, fat, man* and *fast.* This has the following range of variants: the local prestige form associated with middle-class speakers is [a], but among working-class speakers [ɛ] (i.e. relatively raised and fronted) is used before velar consonants (*bag, back*), while other contexts show a variant further back than [a], and also sometimes raised, with or without a centring off-glide, giving for instance [ɔ·ə]. The interest of this example is not only that several different phonetic contrasts are involved (front/back, low/raised, with/without off-glide), but that it is hard to see how the variants could be reduced to a single ordered list on phonetic grounds, since there are no obvious extreme sounds to provide end-points for the lists. There are extremes, of course, but too many of them, since [a], [ɛ] and [ɔ·ə] could all justifiably be treated as extremes. The problem is that the Labovian method requires a single ordered list of variants, whereas a triangular pattern, like the one for Belfast (a), cannot be reduced to such a list. (Berdan 1978 describes a statistical technique for representing results on a number of different variables in terms of a single, more abstract variable, but even with this technique it may be necessary to have more than one such abstract variable.)

5.3.2 *Calculating scores for texts*

The classical Labovian approach offers an attractively simple method for assigning scores to texts, to show similarities and differences between speakers' use of linguistic variables, but we shall see that it also has serious weaknesses. A score is calculated for each variable in each text, which allows texts to be compared with respect to one variable at a time, which is the prime aim of quantitative studies of texts. To calculate the text scores for a given variable, a score is assigned to each of its variants; the score for any text is then the average of all the individual scores for the variants in that text. To take a simple example, let us say we have a variable with three variants, A, B and C, and we have calculated the score as 1 for each instance of A, 2 for each B and 3 for each C. Now assume that we have a text containing 12 A's, 23 B's and 75 C's. We calculate the text score by calculating the scores for all the A's ($12 \times 1 = 12$), all the B's ($23 \times 2 = 46$), and all the C's ($75 \times 3 = 225$), then adding all these together ($12 + 46 + 225 = 283$) and dividing the answer by the total number of variants found (i.e. $12 + 23 + 75 = 110$), giving $283 \div 110 = 2.57$. This is the score for the text concerned for this variable, and it will of course be easy to compare it directly with scores for other texts for this same variable.

This method has two failings, both of which are important. The first is to do with the RANKING of variants, on which we touched in 5.3.2. Assigning separate scores to individual variants (1 for an A, 2 for a B, and so on), has to be based on some kind of principle, otherwise the results may be nonsense. Scoring is not simply arbitrary, since the apparent relations among texts could be completely changed by using a different scoring system. There is no problem if a variable only has two variants, since it makes no difference which one is scored 'high' and which 'low' (provided, of course, that the same scores are given throughout the analysis). The problem arises where there are three or more variants, since the scoring system reflects a particular *ordering* of the variants, with two variants picked out as maximally different and the others arranged between them as intermediate values. This means that whenever three or more variants are recognised on a single variable, the analyst has to be able to pick out two of them as the extremes and to arrange the remainder between them. This can be done in many cases on the basis of the phonetic relations among the variants, in the case of a phonological variable, since often the variants can be arranged on some phonetic dimension such as vowel height. However, we have seen that this is by no means always the case – there may be more than one such dimension involved – so the phonetic facts do not tell the researcher how to order the variants. Another basis for ordering is the social prestige of the variants, which allows the most standard and the least standard variant to be picked out as the extremes and the others ranked in between according to relative 'standardness'. The problem with this approach is that it assumes in advance that society is organised in a single hierarchy reflected by linguistic variables, whereas this often turns out not to be true, so the method biasses the research towards incorrect conclusions.

The second weakness of the Labovian scoring system is connected with the distribution of variants, since the final figure for a text gives no idea of the relative contributions made by individual variants. A score of 2 for a text in our hypothetical case could reflect the use of nothing but B (scoring 2 each time it occurs), or of nothing but A and C, in equal numbers, with no instances of B at all. Let us take an actual example, using data from a study of the (r) variable in Edinburgh by Suzanne Romaine (1978). This study is unusual in providing separate figures for individual variants, rather than aggregate scores for the whole variable. The variable (r), like the one which Labov studied in New York, applies to words containing an *r* (in the written form) not followed by a vowel in the same word. However, these particular figures apply only to (r) occurring at the end of a word, and show the influence of the linguistic context: whether the word is followed by a pause, or by another word beginning either with a consonant or a vowel. The variants are not quite the same as those distinguished by Labov, since there are two possible types of consonantal constriction for (r) in Edinburgh, a frictionless continuant, as in RP and most American accents [ɹ], and a flapped [r]. The distribution in the three contexts described above of these two variants, plus the zero variant (ø), is shown in table 5.1. Context shows some quite complex patterns of influence on the choice of variant. A following vowel greatly favours the flapped [r] in comparison with either of the other variants, but other contexts favour both consonantal variants about equally, though the zero variant is more popular before a pause than before a consonant. If the figures in this table were reduced to text scores in the usual way, most of this information would be lost. Say we score 1 for [r], 2 for [ɹ] and 3 for ø,

Table 5.1. *Edinburgh (r): three variants as percentages of (r) in three linguistic contexts (based on Romaine 1978:149)*

	Before vowel	Before consonant	Before pause
[r]	70	40	34
[ɹ]	26	48	38
ø	4	12	28

a typical text would score 1.34 for (r) before a vowel, 1.72 before a consonant and 1.94 before a pause, so we might guess that [r] is more common before a vowel than before a pause, and perhaps that ø is more common before a pause than before a vowel, but this would be just a guess, and there are many other ways of interpreting the figures, including of course the complex interpretation they in fact demand.

It therefore seems preferable not to reduce figures to a single score for each variable, but to keep those for each variant separate, as percentages of the total cases where the variable occurred, so making it unnecessary to assign separate scores to variants, and also solving the problem of ranking.

5.3.3 *Calculating scores for individuals and groups*

In a sociolinguistic study of texts the investigator has material produced by different individuals, and often more than one text from each, produced in different circumstances (as in the case of Trudgill's tape-recordings, where each interview comprised four different texts, one for each style). A typical research project might involve the study of 10 variables in the speech of 60 people under 4 types of circumstances, producing $10 \times 60 \times 4 = 2,400$ separate scores for texts, if the classical Labovian method were used. The figure would of course be much larger if the alternative of quoting separate scores for individual variants were adopted. The problem is how to handle such a large amount of data without being swamped. By far the most satisfactory solution is to use a computer with a sophisticated statistical programme, which is now widely done where sufficient funds and manpower are available.

However, another solution is to reduce the number of figures by producing averages for individuals or groups of individuals, and this is still common practice among sociolinguists. For instance, if we can reduce 60 speakers to 8 groups defined, say, by sex and socio-economic class, we immediately reduce the total number of figures from the 2,400 given above to 320, which means just 32 figures for each variable taken on its own. Moreover, the number of cases covered by each of the figures is increased, since each score for a variable will represent a whole group of speakers instead of a single one. This has the advantage of increasing the statistical significance of any differences between scores, since this depends not only on the size of the difference but also on the number of cases involved. There are thus great gains from merging separate figures into averages.

163

The quantitative study of speech

All the actual figures quoted so far (figures 5.1–5.3, table 5.1) have been group averages and not scores for individual speakers. This is typical of the literature, where it is in fact rare to find figures for individual speakers. (Some recent exceptions are Douglas-Cowie 1978, Macaulay 1978, Reid 1978; other studies, such as Labov (1972a: 100–6, 168, 288, 306) and Le Page et al. (1974), quote figures for selected individuals but not for their whole sample.) However, the practice of reducing individual figures to group scores has two regrettable consequences, rather similar to those that stem from reducing variant scores to variable scores (p. 161).

A reliance on group scores alone conceals the amount of variation within each group. A group score of, say, 2 for some variable ranging from 1 to 3 could be produced either by all the members of the group having scores very close to 2, or by some scoring 1 and others 3. In the former case, the group average of 2 represents a norm around which the speech of the group members clusters, whereas it is completely meaningless or misleading in the second case. There is no way of knowing whether any given group average is meaningful or not, without some indication of the amount of variation within the group, which is admirably provided by a widely used statistic called the 'standard deviation', which is low when there is little variation and rapidly increases in size with increasing variability in the group of figures. The kind of pattern

Table 5.2. *Tehran Persian vowel-assimilation: percentage of vowels assimilated in the casual speech of 40 speakers of 8 groups based on education and sex*

Sex:	Male				Female			
Education:	univ.	second.	prim.	none	univ.	second.	prim.	none
Scores:	7	24	46	71	5	21	33*	55*
	12	28	48	77	5	22	38*	60
	13	32	53	81	6	23	39*	67
	14	36*	56*	81	6	28	43	68
	18	41*	57*	82	6	29	48	73
Average:	13	32	52	78	6	24	40	65
Standard deviation:	3	6	4	4	0	3	5	6

which may be found where variation is small within groups is shown in table 5.2, demonstrating that predefined groups of speakers may turn out to be remarkably homogeneous as far as their speech patterns are concerned, in contrast with the case illustrated in table 5.3, where predefined groups are relatively heterogeneous linguistically.

The figures in table 5.2 were supplied by Nader Jahangiri from data collected by Labovian interviews with 40 speakers of Persian in Tehran (see Jahangiri 1980). The variable is concerned with the assimilation of one vowel to another in the following syllable in words like /bekon/ 'Do!', whose first vowel varies between [e] and [o]. Each figure represents the percentage of assimilated vowels in the speech of one speaker, and the speakers are arranged in eight columns, each representing a separate group. The groups are defined on non-linguistic grounds, on the basis of education (university, secondary, only primary, or none at all) and sex. Two things are particularly remarkable about the figures in table 5.2, namely the homogeneity of the groups and the lack of overlap between them. The overlap is shown by the asterisks, which are attached to scores in one educational group which overlap with those in the adjacent one. For instance, the two scores of 36 and 41 at the foot of the 'Male, secondary' column overlap with the figures 33, 38 and 39 at the top of the 'Female, primary' column. It will be seen that there is no overlap at all between educational groups of the same sex, and all the asterisks represent cases where the males of one group overlap with the females of the next group 'down'. As for the homogeneity of the groups, this is shown by the standard deviation figures, which reflect the extent to which the individual scores deviate from the group average. The standard deviation figures are surprisingly low, none of them being above 6, and one of them being the amazing 0 representing the virtual identity of the scores for female university graduates. This figure is all the more impressive when one remembers what it represents: the percentage of words like /bekon/ whose first vowel is assimilated to the second in casual speech. Results such as these offer a real challenge to anybody looking for a psychological and sociological model to explain linguistic variation.

A study of the pronunciation of sixteen 11 year old boys from three different schools in Edinburgh is the source of the data in table 5.3. The children wore radio microphones while playing in the playground, and the data collected were thus expected to be close to the kind of speech the children used naturally. The three schools were chosen so that each

Table 5.3. *Edinburgh (t): percentage of (t)*
realised as [ʔ] *or* [ʔt] *by sixteen children in*
'playground style' (based on Reid 1978: 160)

School 1	School 2	School 3
30	60	65
69†	80†	71
69†	85	80
100	85	88
100	89	
100	90†	

would cover a different range of social backgrounds, but it can be seen that grouping boys according to their school produced very hetero-geneous results from the point of view of the (t) variable, with a great deal of overlap between groups. Reid also gave information about the occupation of the boys' fathers, but even this supposedly more accurate measure of social status did not produce much more homogeneous groupings. All the boys from school 1 had fathers classified as 'foremen, skilled manual workers and own account workers other than profes-sionals', with the exception of the two marked with daggers, whose fathers were 'semi-skilled or unskilled manual workers or personal service workers'. The two boys marked with a dagger in the column for school 2 also had fathers in the 'foremen, etc.' class, whereas all the rest were in the class of 'professionals, managers and employers'. Whether we base groups on school, or on father's occupation, or on both, it seems clear that group averages for the use of (t):[ʔ] would be rather meaningless.

The other problem which arises from group scores is related to the first, and in fact arises out of it. If grouping speakers or texts is simply a matter of convenience for the analyst faced by an otherwise unmanage-able mass of data, there is probably no problem. No doubt the grouping will help him to see various broad trends in the data which he might otherwise miss. But there is a danger of moving from this position to a very different one, where one believes that groupings are socially 'real', part of the objective structure of society, and therefore part of the theoretical framework that is referred to in interpreting the results. This may be justifiable in some cases, but it is important to consider alterna-tive ways of interpreting the data without assuming the existence of discrete groups in society. We have already mentioned one such alternative (p. 30), according to which society is structured at least partly in terms of networks of more or less closely connected people, who are influenced to different degrees by the norms of the various networks. The weakness of group analysis is that it makes no allowance for people who belong to groups to different extents; and when individual scores have been merged in group averages there is nothing to indicate whether or not this should have been taken into account. We shall return to the use of networks below (5.4.3).

To summarise this section, we have criticised the Labovian method of identifying variants and calculating scores because it loses too much information which may be important. Information about the use of individual variants is lost when these are merged into variable scores, and information about the speech of individuals is also lost if these are included in group averages. At each stage the method imposes a structure on the data which may be more rigid than was inherent in the data, and to that extent distorts the results – discrete boundaries are imposed on non-discrete phonetic parameters, artificial orderings are used for variants which are related in more than one way, and speakers are assigned to discrete groups when they relate to each other in terms of networks rather than groups. It is not always easy to make the analysis less rigid, but we may hope that new methods will produce even more enlightening results than the classical Labovian approach.

5.4 Influences on linguistic variables

5.4.1 *Linguistic context*

This section reviews the kinds of factor which have been found to influence the choice of variants on linguistic variables, starting with the effects of linguistic context. Strictly speaking this is not a matter for sociolinguistics at all, but for a purely 'internal' study of language structure without reference to society. However, linguists interested in relations internal to language have tended not to study texts, but to use introspective methods, so that the quantitative study of the influence of one item on contiguous ones has been left to sociolinguists. Once again, William Labov was the first to make a detailed study of such patterns, in his study of the 'deletion' or contraction of *is* in the speech of black American adolescents (Labov 1972b: ch. 3).

On the whole, this work has shown that the influence of linguistic context on the selection of some variant may be probabilistic rather than categorical, as some previous work had tended to assume. For example, table 5.1 showed that the influence of the sound following a word potentially ending in /r/ made a variant more likely to occur in some contexts than others, rather than eliminating it entirely from some contexts and making it obligatory in others. Most descriptive linguists and phoneticians have probably always been aware that some areas of language worked like this, but their theoretical frameworks have no place for probabilistic differences.

As for the contexts that have been referred to, they are mostly of quite familiar kinds. For pronunciation variables we may refer to the type of sound following the variable, or to its place in the word, and so on. A number of variables involve the presence or absence of some word, and frequently both phonological and syntactic aspects of the linguistic context are relevant. An example is the variable (*is*) which Labov studied (Labov 1972b: ch. 3), covering the forms *is*, *'s* and ø. This was found to be influenced by the grammatical class of the subject (NP or pronoun), that of the complement (adjective, noun phrase, locative, or verb), and the nature of the next sound (vowel or consonant). There is at least one instance of a purely syntactic variable influenced by the syntactic context, namely the variable (*bai*) in Tok Pisin (Sankoff 1973b). *Bai* (derived from 'by and by') is a future-tense-marker, and occurs either before or after the subject, depending on whether this is a noun phrase or a pronoun. If it is a pronoun, *bai* is more likely to precede than to follow it, but neither order is totally excluded in either case.

Probably the most interesting aspect of the study of the linguistic context is the question of *lexical* differences between contexts. It is becoming clear that the probability of a particular variant occurring in a word may vary according to what that word is, and not on general phonological or syntactic properties of the word. For example, in Belfast one of the variables is the vowel in words like *pull*, *put*, *took* and *could*, which we can call the (ʌ) variable. This varies between [ʌ] (as in RP *cut*) and [ʉ] (similar to RP *put*, but somewhat closer). As part of the analysis of data collected by the Milroys, a list of individual words containing this variable vowel was drawn up, and a score calculated for each word (Maclaren 1976, J. Milroy 1978). The occurrences of words containing (ʌ):[ʌ] (table 5.4) illustrate the general point that gross differences in the probability of a variant may occur from one word to another without it being possible to account for them in terms of general phonological differences between the words.

The reason why figures such as these are interesting is that they

Table 5.4. *Belfast* (ʌ): *percentage of* [ʌ] *in eight words* (*based on Maclaren 1976*)

	Percentage of [ʌ]	Total no. of occurrences
pull	74	69
full	47	32
put	39	309
took	33	148
could	31	266
look	27	191
would	16	541
should	8	59

provide support for the theory of LEXICAL DIFFUSION – the theory that a diachronic sound-change may spread gradually through the lexicon of a language, rather than affecting all the relevant words at the same time and to the same extent (see Chen & Hsieh 1971, Chen & Wang 1975, Hsieh 1972, 1975, Wang 1969, Wang & Cheng 1970). There is evidence that the [ʌ] pronunciation of words like *pull* in Belfast is an innovation, so table 5.4 shows that this innovation has affected different lexical items to different extents. According to J. Milroy (1978), the overall differences in table 5.4 reflect the fact that some words are given the [ʌ] pronunciation (more or less consistently) by different proportions of the population – three-quarters of their sample of speakers say [pʌl] for *pull*, but less than one in ten says [ʃʌd] for *should*. In other words, for any given speaker each word is in one or the other of two lexical classes, the [ʉ] class and the [ʌ] class, and the change from [ʉ] to [ʌ] involves the gradual transfer of words from the [ʉ] class to the [ʌ] class.

How does the theory of lexical diffusion relate to the wave theory discussed in 2.3.2? According to the latter, changes spread gradually through the population, just as, according to the former, they diffuse through the lexicon, so we might expect a connection between them. A reasonable hypothesis is that changes spread cumulatively through the lexicon at the same time as they spread through the population, so that the words which were affected first by the change will be the first to be adopted in the new pronunciation by other speakers. From table 5.4 we cannot tell whether this is actually the case – it could be, for example, that the few people who use the new pronunciation of *should* still use the old pronunciation of *pull*, and vice versa, whereas our hypothesis

predicts that the new form of *should* will be used by people who use the
new form for all the other words in the list as well. A small amount of
evidence in favour of this hypothesis comes from table 5.5, which relates
again to the phenomenon of vowel-assimilation in Tehran Persian (see
table 5.2). It gives two separate sets of data for six words which are
capable of undergoing the process. The figures on the right show how
often each word was assimilated in the free speech of all the speakers
studied, revealing a gross difference between words like /bekon/ which
assimilate nearly every time they are used, and /bebor/ which hardly
ever assimilate. The plus signs on the left show which of these words
were assimilated by seven selected speakers who were asked to read a
list of words which could assimilate. It can be seen that speaker A used
assimilated forms for all the words, in contrast with G who assimilated
none of them, and that any word assimilated by one speaker would also
be assimilated by all those to his left in the hierarchy. (This kind of
pattern is known as an 'implicational hierarchy', and will be discussed
in 5.5.2.) As far as the selected words and speakers are concerned, then,
table 5.5 shows that the innovation of vowel-assimilation is diffusing
cumulatively through the lexicon and the population, as predicted by

Table 5.5. *Tehran Persian vowel-assimilation: use of assimilated forms
of six words by seven speakers reading word list, and by all speakers in
free speech (based on Jahangiri 1980)*

	Assimilation by seven speakers reading word list							Assimilation in free speech by all speakers	
	A	B	C	D	E	F	G	% assimilated	Total
/bekon/ 'Do!'	+	+	+	+	+	+		91	331
/bedo/ 'Run!'	+	+	+	+	+			78	23
/bexan/ 'Read!'	+	+	+	+				40	139
/begu/ 'Tell!'	+	+	+					22	132
/bekub/ 'Hit!'	+	+						4	122
/bebor/ 'Cut!'	+							3	124

our hypothesis. However, it has to be admitted that the words and speakers were specially selected in order to illustrate this point as clearly as possible, and that the pattern for the research as a whole, which used ten speakers who were asked to read sixty words in all, is much messier, suggesting that the hypothesis is probably too simple. For instance, it is hard to see any reason a priori why an innovation should not be applied to new words by people other than the originators of the innovation (or their descendants), but this possibility is excluded by the hypothesis.

5.4.2 *The speaker's group membership*

The most obvious source of influence on linguistic variables is the speaker himself, i.e. the kind of person he is and the experiences he has had. (Another obvious source of influence, which has already been mentioned, is the formality of the situation.) Various kinds of difference between speakers have been widely and exhaustively studied by sociolinguists, including region of origin or of present home, socio-economic status, sex, race and age. According to the theory of acts of identity, such factors will influence people's speech only to the extent that they represent social groups with which speakers can identify themselves – in other words, what counts is not so much one's experience of a particular variety of speech, but rather one's willingness to identify oneself with the kind of person who uses it. However, it is worth mentioning that there is a small amount of evidence that sheer exposure to a standard variety on television *can* affect the speech of people who show no other sign of identifying with the upper social class (Naro 1978). The effect of the mass media on people's speech deserves careful study, but has received virtually none.

We have already quoted examples of differences due to socio-economic status (pp. 148, 165), age (p. 148) and sex (p. 165), and there is no need to multiply such examples, but two factors have not yet been illustrated and are worth discussing here since they will be relevant to 5.4.3. They are the influence of place and race.

The influence of the *place* where a person lives has been studied by Peter Trudgill (1975b), who took a linguistic variable in southern Norway, the vowel (æ), which varies between [ɛ] and a slightly raised and backed [a]. The latter is an innovation which is currently spreading from the local town, Larvik, to the surrounding region. The only other settlement of any size in the area is Nevlunghamn, which is connected to Larvik by road, and Larvik and Nevlunghamn are on opposite sides

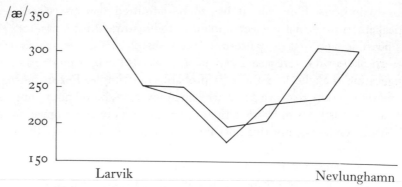

Figure 5.4. Southern Norway (æ): scores for selected households in and between two centres of influence. High score = high incidence of (æ):[a] (based on Trudgill 1975b)

of a peninsula (which is in fact the southern tip of Norway). Trudgill and a Norwegian colleague interviewed people living in selected houses at regular intervals along two lines between Larvik and Nevlunghamn, as well as others living in these towns themselves. Figures for (æ) in the speech of the people interviewed are shown in figure 5.4, in which the horizontal axis represents distance between the towns, the vertical axis represents the proportional use of (æ):[a], and the two lines represent the two routes between the towns. The curves in figure 5.4 are exactly as we should expect them to be according to the wave theory (2.3.2). The highest scores are in Larvik, where the innovation started, the next highest in Nevlunghamn with its easy road link and regular commercial and other contacts, and the lowest scores are in the home-steads furthest away from either of these centres of influence. Once again it is hard to know exactly how to interpret the figures in linguistic terms – are the differences due to differences in the number of lexical items affected by the innovation (see p. 169), or in the general rate of application of a rule replacing [ɛ] by [æ]? However, in either case we can see how the linguistic influence of Larvik is proportional to the amount of social contact with people in Larvik.

The factor of *race* has been shown to be relevant by William Labov and his associates in New York, working on distinctive features of the speech of black adolescents. A number of patterns of speech are charac-teristic of black, rather than white or other, speakers in the northern states of the USA, including use of the so-called 'zero copula', i.e. using nothing at all where white speakers would use *is*, as in *John tired* 'John is tired'. (More precisely, Labov has shown that the zero variant is used by blacks where whites would use the contracted *'s* – see Labov 1972b: ch. 3.) It appears that whites in the northern states virtually never use the zero copula, whatever their socio-economic status, but whether blacks use it or not, and how often, depends on how close they feel to the black sub-culture. Evidence for this comes from Labov's study of one particular black gang (or 'peer-group') in Harlem, called the Jets. Having established regular contact with this group, he was able to study its internal structure and relations to the other black adolescents in the neighbourhood. By asking who associated with whom, he identified four separate groups: core members of the Jets, secondary members, peripheral members, and non-members. (The latter are called 'lames' by black adolescents, and are those least closely associated with black culture, although they may of course be just as dark-skinned as the core Jets.) When Labov calculated scores for each of the four groups showing what percentage of their use of (*is*) was made up of zero copulas, he found a steady decline from the core to the edge of the gang. Core Jets scored 45 per cent zeros, secondary Jets 42 per cent, peripheral Jets 26 per cent and lames 21 per cent. (The totals of (*is*) were respectively 340, 223, 82 and 127, i.e. large enough samples for the differences to be taken seriously.) This illustrates the way in which linguistic variables may be exploited by speakers as subtle symbols of the extent to which they identify with some group, in this case one based on race. Even the lames identified themselves as black by their occasional use of (*is*):ø, since whites never use the zero copula, but distanced themselves from the central core of the black community by using the zero copula less often than core members. (This account is based on Labov (1972b: ch. 7), and the figures are derived from those on p. 279.)

We have already discussed examples of *socio-economic status* affecting speakers' scores, but now it is necessary to ask some fundamental questions about the concept of 'socio-economic status' itself. First, is it a unitary concept? That is, is there a *single* hierarchy for each society which has a hierarchical structure, to which various factors such as wealth, education and occupation contribute as defining characteristics, or is it just a loose term for a range of different hierarchical structures which are more or less independent of each other – one for wealth, another for education, and so on? Most work in sociolinguistics has tended to accept the first position, and has used a scoring system for speakers which accounts for a variety of factors. For instance, Trudgill took account of occupation, income, education, housing, locality and father's occupation, reducing these factors to a single scale. On the other hand, it is rightly considered an empirical question whether such a procedure is correct, and sociolinguists feel that they have unusually clear data for answering the question, since it reduces to a matter of statistics. Given the scores for speakers in any body of texts and background information about speakers' income, education and so on, which social factors, alone or in combination, provide the best basis for predicting the scores?

Interestingly, Labov himself provided an indication of the answer, namely that different factors are relevant to different variables, which is perhaps what we might have expected if society is viewed as a multi-dimensional matrix in which the individual locates himself. In Labov's main interview-based survey in New York, the best basis for predicting scores for some variables, e.g. (r), was a combination of occupation, income and education whereas, for others, it was a combination of just education and occupation (Labov 1972a: 115). An instance of the latter kind of variable is (th), pronounced as either [t^h] or [θ] in words like *thing*. Other sociolinguists have produced social hierarchies that correlate remarkably well with the scores for linguistic variables on the basis of just one factor, such as education (table 5.2). Sociolinguistic data seem therefore to suggest that factors such as occupation and education ought to be recorded separately but allowed to interact with one another, in just the same way that they can interact with factors such as age and sex. In other words, the data give relatively little support to the notion of social status as a unitary phenomenon.

A second fundamental question is whether society can be allocated neatly into separate groups defined on the basis of social status, which we might call 'socio-economic classes'. In view of the answer to the first question, it seems unlikely that this is how societies are organised, since the different possible bases for defining the classes are likely to conflict, which means in effect that each criterion defines a different set of classes. Moreover, there is increasing evidence that the notion of discrete groups in society is generally less illuminating than the view that society is organised round a number of distinct focal points, each defining a separate norm for behaviour, and attracting to varying degrees allegiance from members of the society. There is no a priori reason why socio-economic classes should constitute an exception to this principle, so the notion of such classes should probably be reinterpreted in terms of focal points rather than discrete entities (in the same way that the meaning of *red* can be defined as a point on the spectrum rather than an area – see 3.2.2).

Interesting questions can then be asked in a meaningful way on the basis of sociolinguistic data. In particular, where a variable is sensitive to 'social-status' factors such as education or occupation, do the scores always suggest that the norm-setters are at the extremes of the scale, i.e. are those with the highest or lowest status? This is clearly the case, for instance, with vowel-assimilation in Tehran Persian, where the highest and lowest incidences of assimilation are among the lowest- and highest-status speakers respectively (table 5.2). Similarly, (ng) polarises society in Norwich into the 'middle-class' norm of (ng):[ŋ] and the 'working-class' norm of (ng):[n] (figure 5.3). Figures 5.1 and 5.2 suggest a similar interpretation for New York (r).

On the other hand, there are cases in the literature where a norm seems to be defined by a group in the *middle* of the hierarchy, supporting the idea that society is not necessarily polarised between 'top' and 'bottom' as far as speech is concerned. An example is the variable (e) reported by Trudgill (1974a: 104), which occurs in a rather small class of words like *tell* and *better*, where /ɛ/ is either followed by /l/, or is preceded by a bilabial consonant and followed by /t/ (which must be glottalised) in a stressed penultimate syllable – a nice example of the possible complexity of linguistic variables! (e) varies between close [e]

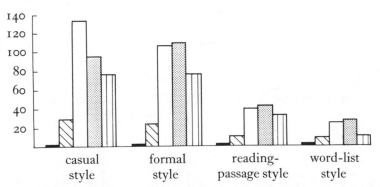

Figure 5.5. Norwich (e): highest scores for five socio-economic classes and four styles. High score = high incidence of (e):[ɐ]. Classes: middle-middle (solid), lower-middle (hatched), upper-working (white), middle-working (dotted), lower-working (vertical stripes) (based on Trudgill 1974a: 105)

and open [ɛ], and the highest incidence of the open variant (which, incidentally, is an innovation in Norwich) is among the *upper*-working-class speakers (figure 5.5 below). Middle-class speakers seem to be relatively unaffected by this variant, but both middle- and lower-working-class speakers aspire to it. Interestingly, the middle-working-class speakers actually increased their use of the open variant in formal interview style compared with casual style, although this meant moving *away* from the norm defined by the middle class, whereas the upper-working-class speakers in formal style were moving away from their own norms in the direction of the middle-class one. To make matters even more complex, all speakers from all classes moved towards the middle-class norm when they were reading, abandoning the other norms altogether.

To make sense of these patterns, it seems that we must postulate no less than three norms: a middle-class norm (e):[e], a lower-working-class norm, which is phonetically the same as the middle-class one, and an upper-working-class norm (e):[ɛ]. Different norms applied in different circumstances (figure 5.6). All three norms applied in casual speech, and their influence is shown by the arrows. In formal style, the scope of the influence of the norms changed, with the middle-class norm now reaching as far as upper-working-class speakers, whereas the lower-working-class norm did not influence any other class. In the reading-styles, only the middle-class norm is operative at all.

To conclude, we have surveyed a number of social factors on the basis of which people may associate themselves with one another – place of origin or home, age, sex, race and various factors involved in socio-economic status, such as education and occupation. Each of these factors

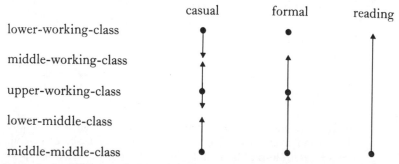

Figure 5.6. Norwich (e). Scope of influence of three norms in three styles

may influence people's use of linguistic variables, either directly or in combination with other factors. This is not to say that any one of the factors must be relevant to speech in every society – for instance, in the whole of Australia there appears to be amazingly little variation due to place of origin or of present home (see e.g. Mitchell & Delbridge 1965). Nor are these the only factors which can influence speech – they are just those which most sociolinguists have studied, and many other factors, such as politics and religion, are also potential sources of influence. Indeed, it would be unwise at this stage to rule out any social factor at all as a possible source of influence. Why one set of factors is relevant in one community and a different set in another is as yet unexplained. We might guess that the relevant factors are those that, for the community concerned, were most important from a social point of view, but it is hard to see much support for this hypothesis from the available facts. For instance, religion might be expected to be a source of influence in Northern Ireland, given the importance of religious divisions in that community, yet the Milroys' data do not appear to show significant differences between the Protestant and Catholic areas they studied which could not be explained in other terms. It would be interesting to have explanations for these (and many other) facts which the quantitative study of texts has produced.

5.4.3 *The speaker's degree of group membership*

This section develops the notion that an individual's use of a linguistic variable depends on the *degree* to which he is influenced by one or more norms in his society. We have already looked at some research which gives strong general support to this idea, such as Trudgill's data on the gradual spread of (æ):[a] in Norway and that of Labov on the use of zero copulas by black adolescents in Harlem, in addition to the many examples we have cited of the influence of differences in social status. The Milroys have specifically investigated this aspect of variation, and we shall outline the theoretical interpretation which they put on their findings, which fits very easily into the general model of language which has been developing through the previous chapters. (See also Gal (1978) for similar data from a rural community in Austria.)

The Milroys selected their speakers through personal introductions within a network of contacts, and they were able to spend a great deal of time in the households concerned, getting to know the structure of their social relations (see 5.2.4). The three communities studied were all typical poor working-class areas, and many of the families involved were typically working-class in being part of a 'closed network', i.e. a network of people who have more contacts with other members of the same network than with people outside it. This affects the *kinds* of relations they have, for, in a traditional working-class area, ties of friendship, work, neighbourhood and kinship will all reinforce one another. One effect of belonging to such a closed network is that people are very closely constrained by its behavioural norms and there is consequently little variation between members in their behaviour (or at least in the norms which they accept). This being so, we might expect to find a relatively high degree of conformity in speech, which is one type of behaviour governed by norms. Conversely, people who do not belong to a closed network, or who belong to a network united by fewer types of bond, might be expected to show a relatively low degree of conformity to the speech norms of any closed network. This hypothesis was tested by the Milroys against their data, and their findings are reported in Milroy & Margrain (1978).

Briefly, the hypothesis was confirmed. Some of the people the Milroys recorded were from extremely closed networks, but others had looser relations to the community. Each speaker was therefore scored for the 'strength' of the network connecting him or her to the other members – a 'network strength score' (NSS), which was calculated by taking account of five factors, for example, whether or not the person concerned had substantial ties of kinship in the neighbourhood, and whether he worked at the same place as at least two other people from the area. It was then possible to make statistical tests on the scores for linguistic variables to see whether any of them correlated with the speaker's NSS. Many of the variables did so, supporting the hypothesis, but the findings went beyond this.

Five of the eight linguistic variables studied showed an overall correlation with NSS, i.e. were influenced by NSS in all subsections of the communities studied – whereas the other three were influenced by network strength in some subsections, though not in all. This is an impressive finding, especially in view of the fact that the variables studied were not chosen in advance with a view to their relevance to network strength.

Secondly, following from the first point, different sections of the community recognised different ranges of linguistic variables as 'membership badges' of their core network. For instance, one variable, (ai), is only used in this way by people in Ballymacarrett and another, (I), only in The Hammer. Similarly, a third variable (called (Λ^1)) is used only by older people as an index of membership strength. This is not to say that other sections of the community avoid using the variants which are associated with core membership of the network, but only that they do not use the variable as a way of showing their group membership. To illustrate this point we can refer to differences between men and women. On two of the variables, (a) and (th), men used a higher proportion of the 'core' variants overall than women, but men's scores for these variables were less closely correlated with their NSS than women's. There is thus some tendency for men (but not women) to use the core variants often irrespective of how close they are to the core of the community. For a woman, however, a high frequency of core variants is a more reliable indicator that she is near to the core, as measured by the NSS.

Thirdly, it is possible to use the NSS to connect scores on some linguistic variables with known facts about social structure. For instance, there are clear differences between males and females for most of the variables in Belfast (just as there are in many other communities – compare, for instance, the figures for Tehran in table 5.2), and equally there are differences in NSS, where men score higher than women. Since the sex differences on linguistic variables show that men use more of the core variants than women (with one exception to which we shall return), sex differences on the linguistic variables can be *explained* as an automatic consequence of differences on the network-strength variable, and consequently we need no longer postulate sex as an independent social factor influencing this linguistic variable. The question is, then, why men score higher on network strength than women. The theory of networks provides an easy answer: assuming that men go out to work more than women do, and that they work with men from their own neighbourhood, men form more work bonds than women, but have roughly the same number of other bonds. Overall, therefore, their networks have more bonds and their NSS will thus be higher. The differences in speech can therefore be explained, more or less directly, with reference to differences in employment patterns.

However, if the employment patterns are not like this, and men do not go out to work with others from their neighbourhood any more than women do, speech differences seem to disappear, to judge by the Belfast data. Of the three areas studied, Clonard has lost its traditional source of male employment, the linen industry, but has stayed relatively undisturbed by the large-scale movement of population which occurred in the other area affected by the decline of the linen industry (The Hammer). The third area, Ballymacarrett, still has a ship-yard to employ its men. Consequently we should expect to find the traditional differences between men and women only in the Ballymacarrett community, while at the other extreme the difference will have been neutralised by the men's loss of local employment. The NSS for the Clonard area confirmed this prediction. Indeed, on the whole women had higher NSS than men in this area, reversing the usual pattern. (It is not clear why the difference should have been reversed, rather than simply neutralised.) The scores for some linguistic variables in the Clonard area also showed that women often used the core variants as often as men (compare, for instance, the figures for the variable (Λ) in J. & L. Milroy 1978: 26). Many facts about the Belfast patterns remain to be explained, but at least the use of network strength as a social variable seems to take us a useful step nearer to understanding them.

The three Belfast communities studied by the Milroys were all low-prestige and relatively tightly knit, but of course not everybody belongs to such a community, especially in modern urban society. What norms govern the speech of these others? They may have access to a standard dialect to use as norm, in which case they are likely to use it because of its prestige. The only thing which might restrain them in accepting this norm is the knowledge that there are other local, less prestigious, ones and that, by accepting the standard, they would be rejecting the others which, for various reasons, may have some value for them. Those who are influenced totally and whole-heartedly by the standard (in Britain, those who speak standard English with an RP accent) may be just as similar to each other in their speech as members of one of the closely knit communities in Belfast, but for quite a different reason: not because they have a dense network of social contacts with each other, but because the norm to which they adhere has been standardised, with all that implies in terms of codification in grammar books and dictionaries, teaching in schools, use in the media, and so on (see 2.2.2).

A person whose norms are provided neither by a closely knit community nor by a standard dialect must, presumably, be able to choose from a wide variety of models, and will himself contribute yet another, unique, model to the world for others to take account of. The community in which he lives will therefore show a relatively high degree of diversity, or *diffusion*, in its linguistic patterns compared with the two other types of community, whose linguistic norms are relatively *focussed* (see Le Page 1968a). Linguists have tended to select relatively focussed communities for their studies (p. 34), and have consequently constructed theories of language which have relatively little room for variability. Even in the small, closely knit communities studied by the Milroys, there was a considerable amount of variation in detail, so we may expect relatively gross variation in more diffuse communities. This prediction seems to be borne out by studies of pidgin languages, which are interesting precisely because of their diffuseness (see 2.5.3), but there remains a great shortage of relevant data on ordinary diffuse language. For instance, it would be of considerable interest to know how much variation there is in Trudgill's Norwich 'upper working class' which appears to have been able to introduce a new norm of pronunciation (figures 5.5, 5.6). What social forces keep this norm alive and even make its influence extend to the middle and lower working classes? We may look forward to understanding these processes better after a few more decades of sociolinguistic research.

5.5 Interpreting the results

5.5.1 *Variable rules*

So far in this chapter we have taken the linguistic interpretation of variation somewhat for granted, leaning heavily on the notion 'linguistic variable' and ignoring the problems of relating such variations to elements of language in a way that could be justified on theoretical grounds (see the discussion in 5.3.1 for some of these problems). How then can the results of a quantitative study of texts be interpreted in terms of linguistic theory? Both William Labov and Derek Bickerton have attempted to answer this question, and we shall consider their answers in turn, indicating some of the weaknesses in their arguments. Both agree (and it is hard to disagree) that it is not possible to explain variability in speech either in terms of some kind of general 'performance' factor, such as laziness or limitations of memory, or in terms of 'dialect mixture', whereby two homogeneous dialects are mixed up in different proportions in a person's speech. These hypotheses both fail to explain how it is that different linguistic variables can be affected in different ways by the same performance factors or dialect mixture, as they surely can.

Labov's answer (e.g. Labov 1972a: 216ff) is quite straightforward in principle, since he accepts the general correctness of transformational-generative grammar (as it was expounded in the late 1960s), and also that every linguistic variable corresponds to a rule of grammar. His variables correspond either to phonological rules or to syntactic transformations, the two kinds of rule which can refer to a linguistic context. Having made these assumptions, the only further step needed to make the grammar compatible with variability was to introduce the notion of VARIABLE RULE, to stand alongside 'obligatory' and 'optional' rules. Whereas obligatory rules have to apply wherever the conditions for applying them are satisfied, and optional ones may or may not apply under such circumstances, a variable rule has a specified probability of applying when its conditions are satisfied, ranging from complete certainty (when it is effectively an obligatory rule) to complete impossibility, For the purpose of notation, Labov introduced the convention of writing the right-hand side of a variable rule between the 'less than' and 'more than' signs < and >, in order to show that the rule was 'more or less' likely to apply. Thus, for instance, the (h) variable could be represented by a rule of '[h]-deletion', written like this:

$$h \rightarrow \; <\!\varnothing\!> .$$

Each variable rule is accompanied by some kind of statement about its probability of occurrence under whatever circumstances affect that probability, giving that information in one of two ways. If the only relevant factors are linguistic, those contexts which favour the variable may be listed as part of the environmental statement about the rule, showing their relative influences on the rule's probability by the order in which they are listed, or by special indices. The other method, used where the influences are social rather than linguistic, is to specify a formula for working out the probability of the rule, given values for whatever social variables are specified. (The details of these two methods need not be elaborated here; the interested reader is referred in particular to Cedergren 1972 (a good introduction), Cedergren & Sankoff 1974, Labov 1972b: ch. 3, D. Sankoff 1978.)

Labov's answer has a number of serious weaknesses. The assumption that every linguistic variable corresponds to a *rule* in a transformational grammar must be rejected. Take for instance the (h) variable, representing the presence or absence of [h] in words like *house* in so many English accents. Translating linguistic variables directly into variable rules, we must arrive at the rule quoted above, which presupposes that words like *house* contain an underlying [h] in their lexical representation for every member of the community to which this grammar applies – in other words, that every member of the community knows that *house* potentially contains [h], whereas *owl*, for instance, does not. But the problems are that many communities, especially among the least educated, do not normally use [h] in *house*, etc., so the child would find it difficult to learn which words contain [h], and also that many such speakers do *not* know which words contain [h], so that they use [h] in words like *owl* or *office* where standard speakers do not. In other words, for such speakers there must be a special rule of '[h]-insertion', for use on formal occasions, to be applied to any word starting with a vowel, in the hope that at least sometimes the [h] will be appropriate and will give a more educated impression of the speaker. For others, the [h] is of course clearly present in their lexical representation of *house*, but not of *owl* or *office*, so that if they pronounce words like *house* without [h], this is the result of a rule for deleting [h]. The variable (h) therefore turns out to correspond not to one rule but to two different ones, each appropriate for a different section of the community. (It is even conceivable that some members have *both* rules, if they have some words with [h] in their lexicon, but know that there are more such words in the standard, without of course knowing which these are.) Similar arguments could be applied to the (r) variable in New York and parts of Britain where the use of /r/ is variable, such as Edinburgh (table 5.1).

It might be objected that there is no problem in principle in assigning a variable to two different rules. There would need to be some recalculation of probabilities (e.g. in order to prevent middle-class people from applying the [h]-insertion rule), but it would otherwise just be a question of adding the necessary variable rules to the grammar. However, this is not so, since there would also need to be two separate lexicons, one with and one without the [h]'s in the entries for underlying forms. There would then need to be some way of choosing between two separate lexicons, with a degree of probability attached to the choice, something which the mechanism of variable rules is certainly not able to do.

Another weakness of Labov's variable-rules apparatus is that it is intended to be used in grammars for whole *communities*, rather than for individuals (as transformational grammars are normally written). This is because the probabilities are intended to reflect differences between speakers, taking account of factors such as socio-economic status. This presents a serious difficulty, since, as we saw above, different members of the community may require different grammars, notably when there are differences in the lexicon (for further discussion and exemplification of this problem see Kay 1978, Milroy & Margrain 1978, Matthews 1979: 45). Moreover, speech communities are hard to delimit satisfactorily (see 2.1.4), and, without an absolutely precise definition of the speakers for whom a given grammar is intended, any claim will be untestable and essentially empty.

It is perhaps significant that Labov's theory of variable rules has had little or no influence on the writing of grammars since it was first propounded in the late 1960s, although linguistic variables have been studied on a large scale. Labov himself, after his first attempts to write grammars containing such rules (1972a, b), has apparently proceeded no further in this direction.

5.5.2 *Implicational relations among grammars*

Building on the work of Charles-James Bailey (1972, 1973) and David DeCamp (1971b, 1972), Derek Bickerton's attempt to fit variability into a linguistic theory (Bickerton 1971, 1972a, b, 1973, 1975) refers explicitly to the wave theory developed as part of comparative linguistics and linguistic geography (see 2.3.2). The theory is quite simple in outline, which is one of its main attractions. Bickerton claims that all linguistic variability is either random or the consequence of different grammars being used on different occasions (and often by different speakers). Where the variation is random, it can be handled by means of the well-established apparatus of optional rules, and there is no need to build probability differences into the grammar, as Labov does; and where the variation is systematic it can be handled by simply postulating different grammars of a conventional sort (which he, like Labov, assumes to be some variety of transformational grammar).

This could equally well have been said of any version of transformational grammar of the ordinary, asocial, kind, but Bickerton goes well beyond this position to take account of a large amount of socially oriented data which he had accumulated, mostly during work in Guyana (South America) on the 'creole continuum' (i.e. the continuum of varieties which exists in communities like Guyana between the creole 'basilect' and the standard 'acrolect' – see 2.5.4). In order to make a place for the very considerable amount of variation to be found in a creole continuum Bickerton made two main suggestions.

He distinguishes between the 'idiolect', in the sense of the total range of speech of a single individual, and the LECT, or ISOLECT, which is a grammar made up of a set of rules compatible with one another but excluding any alternatives (except for those leading to random variation). This distinction between the 'grammar' and the 'individual speaker's competence' means that a given speaker could be allowed to include more than one lect in his competence, and his performance could be correspondingly variable. The total amount of variability found in a community would thus be handled in three steps: (i) by distinguishing between random and significant variation; (ii) by writing individual lect grammars covering all possible combinations of forms; and (iii) by finding out which individuals use which lects, taking it for granted that many, or even all, of them will use more than one. This approach clearly makes the analyst's job harder than would Labov's, since one cannot take either the common community grammar or the unity of the individual speaker's grammar for granted. However, the existence of a shared basic grammar in every community has already been questioned (p. 183), and the importance of allowing each individual to be treated separately in the analysis emphasised, so in these respects Bickerton's seems a more realistic approach than Labov's.

Bickerton's other main suggestion was that relations among the lects, at least in the community he had studied, were sufficiently systematic and constrained for the analyst to write an ordered set of rules for converting one lect into another (on similar lines to transformational rules, but their formalisation is a matter of detail which need not concern us). The fact that such rules are ordered means that the lects can be arranged in an IMPLICATIONAL HIERARCHY, in the same way that we saw that speakers can be ranked relative to lexical diffusion (table 5.5). An implicational hierarchy is a kind of relation between properties and individuals such that the possession of one property from the hierarchy entails the possession of all the others below it in the hierarchy. The properties concerned might be different rules of grammar, or the same rule applying in different environments, as in the example below (from Bickerton 1971). In Guyana, there are two forms for the particle which introduces an infinitive (standard English *to*): the basilectal *fu* (or *fi*), and the acrolectal *tu*. The rule for choosing between these selects *tu* in certain environments which are in an implicational hierarchy as follows:

environment I: after 'inceptive' verbs like *staat* 'start', *begin*,

environment II: after 'desiderative' verbs and other 'psycho-logical' verbs such as *want*, *disaid* 'decide', *trai* 'try', *beg*, *alau* 'allow', *fuget* 'forget',

environment III: after other verbs – e.g. *ron* 'run', *kom* 'come', *bara* 'borrow', i.e. when the infinitive expresses purpose.

There are lects in which *tu* is used in environment I but in neither of the others, and lects in which it is used in I and II but not in III, and others in which it is used in all three, but sufficiently few instances of *tu* occurring in II without occurring in I, or in III but not in II or I, to justify postulating a hierarchy with I as a prerequisite for II and II as a prerequisite for III.

By moving the locus of variability out of the individual grammar into the relations between grammars, we in effect move the study of it out of descriptive linguistics into comparative linguistics. In particular, it becomes a branch of comparative historical linguistics, since one is asking 'How do the relations among contemporary varieties (i.e. lects) reflect the historical changes through which these varieties have come to be as they are?' Bickerton claims that the synchronic relations within a creole continuum reflect the diachronic changes very closely indeed, since for him the implicational hierarchy of rules or environments con-stitutes the only possible 'ladder' up which speakers may climb in moving from the basilect towards the acrolect. Thus the rules which convert one lect into another are simply the synchronic relics of actual historical changes, which took place in the past as low-ranking speakers edged their speech in the direction of the acrolect, setting an example that was followed by other speakers. If we think of these moves as introducing acrolectal (or at least non-basilectal) forms as innovations into basilectal speech, it is easy to see this approach as an attempt to introduce the wave theory (2.3.2) into synchronic linguistics.

Another obvious parallel can be drawn between Bickerton's theory and that of lexical diffusion (discussed in 5.4.1). Unlike Labov, Bickerton has concentrated on syntax and semantics rather than on pronunciation, but like Labov his discussions are about relations between rules rather than between lexical items. However, it is easier to see how Bickerton's theory of variability could be used to describe variability in lexical items, since lects may differ in their lexical items just as easily as in their rules. In either case, all that is needed is a conversion rule for changing an item in one lect into a different item existing in another. The theory of lexical diffusion could thus be treated as a special case of Bickerton's theory of the relations between lects.

It is perhaps important to distinguish in this theory between its most general features and potential and its particular applications to the Guyanese data, because the latter could in some respects represent an atypical sociolinguistic situation, with a relatively clear hierarchy between basilect and acrolect. Bickerton himself denies that there is a single implicational hierarchy for all aspects of the grammar (a point made even more explicitly in DeCamp 1972). For instance, some aspects of the phonology may vary independently of the variations in the form of *tu/fu* and of other aspects of the syntax. Indeed, it seems highly likely, a priori, that this is so. Thus the relations between lects must not be described by means of a single implicational hierarchy, but by a larger number of small hierarchies, each containing a fairly small number of rules or environments. This considerably increases the flexibility of the model compared with the simple interpretation where there is just a single hierarchy, and in particular it allows the model to be applied to the *multi-dimensional* kind of situation which exists in many communities. We may see each implicational hierarchy as reflecting a separate dimension in the social world, and implicational hierarchies could even be envisaged as working in opposite directions along the same social dimension – for instance, one change spreading from town to country and another spreading from country to town.

For all its attractions, Bickerton's theory has two serious short-comings, the first of which is that no allowance is made for probabilistic differences between lects, of the kind which are surely shown to be a reality by the data quoted in this chapter. For instance, how would the relations between the various lects in Tehran Persian (table 5.2) be described? (Incidentally, it is worth pointing out that the differences in the Persian data are not a matter of lexical diffusion, since lexical differences have explicitly been allowed for in the data by excluding frequent lexical items.) For any given rule, Bickerton only allows three possible relations to a lect X: it must be obligatory, optional or non-existent in X, but all the lects in table 5.2 have vowel-assimilation as an optional rule, so Bickerton's theory does not allow us to distinguish them.

The second shortcoming also concerns probabilities, namely that Bickerton's rules for relating lects to each other are themselves probabilistic statements about the most likely relations among them. His own data give plenty of examples of individual lects which infringe the implicational hierarchy, although these deviant lects are sufficiently outnumbered by the regular ones to suggest a significant trend. Thus we can take Bickerton's lect-relating rules as interesting and revealing statements about the *most likely* route for individuals to follow between basilect and acrolect, but they do not cover the full range of variability found in the community, since the deviant lects are excluded. It seems, then, that, in describing the speech of a community, it is not sufficient to have a description of one or more 'base-point' grammars and then a collection of lect-relating rules (in implicational hierarchies). Instead one needs a complete description of every lect found in the community, including the deviant ones, supplemented by a comparative commentary on the relations among these lects. In other words, the distinction between descriptive and comparative linguistics re-emerges, and the problems of the descriptive linguist are exactly the same as they were before – how to identify the object of his description (what Bickerton calls the 'lect', which will surely be just as hard to pin down as the idiolect, given that it relates to more than one implicational hierarchy), and how to identify the patterns in speech and their interrelations.

5.5.3 *An ideal theory*

It is now perhaps possible to identify the features which a linguistic theory ought to have in order to include the strengths of the two theories outlined above while avoiding their weaknesses. No current theory has all these features, but it is by no means impossible to imagine such a theory being developed in the next decade or so.

Firstly, the theory must include both descriptive and comparative linguistics. The description of the grammar of the individual speaker will be based on the theoretical principles of descriptive linguistics, while the range of speech found in a given community will be described in terms of the theory of comparative linguistics. In this way we shall travel safely between the Scylla of assuming that everybody has the same individual grammar and the Charybdis of leaving possible differences between individual grammars completely unconstrained. The descriptive part of linguistics will cover the familiar range of questions about the exact structure of particular grammars, or of grammars in general, and the comparative part will have a number of interesting and important questions to answer, including those which have come up in this chapter. They might be succinctly summarised as 'How and why do individual grammars differ?', or alternatively 'How and why do individual grammars agree with each other?'

Secondly, the theory must be compatible with one relating to language learning, so that whatever similarities are postulated between individual grammars are the result either of chance or of the individual learning from what he hears. (I am taking it for granted that there will be similarities of a general kind, corresponding to linguistic universals.) This means that the theory must be able to accommodate individual grammars in the same community which differ, for instance, in their lexical items or in their fundamental syntactic rules – it must not be necessary, for instance, to assume that everyone in the community in question has the same underlying phonological forms for words like *house*, so that variations in pronunciation may be located in the phonological rules. For the descriptive linguist this requirement raises a very serious problem, since it is quite likely that the observable data will not be sufficient to allow him to decide, for any given individual, which is the appropriate analysis, and he may have to resort to psycholinguistic experimentation in order to decide, say, whether a given speaker has an underlying [h] in *house* or not. (This general problem is described in a somewhat different context by James McCawley 1977.)

Thirdly, the theory will be based on a model of language structure in which there is much less difference between lexical items and the syntactic structures into which they fit than in most current theories. Following the terminology of 2.1.2, we can refer simply to 'linguistic items', using this term to cover not only lexical items but also syntactic constructions and morphological and phonological patterns of any type. In other words, a linguistic item is simply a pattern which may be identified, at any level of abstraction, in the structure of a sentence. The reason for wanting to reduce the differences in the treatment of different kinds of item is that the facts of social distribution are of much the same type whether the item concerned is a lexical item (like *pussy* in contrast with *cat*), or a construction (like *Teddy fall down* in contrast with something like *Let Teddy fall down*), or a phonological pattern (e.g. [t] instead of [st]), or a morphological one (e.g. *goed* instead of *went*). The more these patterns are treated differently in a grammar, the harder it is to develop a unified method of relating them to social context, and also the harder it is to explain why they are all related to social context in the same kinds of way. From this point of view, transformational-generative grammar is an unpromising theory, because of the fundamental distinction that it makes between patterns which are stored in the grammar, as lexical items, and those which are defined indirectly by means of phrase-structure and transformational rules. (There are other reasons for rejecting transformational-generative grammar as a theory of language structure – see e.g. Hudson 1976.)

Finally, the theory must be compatible with probabilistic statements of some kind. These statements will need to refer not only to items in their social context ('item X is n per cent probable in social context Y'), but also to items in given linguistic contexts, given the importance of linguistic context as an influence on linguistic variables (see 5.4.1). Moreover, it would be an advantage if the theory were compatible with the notion of prototypes. The connection between probabilities and prototypes is that both make use of non-discrete categories – just as item X is more or less likely than item Z in context Y, so item X may be more or less similar than item Z is to some prototype. It is conceivable that any mechanism allowing for the description of prototypes might also allow for probabilistic differences among items, but at this point we are probably looking too far into the future.

The most general and important point that has come out of this chapter is probably the close connection between data and theory. Until the data on quantitative variations on linguistic variables became available through the work of Labov, it was unnecessary to take seriously the need for quantitative statements in a linguistic theory, and conversely the lack of a place for such statements in linguistic theory prevented most linguists from bothering to look for the relevant data.

6

Linguistic and social inequality

6.1 **Linguistic inequality**

6.1.1 *Introduction*

One of the most solid achievements of linguistics in the twentieth century has been to eliminate the idea (at least among professional linguists) that some languages or dialects are inherently 'better' than others. Linguists are willing to recognise that some varieties of language are considered by the layman to be better than others, but they point out that each variety displays characteristics common to all human language, such as being rule-governed, and that even the least prestigious language varieties may reveal an impressively complex set of structural patterns. Linguists would claim that if they were simply shown the grammars of two different varieties, one with high and the other with low prestige, they could not tell which was which, any more than they could predict the skin colour of those who speak the two varieties.

Moreover, most linguists would probably say the same about linguistic differences between *individual* speakers: if there are differences between the grammars of two people, there is no way of knowing which has the higher prestige in society simply by studying the grammars. Admittedly there are individuals who clearly have *inherently* imperfect grammars, such as children, foreigners and the mentally retarded, but these deviations are easy to explain and predict, and leave intact the claim that *all normal people are equal with regard to their grammars*. Of course, there is no shortage of differences between grammars, whether of individuals or whole communities, but there are no purely linguistic grounds for ranking any of the grammars higher than others.

This position is summed up in the well-known slogan, 'Linguistics should be descriptive, not prescriptive.' It is less widely acknowledged that this slogan raises problems. It is harder than many linguists realise to avoid prescriptivism, since the historical development of linguistic theory has been so closely linked to the description of prestigious varieties, such as standard languages. Labov pointed out that the normal method of obtaining information about a person's language is to ask him for judgments on sentences, a method which is virtually useless if he speaks a non-standard variety but is familiar with the standard one, since his judgments will almost always relate to the latter rather than to his own normal speech (Labov 1972a: 214). Moreover, the idea of language as a well-defined set of sentences, on which the theory of generative grammar is based, may be a legacy of the prescriptive roots of linguistics in grammars and dictionaries that are intended to distinguish 'correct' from 'incorrect' speech, since it is notoriously difficult in practice to identify the boundary of the set that is supposedly defined by any given language. Prescriptivism even seems to be a matter of principle for some linguists, such as Noam Chomsky. In a much-quoted passage (Chomsky 1965: 3), we find the suggestion that 'linguistic theory is concerned primarily with an ideal speaker–listener, in a completely homogeneous speech-community, *who knows its language perfectly* . . .'. It is hard not to interpret this as a claim that some speakers – perhaps all non-ideal ones – know their community's language *less* than perfectly, with the implication that there is some absolute standard against which an individual's knowledge of his language may be judged. It should be clear that no such absolute standard exists unless one is deliberately created as a prescriptive exercise. It is all too easy for linguists to write grammars which they believe to be descriptive, but which are in fact prescriptive and are taken as such by the general public.

Another problem arising from the doctrine of linguistic equality is that it deflects attention from language as a possible source of social inequality. If language were something which automatically developed at the same pace and to the same extent in all normal people, then those of the same age or degree of maturity should be at the same linguistic level, and there would be no need to worry about some people developing faster than others, since this would not happen to normal speakers. This comfortable view leaves only two problem areas, one concerned with abnormal speakers (such as foreigners and the mentally retarded), and the other with the effects of prejudice. Prejudice does of course exist (see 6.2), but the doctrine of linguistic equality leads to the conclusion that eliminating prejudice (should that be possible) would leave abnormal speakers as the only people with linguistic problems. Evidence is given in 5.3 and 5.4 that this is not the case; there are identifiable differences between people of the same age in aspects of language such as vocabulary, certain areas of syntax, skill at using speech for certain tasks, and the arts of reading and writing, which can only be described as examples of *inequality* between the individuals concerned – and these are precisely the areas of language which are taught in schools. If linguistic equality were taken literally, there would presumably be no need for schools to include any aspects of the mother-tongue in their curricula, since it could be left to look after itself!

The reason for the conflict between what linguists appear to claim about language and what every layman knows about the need to *teach* the mother-tongue must be that the two groups have very different concepts of 'language'. When linguists make claims about linguistic equality, they are referring to the basic core of language structure, which is the area with which linguistic theory has been most concerned. However, the layman takes this basic core completely for granted, and in saying that people are unequal linguistically refers to more 'peripheral' aspects such as vocabulary (especially learned vocabulary) and register-specific constructions. The layman may overstate his case (as often happens), and claim that certain children have 'no language' at all, in which case it may be helpful for the linguist to point out the error, but the linguist in turn must be careful not to seem to overstate his own case, by implying that 'linguistic equality' applies to the whole of language and its use.

6.1.2 *Three types of linguistic inequality*

The remainder of this chapter is divided into three main sections, each dealing with a different type of linguistic inequality and relating it to social inequality. In each case, linguistic inequality can be seen as a *cause* (along with many other factors, of course) of social inequality, but also as a *consequence* of it, because language is one of the most important factors by which social inequality is perpetuated from generation to generation. The present section introduces these three types of linguistic inequality.

The first might be called SUBJECTIVE INEQUALITY, since it concerns what people *think* about each other's speech (i.e. the area of linguistic prejudice, referred to above). In some societies (but by no means all) people are credited with different amounts of intelligence, friendliness and other such virtues according to the way they speak, although such a judgment based on speech may be quite wrong. Consequently, whatever virtues are highly valued, some speakers are thought to have more of them than they really have, simply because they have the 'right' way of speaking, and others are thought to have less because their speech conveys the wrong impression. Thus language, in the form of variety differences, contributes to social inequality by being used as a yard-stick for evaluating people, and by being a highly unreliable yard-stick.

The second type can be called STRICTLY LINGUISTIC INEQUALITY, to distinguish it from the general concept of 'linguistic inequality' running through the whole chapter. Strictly linguistic inequality relates to the linguistic items that a person knows (in the very broad sense of 'linguistic item' used in 2.1.2). It is scarcely open to doubt that the items one knows reflect the experience one has had, and that people with different experiences will know different ranges of items. This is particularly obvious in the case of vocabulary, where some individuals have a rich set of technical terminology for a particular field – such as fishing, pop culture, or linguistics – whereas others have virtually no vocabulary for those fields. However, the same kinds of differences can be found in other areas of language, such as where vocabulary is restricted to certain kinds of interactants, such as parents and babies; or where syntax is restricted, as at auctions or in radio commentaries on horse races. In each case, some people know the items concerned and others do not, and those who do know them are likely to fare better in the particular social situations where such items need to be used. In one sense, social inequality arises on each such occasion, but some occasions are more important than others in terms of their effects on overall life-chances – performance in examinations or job interviews, for instance, has more far-reaching consequences than how one copes in a discussion on fishing. Accordingly, the interest of sociolinguists has centred on differences relevant to the more significant areas of life, notably the performance of children at school.

The significance of strictly linguistic inequality has been greatly exaggerated in the past (see 5.3), but there is a third type of linguistic inequality whose social importance can scarcely be overstated. We shall call this COMMUNICATIVE INEQUALITY, to emphasise that it is concerned with knowledge of how to use linguistic items to communicate successfully, rather than simply with knowledge of the linguistic items themselves. Communicative inequality refers, for instance, to the kind of knowledge or skill that is needed when using speech to interact with other people (see chapter 4). It also includes inequalities in the ways in which speakers select variants of linguistic variables in order to present a favourable image (chapter 5), which means that communicative inequality subsumes subjective inequality. Communicative inequality also concerns the themes discussed in chapter 3 on the relations of language, culture and thought, since it involves differences at the levels of conceptualisation and culture. In other words, communicative inequality brings together all the major themes running through this book, and relates them to important social questions such as equality of opportunity, and educational policy.

6.2 **Linguistic prejudice**
6.2.1 *The nature of linguistic prejudice*

A good deal of evidence shows that people use language in order to locate themselves in a multi-dimensional social space. From the speaker's point of view, this is a way of communicating information about himself – about the kind of person he is (or would like to be) and his position in society. Correspondingly, the hearer may draw conclusions from speech about the speaker's characteristics and place in society. If nobody paid attention to the social signals that speakers sent out, there would be no point in sending them but, as everyone knows, people do pay a great deal of attention to such signals, and this habit of using social signals as sources of information we shall call LINGUISTIC PREJUDICE. The term 'prejudice' may seem odd where neutral questions, such as where the speaker was brought up, are concerned, but judgments based on speech are commonly evaluative, so it would appear justifiable to call them instances of prejudice, entirely comparable with the favourable or unfavourable judgments that people base on observable factors such as clothing. We shall return to the question of how value-judgments come to be based on speech, but for the moment we shall assume that judgments are simply factual.

It is not hard to understand why people use speech as a source of information about the speaker's social characteristics. The need for such information arises on meeting a stranger when one has to interact with him or assess his credibility (as in a public address by a politician). In either case, it is important to know something about the other person in order to plan one's own behaviour. In talking to him, what kinds of information can one take for granted? What are his values likely to be, and how are they likely to influence what he is saying and his reactions to what others say? And so on. This basic need for information about the other person has been called COGNITIVE UNCERTAINTY, and a theory has been developed around it by a group of social psychologists (Berger & Calabrese 1975, Berger 1979; see simple explanations in Giles, Smith & Williams 1977, Smith & Giles 1978).

We can locate this theory in a much more general one, concerning *prototypes* (see 3.2.2). One reason why humans are so prone to make use of prototypes is that they need otherwise inaccessible information *quickly*, so that they can use it in planning their behaviour. For instance, when a person is given a plate of food to eat, he jumps to a large number of conclusions about the characteristics of the various objects on the plate without any more evidence than his experience that objects with certain observable properties and relations to their environments normally turn out to have various other properties. Things that look like potatoes generally taste like them and have the consistency expected of a potato, and so on. Thus if there is something on one's plate that looks like a potato, and the other circumstances are compatible with its being a potato (e.g. it is the meat course not the dessert), then one can safely guess what to do with it (slice it with a knife, mash it with a fork, etc.) and what taste to expect. This guess *could* be wrong – the cook might have disguised an egg to look like a potato – and it might be seriously inappropriate to take it on trust, but it is worth running that risk in everyday life. The alternative would be to test every hypothesis before acting on it, though it is hard to see how this would help, since the testing of a hypothesis is itself a risky undertaking (how, for instance, would you find out whether the postulated potato had the expected taste?). The need to reduce cognitive uncertainty in social interaction has just the same kind of explanation, and there is an exact parallel between the way in which people accumulate information about proto-typical potatoes on their plates and the way they develop a picture of the characteristics of a prototypical user of a particular linguistic form.

This discussion has an important practical consequence. It may occur to the reader that people *ought not* to jump to conclusions about other people's non-linguistic characteristics on the basis of their speech, and that in some way sociolinguists and the school system should try to train people not to do so, but this position is untenable. It is important that people should use speech in this way (as one potential source of information), since social interaction cannot otherwise take place between people who do not already know each other well. Of course, something can and should be done about linguistic prejudice where there are serious problems to be tackled (p. 207), but it cannot be eliminated altogether, since it is an essential ingredient of all social interaction.

We now turn to the question of *values*. Why do people evaluate each other, favourably or unfavourably, on the basis of speech? Part of the answer is simply that values are attached to the *non*-linguistic characteristics concerned, so that anyone whose speech suggests that he has a highly valued characteristic will naturally be highly valued, and conversely for characteristics which are held in low esteem. The characteristics that are highly valued can vary from society to society – for instance, toughness may be highly valued in one society, and rated negatively in another. Consequently, if a characteristic like toughness is associated with a particular form of speech (such as a dialect), people who use that form of speech will be highly valued where toughness is respected, and rated negatively where it is not. Toughness is in fact a characteristic commonly associated with working-class speech in countries like Britain and the United States, so the example is not unrealistic.

However, the question of the values attached to speech must also take account of the fact that language is used as a *symbol of group-membership*. People use their speech in order to identify the particular social groups to which they belong (or would like to be thought to belong), so they are evaluated by others according to how the latter evaluate the groups concerned. To some extent, this is simply another way of describing the relation discussed in the last paragraph, since the characteristics we attribute to another person are simply aspects of the prototype-member of the group to which we think he belongs; and the way in which we evaluate these characteristics depends in part on the values of the group to which we ourselves belong. However, social psychologists have claimed that people like to think the group to which they belong is, in at least some respects, better than others with which it can be compared (Tajfel 1974; see the explanation in Giles, Bourhis & Taylor 1977). In other words, part of each individual's view of himself is derived from his view of the social group, or groups, to which he belongs, and self-respect depends in part on respect for the group as a whole. Although this theory seems to be stating the obvious, it has important consequences which are worth noting.

It helps to explain why a person's speech pattern is such a permanent aspect of his behaviour, and provides such a reliable clue to his social identity. By making an 'act of identity' with a group, and adopting its speech patterns, a member's view of that group becomes part of his view of himself, and it becomes correspondingly difficult to switch allegiance to other groups. Fortunately, the multi-dimensional nature of linguistic variation allows one to identify to some extent with a number of different groups at the same time – for example, by keeping a working-class accent while adopting middle-class syntax and vocabulary. However, there are limits to this flexibility, and the psychological ties of the present group are usually strong enough to guarantee adherence to its speech patterns until there is some prospect of moving into a more attractive group. (Giles, Bourhis & Taylor 1977 contains a good discussion of the factors which lead people to shift allegiance between groups.)

The claim that people like to think they belong to a valuable group has direct relevance to the question of linguistic prejudice. One of the ways in which people persuade themselves that their group is better than others is by finding characteristics of their own group which appear in some ways inherently preferable to those of other groups used as points of comparison. For instance, a group might be better at some competitive sport, in which case its members can emphasise this as an important characteristic of the group, thereby adding to their self-respect. However, it may be hard to find such a positive characteristic, so groups often resort to the use of inherently *neutral* characteristics as evidence of their own superiority. For example, group A drinks beer, and knows that group B drinks wine, so members of A persuade themselves that beer-drinking is inherently better than wine-drinking; then they use this as evidence for their superiority over B. (Of course, B can use precisely the same tactic to prove the inferiority of A.) It is not hard to think of examples of this tendency outside language, but the tendency is particularly clear in language, where there are abundant neutral differences between any two groups. If parents tell children that their own way of speaking is the 'right' one, then it will automatically follow that other groups speak less well. This seems to be a very widely used practice. For instance, Gillian Sankoff reports (1976) that each Buang-speaking village in New Guinea believes that its dialect of Buang is the best. It is certainly not the case that *every* group in the world thinks its own way of speaking is the best, but that is at least one available way of boosting any group's self-esteem, thus taking the explanation of linguistic prejudice a step further.

Let us see how far the explanation has in fact been developed. We

can understand why people guess other people's non-linguistic characteristics on the basis of their speech. We can also see that where these
non-linguistic characteristics are evaluative, judgments based on speech
will be value-judgments, and so may reasonably be referred to as
'prejudice'. Groups may arbitrarily define their own speech-forms as
better than those of other groups, especially those with which they are
in close contact, so that language *itself* becomes open to value-judgments,
rather than just a source of them. This explains why societies can consist
of groups which each think their own way of speaking is the best. Of
course, there is a good deal of scope for rationalising the arbitrary
elevation of one linguistic form over another. For instance, one can
point to the fact that people who use some form also generally have
some particular highly valued characteristic, such as toughness, and use
this as evidence for the superiority of the linguistic form in question.
The main point of such arguments is to reinforce the morale of the
group, so they pay little attention to such logical niceties as the fact that
the highly valued characteristics in question were themselves selected
to enhance the group's image in comparison with its neighbours.

The explanation is still not complete, however, as we still have to face
up to the challenge posed by Gillian Sankoff (1976): 'Perhaps the major
task of sociolinguistics is to reconcile the essentially neutral, or arbitrary,
nature of linguistic difference and of linguistic change, with the social
stratification of languages and levels of speech unmistakeable in any
complex speech community.' The problem is that we cannot explain
one of the most widely reported phenomena of sociolinguistic studies
in countries like Britain and the United States, where some groups do
not believe that they speak better than others but, on the contrary, think
that they speak badly. This is generally known as LINGUISTIC INSECURITY,
following Labov (1972a: 133). The existence of such groups might be
taken as evidence against the claim that groups tend to use language as
a way of enhancing their self-respect, as clearly such groups have no
such benefit, but we may be able to salvage this claim in the following
way.

Members of a complex society belong to groups at many different
levels – the household, the peer-group, the region or city, the 'socio-
economic class' and the nation, to mention but a few of the groupings
involved (which may cut across each other as well as being arranged in
a part–whole relationship). If there is a conflict between the values of
two groupings (e.g. if the values of the nation conflict with those of

regionally and socially based groups), the values of the nation may triumph at the expense of those of the less powerful group. Thus, William Labov reports that New Yorkers in general accept the values of a wider American community which leads them to devalue many of the linguistic forms characteristic of New York. He goes as far as to describe the New York speech community as 'a sink of negative prestige' (1972a: 136), and a similar lack of self-confidence has been reported from other communities, such as Glasgow (Macaulay 1975). In these communities people believe that they 'ought' to use different forms from those they in fact do use, because the former are highly valued and the latter are rejected by the wider community.

This explanation disposes of the problem of linguistic insecurity, but raises another question: 'Why don't all people speak in the way that they obviously believe they should?' (Labov 1972a: 249). If all New Yorkers or Glaswegians were to give up talking like residents of those areas and started to talk like Americans or Britons instead, they would be able to congratulate themselves on speaking 'properly'. We can suggest an answer to this question, though it leaves many loose ends. To reach the answer, we must first consider the mechanism by which values get established, and recognise that on the whole the values accepted by the wider community will be those of the most powerful group within it, since this will be the one that controls such channels of influence as the schools and the media. If enough school-teachers tell enough New York or Glasgow children often enough that their speech is 'slovenly', 'ungrammatical', 'ugly', or just 'wrong', and tell them what they ought to say, then the children will presumably believe them, especially if they hear no contradictory opinions from their parents.

Secondly, we must consider the problems of actually doing what the teachers recommend. The most highly valued speech-forms are those of one particular group in a society (the most powerful), although they are widely accepted throughout the society as a result of the influence of schools, etc. A child who gives up the forms of his local group and adopts those that are widely accepted in the nation would in fact be adopting forms that are the identifying symbols of another group, the 'upper' class (assuming that this term can be used to refer to the group from whom the values originated, and for whose benefit they were originally developed). The option is not a real one. On the one hand, the child may recognise that he is likely to lose more than he gains in the process, since he will almost certainly lose the respect and affection of his friends and possibly his family, and may in any case not succeed in adopting the prestige forms sufficiently well to pass himself off as a member of the upper class – not to mention the problems of reconciling all the other aspects of his behaviour and background with membership of that class. On the other hand, he may have a negative image of at least some aspects of the personality of the prototypical member of the upper class, and a correspondingly positive image of his own group. For instance, members of the upper class are commonly seen as cold, unfriendly and unreliable (Giles & Powesland 1975: chs 4 and 5), and a member of another class may prefer to stay as he is, emphasising the positive virtues of his own group, while nevertheless recognising the upper-class forms as in some absolute sense 'right'. This kind of contrast is often referred to in terms of OVERT PRESTIGE (the prestige of the high-status group representing, symbolically, the whole community) and COVERT PRESTIGE (that of the local, non-prestige group) (Trudgill 1974b: 96).

It may be helpful to summarise this discussion by comparing three ways in which speech may be used as a source of information about the speaker, quite apart from the content of what he says. Firstly, it may be used as a source of non-linguistic information about the speaker, exploiting the connections which one believes normally exist between linguistic and non-linguistic variables ('If he uses form X, he most probably has social characteristic Y'). The non-linguistic characteristics themselves may also be subject to value-judgments, in which case speech counts as a source of such judgments about speakers. Secondly, a group may believe that its way of speaking is inherently better than that of other groups, in which case a person's speech is a source of *linguistic* value-judgments ('If he uses form X, he must be a good/bad speaker'). This belief is not shared by the other groups concerned, so everyone feels that his group is a little superior because it speaks better. This is the situation reported for the Buang, where the villages determine both the forms people use and the values they attach to them. The third use of speech is found in countries like Britain and the United States, where (except for the upper class) the groups determining people's choice of forms are not the same as those that decide the values of such forms. Here, speech is again used as a source of both linguistic and non-linguistic judgments, but those who do not belong to the upper echelons of society may judge their own speech as inferior, thus making it correspondingly difficult for them to build a favourable image of their own group.

6.2.2   *Stereotypes and how to study them*

    People thus use the speech of others as a clue to non-linguistic information about them, such as their social background and even personality traits like toughness or intelligence. This is an example of the way in which people use information stored in terms of prototypes: if characteristics A and B are typically ('prototypically') associated with each other, we *assume* the presence of B whenever we *observe* the presence of A, or vice versa. If A issome characteristic of speech and B is some characteristic of personality, speech will be used as a clue to personality, which is generally harder to observe directly than speech. Similarly, if some speech characteristic is linked in a prototype with a social characteristic, such as some particular type of education, the former will be used as a clue to the latter. In the sociolinguistic literature, this kind of prototype is generally referred to as a STEREOTYPE, so it may be helpful to change our terminology accordingly. However, the reader should be warned that Labov (1972a: 248) has used the term 'stereotype' in a more restricted sense, to refer only to connections between linguistic and non-linguistic characteristics of which people are AWARE at a conscious level, in contrast with the majority of such connections.

How then is it possible to study these subjective connections objectively, and to analyse the stereotypes which people use? It might be thought that true objectivity would require us to by-pass what is in people's heads, and study the connections between linguistic and non-linguistic variables directly, as described in chapter 5, in order to find out precisely how close a connection there is between the variables. But however objective and accurate this information might be, it would be irrelevant if we were mainly interested in the layman's stereotypes, as in this section, since we would still not know how close they came to the objective truth. The only way to study the layman's stereotypes is to study the layman himself and find some way of making his stereotypes more accessible. As we have just noted in connection with Labov's use of the term 'stereotype', most people are not consciously aware of the connections between specific linguistic and non-linguistic variables, so there is little point in asking people directly about these connections ('What kind of person do you think uses such-and-such a form?'), but there are nevertheless ways of tapping people's knowledge more or less indirectly.

The most straightforward and widely used method is called the SUBJECTIVE REACTION TEST, first developed by social psychologists, notably Wallace Lambert of McGill University, Montreal, and applied by other social psychologists, including a particularly active British group led by Howard Giles, of Bristol University. However, the method has been adopted by Labov and is part of his methodology for investigating linguistic variability. (The standard survey of this and other techniques is Giles & Powesland 1975.) The investigator prepares a tape-recording of a series of people talking, usually keeping the content of what they say constant by having them read a passage of prose, or count from one to twenty, for example. The tape might typically contain a dozen voices, each speaking for a minute or so. The 'subjects', i.e. the people whose stereotypes are being investigated, are then asked to listen to these voices, one at a time, and answer a questionnaire about each. A subject might be asked to make ten to twenty judgments about the owner of each voice, and these judgments can then be compared from one voice to another. Some would be 'objective' (e.g. 'Where do you think this speaker comes from?' or 'Which of the following places do you think the speaker comes from: ...?'), but many of them would probably be evaluative, and the subject would be asked to locate the speaker somewhere on a particular scale, such as 'toughness', 'intelligence', or 'friendliness'. The standard way to obtain such evaluations is to define each scale in terms of two contrasting adjectives, such as 'tough' and 'gentle', 'intelligent' and 'unintelligent', or 'friendly' and 'unfriendly', and then to allow seven points on the scale ranging from, say, 'very tough' through 'tough', 'somewhat tough', 'neutral', 'somewhat gentle', and 'gentle', to 'very gentle'. The subject has to pick one of these points for each voice, but the wide range of alternatives allows him to make quite subtle distinctions (which subjects typically do). On the other hand, the fact that his choice is restricted to the seven points on each scale, which can be numbered 1–7, makes it possible to use quantitative methods in comparing judgments, both across voices and across subjects. Needless to say, many variations on this type of questionnaire have been used by researchers. To take just one example, Labov asked subjects 'Which of the following jobs do you think the speaker might hold: ...?' (Labov 1972a: 128).

The results of subjective reaction tests typically show clear differences both between voices and between subjects. In other words, different voices evoke different stereotypes in the mind of the same person, whilst the same voice may suggest different stereotypes to different people. For instance, in a recent study of attitudes among pupils in a secondary school in Newham, London, Greg Smith (1979) has found quite consistent differences between the ways in which Cockney and standard-accented voices were evaluated, with Cockney voices receiving *negative* evaluations for virtually every scale, and standard-accented voices *positive* ones. This finding may surprise readers who know that in areas of London like Newham virtually everyone has a more or less 'Cockney' accent (except recent immigrants), so the subjects in this research were in fact giving negative evaluations to the stereotype evoked by their *own* accent. It is even more surprising to see that the list of negatively evaluated characteristics include friendliness, intelligence, kindness, 'hard-workingness', good looks, cleanliness and honesty. These results appear to suggest that the values of the most powerful section of society may be spread throughout the rest of society so that other sections not only devalue their own speech (as the subjects in the Newham research did with regard to the scale of 'well-spokenness'), but also most other aspects of their self-image. The results at least support the claim that subordinate sections of society may hold their own speech in low esteem as a result of being influenced by the more powerful sections (6.2.1). This research also showed many other differences between voices and subjects. For example, voices recognisable as those of male West Indian immigrants were rated more positively by white girls than by white boys on most of the scales, suggesting that in Newham at least white girls may be attracted by West Indian boys, and white boys may realise this and resent it.

The subjective reaction method can be made more sophisticated in two ways. The pioneer of this field of study, Wallace Lambert, introduced what is called the MATCHED GUISE TECHNIQUE in order to reduce the effects of differences in voice quality between speakers. The problem is obvious: if one wanted to compare, say, attitudes of people bilingual in Welsh and English to each of these languages, it would be silly to choose as one's speakers a Welshman with a booming voice and an Englishman with a squeaky one, since these voice-quality differences might well override all those due to the languages themselves. The matched guise technique aims to avoid this kind of problem by recording the *same* speaker using more than one 'voice'. In this type of experiment there might, typically, be three speakers, each producing speech in two languages or dialects, and the six voices would be ordered randomly so that hearers would not notice similarities in voice quality. Equally typically, hearers do not realise that different voices belong to the same person, and give quite different answers to the questions about status and personality for the two voices belonging to the same speaker (Lambert 1967). In some cases, a virtuoso speaker can produce as many as thirteen different voices (Giles & Powesland 1975: 28), but there is always the danger that he may be producing an exaggerated version of the accents or dialects he is simulating. It seems, however, that there is little difference between results produced by the matched guise technique and those where the voices were each produced by a different speaker.

Another way in which the subjective reaction method may be made more sophisticated is by controlling the speech used in such a way as to make it possible to identify the particular linguistic features to which hearers were reacting. This is a method developed by Labov (1972a: 128, 146), who compiled a list of twenty-two tape-recorded sentences produced by five different female speakers for a different purpose, selecting the sentences so that each illustrated either just one or no sensitive phonological variable. Hearers were told to guess the job of the person speaking each sentence in the list. It was therefore possible to compare the job-rating for a given speaker on different sentences, and it could be assumed that any differences in ratings were due to differences in the variables represented. For instance, one speaker was rated as a receptionist on one sentence, but as a switchboard operator on another, although the sentences were in fact just different utterances of the same sentence ('He darted out about four feet before a car, and he got hit hard'), with a single difference in pronunciation: in the second utterance, one out of the five postvocalic *r*'s was not pronounced as a consonant, whereas in the first utterance they were all pronounced as consonants. It will be recalled from 5.2.2 that this is an important sociolinguistic variable in New York City (where this experiment was carried out), but these results show how remarkably sensitive hearers are to the occurrence of individual non-standard features in the speech of others.

The subjective reaction test has drawbacks as a way of discovering people's attitudes to speech-forms, not least that it requires people to fall back upon their stereotypes, since they have no other way of answering the questions put before them. It is possible that less use is made of stereotypes in real-life situations, people normally reserving judgment more than in these experimental situations. In order to test this hypothesis, it is necessary to find an alternative test of attitudes, where the focus is not on the experimental task as such and the situation is more normal. Several such alternatives have been devised, some remarkably ingenious. We shall describe one such experiment here (from Giles & Powesland 1975: 102), but another will be described in 6.2.4.

A researcher who could use either RP or a Birmingham accent arranged to talk to two groups of 17 year olds in a school, having already established that school children rate RP high and Birmingham accent low. To each group he gave a short talk about psychology, explaining that he was a university lecturer in psychology and that his department wished to find out what students in schools who expected to go to university knew about that subject. He asked them to write down all they knew about psychology, then went out, leaving his assistant behind with the group. She collected their writings, then explained that there was a second part to their research since they would like to know whether the lecturer who had just spoken would be a suitable person to give lectures on psychology at schools. The students were asked to write down what they thought of the lecturer, and to evaluate his intelligence on a scale. The pattern of the experiment was the same for each group of students except that the lecturer used his RP accent to one, and his Birmingham accent to the other. The differences in the responses of each group were significant. The direct question about intelligence got answers showing that the lecturer was rated higher in his RP 'guise' than in his Birmingham one – in spite of the fact that he gave precisely the same talk, introduced himself as a university lecturer, and in every other way behaved in the same way to each group. Moreover, the students wrote far more both *to* him and *about* him in his RP than in his Birmingham guise (24 per cent more to him and 82 per cent more about him). Assuming that the groups of students who heard the two guises were reasonably similar in their composition (and there is no reason to think otherwise), the explanation for these differences in *behaviour* between the groups must have something to do with their attitudes to the two accents used. One explanation is that they liked the speaker more in his RP guise, and there is some independent evidence that people will write more both to and about people they like than those they dislike. Thus it can be seen that people's actual behaviour can be influenced by their prejudices, and that these are not confined to what they *say* about each other.

Before leaving the general question of the experimental study of the role of speech as a clue to stereotypes, it is worth mentioning another experiment which shows that speech is not the only clue. Indeed the deductive chain may go in the reverse direction, from some other observable feature to the relevant stereotype and thence to the speech type, even when the speech itself is observable. Frederick Williams (1973) devised an ingenious experiment in which videotapes were made of three children viewed from behind, so that it was clear to the viewer that they were racially different (white, black and Mexican–American respectively), and that they were talking, though their mouths and faces were not visible. This made it possible to dub the *same* sound-track onto the film of each child without the viewer realising that the speech did not fit the movements of the mouth. Student teachers acted as judges, and three matched groups were each asked to evaluate the speech of one of the children on the scales of standardness and fluency. When the ratings of the groups were compared, there was a clear difference between those for the different children, in spite of the fact that exactly the same speech was heard in each case. The speech of the black and Mexican–American children was rated less standard than that of the white child, and the speech of the Mexican–American child was rated as less confident than that of either of the others. These differences corresponded exactly to the stereotypes established in other experiments for these three racial types, and the results may be interpreted as showing that the student teachers had used visual clues to identify a stereotype and had then assumed that the speech they heard was as predicted by that stereotype. It is hardly necessary to point out that if this strategy is typical of those used by teachers in assessing pupils' speech, it could be a waste of a pupil's time to try to 'improve' his speech, even if he wanted to do so.

6.2.3 *Prejudice of teachers*

This section and the next focus on the practical social problems connected with education. A great deal of sociolinguistic research has had this particular bias, and it is specially important not only because the education system itself is probably one of the main vehicles by which the upper-class prejudices are disseminated through society (see 6.2.1), but because educators should understand more clearly the potential role of prejudice. School teachers and their pupils both have fixed speech stereotypes, and both sets of stereotypes are potentially the source of serious problems. On the other hand, it is perhaps necessary to remind ourselves that there are many sorts of teacher and pupil, and not all teachers may be influenced by the speech of pupils to the extent implied by what follows (see Taylor 1973). Moreover, the research reported below has a heavy bias towards the English-speaking world, and it should not be assumed that the findings can be generalised to all societies and educational systems (compare, for example, the discussion of 'purism' in Ceylon in De Silva 1976, forthcoming). With these cautions, we can identify a number of ways in which teachers' prejudices may present problems for their pupils.

There is some evidence that teachers base their first impressions of pupils on speech-forms in preference to other sources of information which might appear to be more relevant. However, it is important to remember that much of the evidence is based on reactions of *student* teachers, rather than experienced ones, who may evaluate pupils in quite a different way. A few student teachers, for example, were asked to assess eight hypothetical school children on the scales of intelligence, being a good student, being privileged, enthusiastic, self-confident and gentle (Giles & Powesland 1975: 3). The eight hypothetical pupils were each defined by three types of information: a photograph, a tape-recorded sample of speech and a sample of school-work (consisting of an essay and a drawing). The individual pieces of information were based on real children, but had been recombined to provide equal numbers of instances of each type of information which would be judged favourably and unfavourably. The question to be answered by this experiment was: what would happen if information from one source gave a favourable impression but that from another source gave an unfavourable one? The very clear answer was that information from the speech sample always took priority over that from the photograph or the school-work: a favourable impression on the speech sample overrode unfavourable impressions from the other sources, and conversely.

Similarly, it is well-known that most of the intelligence tests used by educationalists put considerable emphasis on skill with language, and that lower-class children consistently perform worse on such tests than on non-verbal intelligence tests, where there is no such emphasis (Bernstein 1971: 52, Dittmar 1976: 32). The reason why lower-class children do poorly on the tests of verbal intelligence may have little or nothing to do with the kinds of gross and superficial differences with which we are concerned in 6.2 (mainly matters of social dialect involving pronunciation), but it is significant that even the formal tests of ability used by the educational system put much emphasis on language.

It would be wrong to give the impression that all teachers evaluate children according to how 'standard' their speech is. Leaving aside the possibility that some teachers avoid making any evaluations at all on the basis of speech, it has been shown (Giles & Powesland 1975: 42) that teachers are of at least two kinds: those who evaluate on the basis of standardness, and those who pay more attention to fluency, which leads to judgments of confidence and eagerness. It would seem, a priori, that the fluency-oriented teachers are likely to make judgments that are more relevant to the needs of the classroom than those who are oriented to standardness, but it is easy to see how a wrong impression could initially be formed of a particular child, and subsequent counter-evidence resisted, in the way that we have described for stereotypes in general.

Assuming that teachers do form first impressions of pupils on the basis of their speech (among other factors), there are problems for the child whose speech leads to an unfavourable first impression. There is the fact that first impressions are resistant to change, so that the child will have to perform that much better in class compared to a child who makes a favourable impression from the start. There is also the problem of the self-fulfilling prophecy: if a teacher expects a child to perform poorly, her behaviour towards the child may be such as to encourage him to do just that. There is research evidence (Rosenthal & Jacobson 1968) that the converse is true (if the teacher has high expectations, she will behave in such a way as to produce correspondingly good performance in the child), and it seems likely that negative expectations by the teacher will similarly lead to negative performance by the pupils.

An additional way in which teachers' prejudices may act against the interests of their pupils is by reinforcing any negative prejudices which the pupils may already have against their own speech, of the kind we discussed in connection with the research in the East End of London. It would be wrong to assume that all teachers fall into this trap, but it would be just as wrong to ignore the large number of teachers who believe that one of their main roles is to point out to children speaking non-standard dialects or accents that their speech is imperfect, in the hope that they will mend their ways. On the whole the only effect of this kind of criticism is either to make the child's self-image more negative or to strengthen his determination not to conform. Indeed, in some cases it would be extremely hard for the child to learn to speak the standard variety against which his speech is judged, because even the teachers themselves do not use it and he may therefore be short of models. This is reported to be the situation in many primary schools in the West Indies, where the model against which children's speech is judged is Standard British English, but the variety used by the teachers themselves is more or less heavily influenced by the local creole language (Le Page 1968b). In any case, a child's language is so closely linked with his sense of identity (see 6.2.1) that he is unlikely to change his speech simply at a teacher's behest.

6.2.4 *Prejudice of pupils*

The first thing to establish in discussing the linguistic prejudices of school children is that they exist. It might be thought that they would be absent from younger children, say those in primary school, or that they would be restricted at that age to factual, non-evaluative deductions from speech, on the assumption that children only become aware of the hierarchical structure of society around adolescence. There is indeed a certain amount of research evidence supporting this reassuring view. For instance, Wallace Lambert (1967) found that a group of 10 year old French-speakers in Montreal were unaware of the negative rating that French has among adults in French Canada, whereas a comparable group of 12 year olds were aware of it. Moreover, a study of British children by Howard Giles (Giles & Powesland 1975: 31) showed that 12 year olds had realistic assessments of the relative prestige of different accents, but often a very unrealistic idea of the nature of their *own* accent (many of them thought they spoke RP, whereas in fact they had a relatively broad regional accent). Seventeen year olds, in contrast, were shown to have a reasonably realistic idea both of the relative status of different accents and also of their own accent. Generalising from these two pieces of evidence to other societies, we might predict that children below secondary school age would be unaware of the relative status of the local accent and the one the teacher used, and that it would be some way into their secondary school careers before they were aware of differences in status between the teacher's accent and their own.

Unfortunately, there is evidence that this conclusion may be unjustifiably optimistic, and that children may in fact be aware of status differences between accents as early as age 3. The evidence comes from an experiment by Marilyn Rosenthal (1974), who devised a method for investigating the attitudes of children to speech-types (cf. also Local (1978), who reaches similar conclusions about children in Tyneside,

England). Her aim was to compare the reactions of 136 American pre-school children, aged between 3 and 6, to two types of voice, one using Standard English and the other using pronunciation, vocabulary and syntax recognisable as non-standard Black speech. Ninety of the subjects were themselves upper-class white children, but 46 of them were lower-class and black, so it was possible to compare the reactions of these groups to the two voices. The experiment centred on two identical cardboard boxes, with faces painted on them (using the same colours, blue and red, in both cases), and each containing a cassette tape-recorder and a present, neither of which the child could see. The children listened to the taped voices purporting to be those of the two 'heads'. Each voice described the present inside the box and made precisely the same claims about its attractions but used different speech-patterns (Standard versus Black non-standard). The children were then asked to choose one of the boxes and take the present out (the presents in the two boxes were in fact identical), then the researcher asked the children a number of questions about their reactions to the heads.

Considering how young the children in this experiment were, the results reflect the adult prejudices remarkably closely. No fewer than 79 per cent of the children said that the 'Standard' head spoke better, and about 73 per cent said they expected a nicer present from this box. Virtually *all* (92 per cent) of the white children recognised that the voice in the non-standard box belonged to a black person, and 72 per cent of them thought the 'Standard' voice was that of a white person. On the other hand, the corresponding figures for black children were only 73 per cent and 59 per cent, confirming a tendency (established by others – e.g. Shuy 1970) for higher-ranking speakers to be more accurate judges than lower-ranking speakers. The black children, conversely, liked the head with the non-standard voice better, and almost half (46 per cent) took the present from this one, although most of them thought that the other one probably had the nicer present. This trend seems to follow the commonly found pattern among non-standard adult speakers, who see standard speakers as wealthy and generally successful but not particularly likeable or trustworthy (see e.g. Giles & Powesland 1975: 67). Finally, the white children, like their parents, appeared to have 'highly pejorative' attitudes towards the owner of the non-standard Black voice, which they were apparently quite willing to express to the investigator. (Another experiment, conducted in Canada on French-speaking school children, showed that 5 year olds already had quite clear attitudes to French as opposed to English – see Schneiderman 1976.)

It seems, then, that we have to assume that at least some children already have quite well-developed linguistic prejudices by the time they go to primary school, and these approach adult sophistication in secondary school. Do such prejudices present problems for pupils during their school careers? It is not clearly established that they do, and we certainly should not assume that what is true of some children is necessarily true of all; but the results of two pieces of research suggest that the teacher's accent (to say nothing of other aspects of speech style) may affect the children's willingness to be influenced by what she says, and even their ability to remember it.

Edward Cairns & Barbara Duriez (1976), in Coleraine, Northern Ireland, compared thirty Catholic school children with thirty Protestant ones of the same age (around 10–11) with respect to their ability to remember the content of a story read (by the same speaker) using one of three accents: RP, middle-class Belfast (Northern Ireland), and middle-class Dublin (Eire). The choice of these three accents was determined by the connection between Catholicism and Eire and between Protestantism and Britain (represented by RP), with the Belfast accent to some extent neutral with regard to religion. Each child heard the story read with only one of the accents, but the children were divided into groups so that all six combinations of three voices and two religions were represented. The results showed that Catholic children who heard the RP voice remembered significantly less about the story than the corresponding Protestant children – presumably because the latter were more favourably disposed towards the stereotype evoked by RP. Similarly, Catholic children who heard the RP version remembered less than the Catholics who heard the (relatively neutral) Belfast accent, and the latter also remembered more than Protestant children who heard the Dublin accent, with its Catholic associations. To confirm that Catholic and Protestant children did in fact have different attitudes to Britain and Eire, they were asked a number of questions such as 'What is the capital city of your country?', to which 3 per cent of Protestants and 70 per cent of Catholics replied 'Dublin'. In other words, all the children agreed that an RP accent was part of a 'British' stereotype, and the Dublin one reflected a 'Republican Irish' stereotype, but they disagreed sharply on their assessment of these stereotypes, according to which commanded their loyalty. The general prediction which these results seem to allow is that children will pay more attention to things said in an accent which arouses their group loyalty than in one which does not, and will consequently remember more of the former. The implications for schools seem obvious.

The second relevant piece of research was conducted by Howard Giles in South Wales and Somerset (see Giles & Powesland (1975: 93–8) for this and related pieces of research) to test the effects of different accents on the extent to which children were influenced in their opinions by the content of a message. This time the pupils concerned were 17 years old, selected from an initial sample of 500 so that there were five matched groups. They were all asked their opinions on capital punishment via a questionnaire, then a week later each of the matched groups was visited by Giles, posing as a criminologist interested in the opinions of school children on capital punishment. He asked the groups to consider an argument against capital punishment which, he claimed, had been produced by a friend of his. Each group received the argument worded in exactly the same way, but in a different form – one group received a duplicated sheet and the other groups heard the argument read in, respectively, RP, South Welsh, Somerset and Birmingham accents. After reading or hearing the argument, the pupils were asked to evaluate the argument as such, and then to state their views for or against capital punishment. Since they had given their views on this question the week before, it was possible to compare the answers given on the two occasions and to measure any change which had, presumably, been brought about by the argument which had just been presented to them. Ratings on the quality of the argument correlated fairly closely with the prestige of the accent used, with the highest rating for RP. However, it was the regional accents, for all their lack of prestige, which had the greatest effect. This result can be interpreted in a number of ways – perhaps the children paid more attention to the message when it was in 'their' accent (as with the experiment in Northern Ireland reported above), or perhaps they were more inclined to trust the opinion of someone who sounded like one of themselves. Presumably several different factors could be at work, but whatever the explanation, there are again clear implications for teachers, if we assume that one of their aims is to influence the opinions of their pupils. (For similar findings relative to bilingual adults hearing messages in different languages, see Cooper et al. 1977.)

It thus seems that the linguistic prejudices of both teachers and pupils are potential sources of serious problems in the education process. It is by no means clear what can or should be done to minimise these problems, but it is hard to see how anything can be achieved unless teachers themselves have a very clear understanding of the nature of linguistic prejudice, and are sensitive to their own prejudices as well as to those of their pupils.

6.3 Linguistic incompetence
6.3.1 *The deficit theory*

The title of this section makes a deliberate reference to Chomsky's notion of 'linguistic competence', by which he means a person's *specifically linguistic* knowledge. At several points in this book we have raised serious doubts about the validity of any distinction between 'specifically linguistic' and other knowledge, but for the sake of the present discussion we shall assume that some such distinction is possible. The notion of 'linguistic incompetence' concerns the *lack* of the kind of knowledge that is covered by Chomsky's 'competence'. Clearly such a lack is a reality in babies, and in others who for one reason or another do not speak some particular language: with respect to that language, they are incompetent. Moreover, someone who is only part of the way towards learning some language as a second one (or towards forgetting a language which was his first language) is to that extent incompetent in the language concerned.

Controversy enters when it is claimed that some children of school age (or even adults) are incompetent in their first language, compared with others of the same age. This claim has been made with reference to children from lower-class homes, and is known as the DEFICIT THEORY. Some believe that this partially explains the poor performance of such children at school: a child needs certain tools, notably language, in order to benefit from schooling, and the linguistic tools of some lower-class children are just not up to the demands made by the school. Some writers even go so far as to claim that such children come to school with hardly any language at all, unable either to ask questions or to make statements of any kind (Bereiter et al. 1966, quoted in Labov 1972b: 205). Linguists and sociolinguists who have studied these issues seriously agree in rejecting this view as dangerous nonsense – nonsense because it is simply not true that any normal children are so short of language, and dangerous because it can distract attention from the real shortcomings of many school systems by putting the blame for educational failure on inadequacies of the child. Those interested will find ample discussion of these questions in, for instance, Dittmar (1976: chs. 1, 2 and 3), Edwards (1976: ch. 4), Labov (1972b: ch. 5) and Trudgill (1975a: ch. 5).

The influence of the extreme version of the deficit theory might be explained by the fact that many children use very little speech when they are in their classrooms 'working' (as opposed to 'messing about'), and that this is especially true of children from lower-class homes. Some children rarely give anything more than a single word in answer to a teacher's questions, and some teachers conclude that this is because they do not know the rules for putting words together into longer sequences, and that, in any case, their vocabulary is limited. A much more plausible conclusion is that the fault is in the situation, and not in the child's linguistic knowledge or lack of it. The child is either unwilling to cooperate, or unsure what the teacher expects of him, and keeps silent at the very times when the teacher wants him to talk, whereas he probably uses a large amount of language in other situations that are more familiar to him, such as when he is dealing with his family or friends. Another factor which predisposes some teachers to underestimate the amount of language a child has is the tendency to discount those bits that are non-standard. Thus some children's lack of speech may be more apparent than real, but this is not to say that children who are underestimated in this way in the classroom do not face a problem. If a child is unwilling or unable to interact verbally with the teacher, he will gain little benefit from school; and if his accent or dialect is non-standard, his academic ability may well be underestimated by the teacher. However, it is important to diagnose such problems correctly and in depth before trying to solve them.

6.3.2 *Restricted and elaborated codes* (1)

Discussions of the deficit theory generally focus on the work of Basil Bernstein, of London University, and to some extent this seems justified, though his work *also* leads to the much more plausible hypothesis to be described in 6.4. Briefly, in the early 1960s Bernstein claimed that it is possible to distinguish two ways of *using* language, called the ELABORATED CODE and RESTRICTED CODE respectively (or earlier, and less clearly, 'formal language' and 'public language' – see e.g. Bernstein 1971: 63). Elaborated code is a kind of speech which is relatively explicit, making fewer assumptions about the hearer's knowledge, and said to be the kind of speech required in school. In contrast, the restricted code, which is relatively inexplicit, makes greater assumptions about knowledge shared by the hearer. This is said to be the kind of speech used between people who know each other well, and it is claimed that many members of the lower working class (which according to Bernstein constitutes 30 per cent of the population) use *only* this kind of speech, whereas most members of higher classes use either restricted or elaborated code according to circumstances (see the collection of papers in Bernstein 1973).

Thus far, Bernstein's theory is compatible with the approach of 6.4 below, where we shall see that it is quite reasonable to distinguish different ways of using language, though not necessarily in such a grossly dichotomous way. Lower-class children may differ from others in the range of ways in which they can use language successfully. Moreover, Bernstein has always emphasised that his theory is not concerned with social dialects, since a non-standard speaker could use an elaborated code, or a standard speaker a restricted one. This is important, because he argues that it is *inherently* necessary to use elaborated code in schools, since it is obviously important for both teacher and pupils to be explicit about the content of a lesson, whereas it is generally agreed that the connection between standard dialect and school is more or less arbitrary – if some other dialect had come to be accepted as the standard dialect of Britain, it would have served just as well as the medium of school education. Admittedly, speakers of non-standard dialects have more problems in school, but this is because of teacher prejudice (6.2.3), and because children need the appropriate standard forms when they learn to read and write (and possibly talk) in school. If there is any truth in the deficit theory, then the problem is quite different, and much more serious: the typical lower-working-class child does not simply have the *wrong* forms, but *none* at all to match against the standard forms – he would have to learn the concepts before he could tackle the standard ways of expressing them.

Bernstein's early work can be taken as an example of the deficit theory because his theory about the two kinds of speech leads him to claim that both syntax and vocabulary are more 'predictable', being more restricted, in speech controlled by restricted code compared with that of the elaborated code type (Bernstein 1971: 171). If the syntax and vocabulary of restricted code speech is more limited than in the elaborated code, and if most lower-working-class people use nothing but the former (as Bernstein claimed), it follows that the active competence of lower-working-class people must contain *less* vocabulary and *fewer* constructions than that of the higher classes, which is precisely what the deficit theory claims. (It must, of course, be admitted that Bernstein was referring only to the speech people produce, and never claimed that those who only use restricted code speech were necessarily incapable of understanding elaborated code speech when they heard it. One can therefore draw no conclusions about passive competence, in contrast with the extreme version of the deficit theory which claims that lower-class children do not even know the meanings of many words or constructions.)

The empirical evidence which Bernstein uses to support his claim comprises a large amount of speech produced by children of various ages (and their mothers) in relatively formal contexts. The unfamiliarity of such situations, and the children's attitude to the interviewer, could perhaps explain such differences as were found. For instance, when lower- and upper-class children were asked to describe the events shown in a series of pictures, the latter used more modifying adjectives and more nouns rather than pronouns (Hawkins 1973). However, when lower-class children (in a different research project) were encouraged by an interviewer to be more explicit, the complexity of their syntax increased, showing that they were well able to produce more complex constructions than they normally used (Lawton 1968).

The evidence regarding *syntax* that has so far been offered is generally hard to interpret, but seems to suggest that there are considerable differences between children in the rate at which their active use of constructions develops, and that such differences exist not only in the relatively formal interview-type situations created by much of Bernstein's research, but also in less constrained domestic situations. Data from the latter type of situation have been collected by Gordon Wells, of Bristol University, using radio microphones worn by children throughout a day at home and adjusted to pick up not only the speech of the wearer but also what other people said (Wells 1979a, b). This method of collecting data allows the researcher to analyse the speech used to the child, and Wells has found that this may exert considerable influence on the rate at which the child's own speech develops. In particular, the more 'communicatively relevant' a mother's answers to a child's utterances, the faster the latter's speech develops in terms of a number of parameters including syntactic complexity. (Wells' ranking of mother utterances for relevance is as follows, disregarding certain categories: *wh*-question – statement or explanation – *yes/no*-question – *yes* or *no* – correction – irrelevant.)

These results are most suggestive, but should not be taken as evidence for the 'deficit theory' as such, for three reasons. First, the determining factor is not social class but type of interaction in the home (though there may be a connection between this and social class). Second, the extreme version of the deficit theory claims that 'linguistically deprived' children have virtually *no* language, whereas Wells' analysis shows no such thing, but only that there are differences in the rate at which the various meanings of auxiliary verbs are developed in speech. And third, none of the research to date is directly relevant to the question of how quickly a child's *passive* competence (i.e. his ability to understand speech) develops, and we must assume at least that passive competence is always well in advance of active competence. This being so, we cannot conclude from the fact that a child never uses some auxiliary verb in one of its meanings that he does not know this part of the syntax of English. The most we can say is that he has not yet learned how to use it himself. In conclusion, then, there is evidence for quantitative differences in the active command of syntax by different children, but not on anything like the scale predicted by the deficit theory.

This leaves *vocabulary* as a possible locus for a linguistic deficit in lower-class children. Lower-class children tend to score badly on vocabulary tests, but this too could be explained in terms of the situation in which such tests take place, and in any case the tests are only concerned with the area of standard, intellectually oriented vocabulary favoured by schools. They do not tell us anything about the *total* number of words a child knows, only about how many of a particular range and maybe not even about this, given the possible damping effect of the testing situation. In the present state of knowledge about vocabularies it would be safest to assume that there are no significant differences in the overall size of vocabulary of lower- and upper-class children.

Indeed, when syntax and vocabulary are considered simply in terms of *quantity*, it can be argued that the difference could favour many lower-class children who do badly at school, to the extent that they are bilingual. Countries like Britain and the United States give citizens little credit for being bilingual in their minority language and that of the host country, though a monolingual who manages to learn the rudiments of a foreign language in those countries is often given great credit. The minority language of a bilingual is usually regarded only as a source of problems, and not as a resource to be counted along with the knowledge of the host language. A similar argument could be mounted in connection with 'monolingual' lower-class children who are able to switch between the varieties of the home and school (as is said to be the case with many West Indian children in Britain, for instance, though similar switching can presumably be expected among children who speak any non-standard dialect). Since no such switching is expected of upper-class children, and there is generally little motivation for an upper-class child to learn a non-standard dialect in addition to his own, it follows that the average non-standard-speaking child is likely to know more linguistic items than one who speaks the standard language. The results of the research we have discussed would seem to contradict this view, but this is probably because the experimental situation was such that the upper-class child was playing 'at home' but the lower-class one was 'away', where he could not use the bits of language of which he was most confident.

The main conclusion to be drawn from this discussion is that every normal child brings to school a vast amount of language, in the sense of linguistic knowledge. The concept of the 'verbally deprived' child, associated with the deficit theory, is a lay stereotype based on a misinterpretation of the fact that some children are inarticulate at school. The problems for schools seem to be (i) how teachers can learn to take the language of such children more seriously, in terms of both quantity and quality (where the problem of prejudice comes in) and (ii), if it really is necessary for the standard language to be taught (and perhaps even used) in schools, how the child's existing language can be exploited as a basis on which to build, without appearing to reject it and the home culture in the process.

6.4 Communicative incompetence

6.4.1 *Communicative competence*

The term 'communicative incompetence' is in contrast with the term 'communicative competence' established by Dell Hymes (1971b; cf. also Campbell & Wales (1970), who use the same term in the same sense). Communicative competence is knowledge needed by a speaker or hearer, but is much more broadly based than the 'linguistic competence' of Chomskyan linguistics. Instead of referring only to the knowledge of linguistic forms, it includes our knowledge – perhaps 'ability' would be a better term – of how to use linguistic forms appropriately. According to Hymes, the goal of a student of language should be:

> to account for the fact that a normal child acquires knowledge of sentences, not only as grammatical, but also as appropriate. He or she acquires competence as to when to speak, when not, and as to what to talk about with whom, when, where, in what manner. In short, a child becomes able to accomplish a repertoire of speech acts, to take part in speech events, and to evaluate their accomplishment by others. This competence, moreover, is integral with attitudes, values and motivations concerning language, its features and uses, and integral with competence for, and attitudes toward, the interrelation of language with the other code of communicative conduct. (Hymes 1971b)

If communicative competence is to cover all these types of ability underlying successful speech, it must include at least the whole of 'linguistic competence' plus the whole of the amorphous range of facts included under 'pragmatics' (the rules for using linguistic items in context); and it must also make close contact with 'attitudes, values and motivations', with which linguistics generally has had little to do, even in discussions of pragmatics.

As far as academic linguistics is concerned, the main question about the two kinds of competence is whether there is such a thing as 'linguistic competence', which can be separated from the rest of communicative competence and studied in isolation. Some linguists feel that this is possible, and point to the achievements of the structuralist tradition, including transformational-generative grammar, as proof that such a division is not only possible but fruitful. Others feel that the notion of 'linguistic competence' is unreal, and that significant progress in linguistics will not be possible without reintegrating the study of linguistic forms and of the ways in which they are used. The kind of support to which these linguists can point is the difficulty that often arises in deciding whether or not a sentence is well formed, i.e. whether or not it is part of the language being described. The present trend seems to be towards breaking down the barriers between language structure and use, so it seems possible that the second view – that no real distinction can be made between knowledge of forms and of uses – will come to dominate linguistics during the next decade.

Whatever the outcome of this particular debate, there can be little doubt about the reality of the knowledge referred to as communicative competence, or about its importance as a determinant of speech behaviour. One of the main components of an individual's communicative competence is a vast set of 'schemata', or abstract structures, for efficiently handling particular types of problem – how to tell a joke, introduce people to each other, order a ticket on a bus, tell someone the way from A to B, answer an examination question on sociolinguistics, give a lecture on theoretical syntax, break bad news, and so on. (For a stimulating discussion of such matters, using the term 'script' rather than 'schema', see Schank & Abelson 1977.) A schema for a particular problem-type makes use both of the individual's experience ('This worked last time, so let's try it again') and of other people's behaviour and precepts ('Other people seem to do it, or to recommend doing it, this way, so I'll do it this way too'). In either case, we may expect considerable differences between people in the schemata that they develop for solving particular problems, and in the ranges of problems for which they already have specific schemata. We may assume, furthermore, that someone with a specific schema for some particular problem will find it easier to solve that problem than a person who is having to work it out 'from first principles'. We may, accordingly, expect differences between people in their ability to solve particular problems, reflecting differences between their previous experiences rather than in their intelligence. An unskilled novice would need a very high degree of intelligence to match the performance of an average experienced decorator when it comes to hanging wallpaper, and there is no reason to suppose that linguistic behaviour is any different from other activities in this respect.

As far as school children are concerned, it would not be surprising to find that some of them take a much more helpful range of schemata to school than others, and we shall see (6.4.2) that this is probably the case. However, an interesting question arises: if schemata reflect experiences, then might it not be possible for schools to provide experiences for all children which will lead them to form whatever kinds of schemata are necessary for success in school? Differences between children from different kinds of home would then be reduced as the school exerted more influence. However, educationalists seem to think that, if anything, the differences between children are often increased, rather than reduced, while they are at school. Before trying to explain this finding, it will be helpful to mention some research which shows the deep influence which schools *can* have on the schemata of their children.

A considerable amount of research has recently been undertaken to compare people from different cultures with respect to their 'ways of thinking', and the results would seem to indicate that people from relatively 'primitive' societies tend to think differently from those who live in more 'advanced' ones. Sylvia Scribner (1977), surveying a number of research findings concerned with the ability in widely separated primitive societies to reason in terms of traditional syllogisms, reported that at first sight these findings appeared to support this conclusion. For instance, the following problem was presented to a number of people in a rural tribe of Liberia (West Africa):

> All people who own houses pay a house-tax.
> Boima does not pay a house-tax.
> Does Boima own a house?

Many people, even adults, could not solve this problem or, if they did, could not explain how they had come to their conclusion. For instance, some people would explain that Boima had no money to pay a house-tax, so presumably he had no money to own a house either.

Similar problems have been presented to people in Central Asia and in Mexico, with the same kinds of result. However, Scribner points out that when account is taken of the difference between those who have been to school and those who have not, 'non-logical' thinking turns out to be a characteristic of those who have not been to school, whereas those with schooling perform in a way comparable with people in an advanced technological society. In her own work, where people were asked to explain their conclusions, she found that two kinds of explanation were offered: a 'theoretical' type, based on the facts as presented in the syllogism, and an 'empirical' type, based on the subject's own knowledge of the world. Where comparable results were available, there was a clear tendency for the non-schooled to give far fewer theoretical explanations than the schooled. This is a particularly impressive finding considering that, in much of the research reviewed, 'schooling' might refer to as little as two years of schooling in some very rigid system where the emphasis was laid on rote-learning.

Scribner's explanation for these far-reaching differences between schooled and non-schooled people is that the school teaches the child a schema for 'logical discourse', where the child has to make a point of *not* using his existing knowledge and prototypes. For instance, this is the kind of schema needed for solving problems such as 'If Johnny has one red apple and Mary has one red apple, how many red apples do

Johnny and Mary have altogether?' If schools are capable of teaching this schema, why is it not possible for them to teach other schemata to children who do not already have them? Before suggesting an answer, it is important to point out that Scribner does not claim that the schooled people in the surveys *all* had the necessary schemata, but only that they were far more common among the schooled than among the non-schooled. The provision of schooling can therefore be seen as only one factor in the development of the schemata concerned, and an explanation is still needed for the fact that some children do learn schemata from school and others do not.

One possible explanation is that some children do not *want* to learn the school's schemata, for the same reasons that they do not want to start speaking like their teachers. If a member of a subordinate group feels that he would only be able to adopt the language of a dominant one at the expense of his feelings of loyalty for his own group, he will positively avoid doing so (see evidence in Giles, Bourhis & Taylor 1977). The term SUBTRACTIVE BILINGUALISM has been used to refer to the situation that such a person is thereby avoiding, since the new language would 'subtract' from his present one (Lambert 1974). People may see a second language as a threat to their first one when the former is set up as inherently superior to the latter, so that adoption of it might seem to be an admission of its superiority. It is at least possible that what is true of languages is also true of schemata for behaviour, including linguistic behaviour. If a child feels that the schemata of the school threaten those he associates with his own group, then he may positively resist any attempt to teach him the former. It should be emphasised that this is only a hypothesis, which has not yet been tested, but it seems inherently plausible in view of the difficulty schools have in persuading some children to accept some of the more obvious schemata of schools, such as those dealing with talking in class.

In the remainder of 6.4 we shall concentrate on communicative competence in relation to schools and school children, but its importance clearly does not end with leaving school. Everyday experience supports the view that communicative competence is one of the main factors determining how successfully one fares in society. As John Gumperz puts it (1977):

> Communication is power in modern post-industrial society. Control over one's life in all arenas depends on the ability to communicate effectively; private life ... involves dealings with

public agencies, and effectiveness in business, employment and public administration is a function of the ability to justify opinions and settle differences.

6.4.2   *Restricted and elaborated codes* (II)

We have rejected the implicit claim of Basil Bernstein that people who always use restricted code must know fewer constructions and words than those who could use either restricted or elaborated, but we accepted, in principle, the claim that there are different ways of using language, according to the emphasis one puts on explicitness (6.3). This can now be seen as a claim about communicative competence, namely that some people have the ability to be relatively explicit when that is necessary, but to take more for granted under other circumstances. One part of communicative competence is clearly just this kind of knowledge about what can be left for one's hearers or readers to supply for themselves, though there are obviously many other things that we also know, and which make us speak differently in different contexts. Thus the theory of restricted and elaborated codes can be seen and assessed as but a small part of the overall theory of communicative competence.

The importance of the theory from the point of view of social inequality lies, not so much in the claim that people use more or less explicit speech in different circumstances, but that different people may differ in the explicitness of their speech in the same circumstances. Bernstein specifically claimed that children from lower-class homes are likely to be less explicit, under the same circumstances, than children from higher-class homes. To the extent that the circumstances concerned are similar to those found in schools, and that explicit speech is required in those circumstances in school, this hypothesis provides a partial explanation for the difficulties at school of children from lower-class homes.

The evidence for such differences between children from different social classes is quite persuasive. For instance, in one experiment (in the United States), lower- and middle-class 10 year old boys were shown a picture of a large number of animals, each different from all the others with respect to four attributes (its name, the number of spots, whether it was standing or lying, and the position of its head). Each child was asked to describe one particular animal in this picture in such a way that it could be distinguished from all the others by someone who did not know which animal he had selected. When necessary, the child was prompted to give more information than he had already given, and the lower-class children on average needed twice as many prompts as those from the middle class, showing that the latter found it easier and more natural to be explicit than the lower-class children (Heider, Cazden & Brown 1968, quoted in Cazden 1970: 92).

Differences between elaborated and restricted codes involve the quantity of information given by the speaker in another way: the elaborated code not only prevents too *little* information from being given, but also too *much* – another desirable attribute from the point of view of the school (though this must be qualified – see p. 229). Evidence for this claim comes from research conducted by Bernstein where children were asked to describe the events in a series of pictures. At one point they were asked what they thought a man in one of the pictures was saying (he was shown shouting angrily at some children who had just broken a window). The difference between middle- and lower-class children in this case was not that the former said more, but that they said *less* – they refused to answer, or said 'I don't know', whereas the lower-class children made a guess. This seems to suggest that middle-class children are more influenced by Grice's (1975) principle, that one should not say things for which one has no evidence (Turner & Pickvance 1973). (An alternative explanation, of course, is that lower-class children are more familiar with the situation of being shouted at by angry men!)

Perhaps the most important aspect of Bernstein's work is that he provides an *explanation* for such differences in terms of the child's experience of language at home. He claims that the elaborated code is used less in lower- than in middle-class homes, or at least less by lower-class mothers when speaking to their children. This is part of the wider claim (p. 100) that language is used differently as an instrument of socialisation by families of different social classes, as shown by what mothers said to interviewers about the ways in which they would probably react to certain hypothetical situations. However, we now refer to more direct evidence (Hess & Shipman 1965, quoted in Robinson 1972: 183) from research where mothers were asked to perform various tasks with their children, all involving language. One particularly interesting task was to draw a pattern by means of a toy called Etch-a-Sketch that consisted of a mobile marker controlled on each dimension by a separate knob. The mother was told that she had to get her child to control one of the knobs while she controlled the other, and between them they were to copy a number of simple patterns. The middle- and lower-class mothers differed quite considerably in the way and extent to which they used speech to guide their children. Middle-class mothers not only gave their children more explicit instructions than the lower-class ones – the most explicit instruction given by any of the latter was simply 'Turn your knob' – but they also showed their children more of the model patterns which they had to copy. The fact that the differences extended beyond speech in this way is one of the most interesting aspects of this research, since it shows how misleading it would be to focus attention exclusively on the linguistic problems of lower-class children in school, and how far communicative competence extends beyond strictly linguistic competence.

Why should there apparently be such differences between lower- and middle-class mothers in their patterns of communication? Bernstein refers to differences in their ways of life, such as the fact that lower-class people, at least in traditional working-class communities, meet rather fewer strangers and can therefore usually take a good deal of shared knowledge for granted. These differences can in turn be explained, he claims, by reference to the general structure of society, which takes us well beyond the range of a sociolinguistics textbook (see for instance Bernstein 1970: 36, Edwards 1976: 107).

The value of Bernstein's theory is that he focusses on the *communicative* capacities of children (though the effect is unfortunately obscured by his claims about limitations on the constructions and vocabulary used – see 6.3.2), and that he tries to explain differences in terms of a total theory of social structure. However, there are some serious weaknesses in the theory of elaborated and restricted codes and their relations to social structure, which leave the theory still unproven.

The concepts represented by the terms 'elaborated' and 'restricted code' are so vague that it is difficult to know how to identify instances of either (Edwards 1976: 92). They are presented as though there was a clear difference between speech which is explicit and that which is not, whereas it is surely the case that *any* speech is bound to leave the hearer to supply some information. To take a simple example, each time we use a definite article we leave the hearer or reader to work out which particular entity is referred to (as in the case of 'the hearer' in the present sentence). Moreover, it is a common experience of university lecturers to find that students, especially in their first year, are anything but explicit about the steps in some argument, but presumably this would not be taken as evidence that they were using a restricted code. It shows, rather, that they have not yet learned to be explicit in spelling out arguments in the way expected of students. It seems, therefore, that the difference between the codes is a matter of degree, and that ability to use elaborated code in one context does not guarantee that it can be used successfully in another; i.e. 'elaborated code' may not be a general orientation towards communication, as Bernstein sometimes implies, but rather a skill specific to a limited range of situations.

There is also a seductive simplicity in the basic theory (though, to be sure, the explanations are anything but simple), which gives the impression that the communicative problems of lower-class children may be diagnosed and understood in terms of a simple dichotomy – whether or not they are limited to restricted code. It seems much more likely that lower-class children suffer at school from a very complex range of inter-connected problems, each perhaps quite specific. An example of a specific communicative problem from which most readers probably suffer is that of speaking in a situation where there is no feed-back from an audience, such as when dictating into a tape-recorder, or recording messages for friends on a tape-recorder, or, worst of all, recording messages for an unknown audience on a telephone with an automatic answering service. It seems reasonable to suppose that the lower-class child is beset with a multitude of such problems when he is at school (not least the problem of complex motivation, to which we referred above), rather than with the single overall problem of learning always to be explicit.

Another weakness of the theory lies in Bernstein's sociological approach. His description of both lower- and middle-class societies is in terms of stereotypes, or even caricatures, with little reference to the vast range of differences within the so-called 'lower class', etc. (Rosen 1972). Moreover, the concept of social class is itself problematic (p. 173), so we need to be suspicious, at least, of generalisations made about particular social classes, especially when they are made across groups in different nations (such as the United States and Britain). Paradoxically, similar criticisms can be made of Labov, who was one of Bernstein's principal critics (Labov 1972b: 201–40).

6.4.3 *The communicative competence of lower-class children*

It seems fair to say that some people have a 'deficit' in their communicative competence with respect to certain types of situation, but the sting is taken out of the word if it is seen that such deficits are spread right across society, and that each of us has his or her own particular range of deficits – though 'gaps' would be a better term (Cazden 1970). Some people have gaps in dealing with formal experimental or school situations in which they have to be explicit, others have gaps with respect to situations where they are confronted with an angry client, and so on. Having seen what lower-class children do badly, it is only fair to look at some of the things that they often do well.

Probably the best documentation of the speech of lower-class people derives from research studies among American blacks. Various studies have shown that lower-class black children (and adults) have a completely adequate set of culturally recognised speech activities, many of which are highly competitive and serve to fix the speaker's rating among his peers. For instance, 'rapping' is a term used to refer to 'a distinctively fluent and lively way of talking, one that is always highly personal in style. It can be a way of creating a favourable impression when first meeting a person, though it can also become rather competitive and lead to a lively repartee' (Burling 1970: 156). One very successful exponent of the art of rapping was Rap Brown, the black leader, who wrote in his autobiography:

> There'd be sometimes 40 or 50 dudes standing around and the winner was determined by the way they responded to what was said. If they fell all over each other laughing, then you knew you'd scored. It was a bad scene for a dude that was getting humiliated. I seldom was. That's why they call me Rap, 'cause I could rap.
> (quoted in Abrahams 1974: 244)

Clearly, speech is given just as important a place in such a society as in the academic middle class; the difference is just in the rules of the game and the criteria of success.

There is some research evidence which shows that, for some tasks, the performance of lower-class children is better than that of middle-class children. One study required the children to make up a bed-time story; lower-class girls were found to be most fluent, and lower-class boys to be least fluent, with middle-class children in between. The explanation for the difference between boys and girls in the lower-class sample is not difficult to find – the girls were presumably more experienced in telling stories to their dolls and small siblings – but the fact that their performance was better than children from the middle class is worthy of note (Edwards 1976: 100).

6.4.4 *The linguistic demands of the school*

One final question to be considered is whether the linguistic demands of the school really are as Bernstein and others have described them. Do schools in fact place such emphasis on explicitness and thinking for oneself, in particular? The assumption that there is a stereotype applicable to all schools is dangerous, for it may be seriously inaccurate with respect precisely to many of the schools which lower-class children attend. It has in fact been suggested that the sociolinguistic profiles of many such schools fit rather well the description of a typical lower-class home which requires only 'restricted code':

> An underlying restricted code is found where communication is realised through forms of speech where meanings are implicit, principles infrequently elaborated, qualified or explored, infrequently related to the specific experience of the child, or the specific requirements of the local context, where alternative possibilities are infrequently offered, where questioning is less encouraged. (Gahagan & Gahagan 1970, quoted in Edwards 1976: 146)

One of the characteristics of schools which has attracted comment is that they tend to emphasise what might be called 'verbal display', which consists in giving *more* information than is strictly necessary (though preferably not information which is false, or for which the child has no evidence, as we noted in 6.4.2). In interviews lower-class children typically give minimal responses to questions – answering 'yes' or 'no' to a *yes/no* question, rather than expanding on the answer, for instance. In contrast, a middle-class child sees a *yes/no* question such as 'Do you often watch television?' as an invitation to describe his television-watching habits at some length. Perhaps it is these elaborated responses which need explaining, rather than the minimal ones, yet in research projects the latter have been defined as a problem for children (Williams 1970: 393) and, in so far as the elaborated type of response is more appropriate in schools, this definition is correct. But if the teacher wants a description, why does he not simply say 'Tell me about . . .'? This simple example illustrates what some observers feel is one of the main sources of lower-class children's school problems, namely a culture-clash between 'middle-class' culture, which controls the teacher's behaviour, and 'lower-class' culture, to which the children are accustomed. Such observers feel that it should be possible to achieve the objectives of the education system within the child's own culture, making use of the communicative competence which he brings to school, even if part of the aim of education is precisely to broaden this communicative competence.

There are thus many questions to which no satisfactory answers have yet been given, and all we have been able to offer is a very brief survey of some of the ideas and supporting research in the area of linguistic and social inequality. Many are only partly developed, and much of the research is hard to focus directly in assessing the competing ideas. One of the leading researchers in this area, who edited a book called *Language and Poverty* (Williams 1970), made a plea which is worth repeating at the end of this chapter:

> I clearly recognise that these ideas move directly to the call for research. But rather than simply a call for more research, they call for better research and for more coordination of efforts. In a larger respect, they ask of our efforts in *social* technology the standards and coordination demanded of our research in the other sciences. As a technological society, we have paid the price of crowded cities, of depressed rural areas, and of the inverse correlation between economic opportunity and minority group membership. We should bring this same technology to bear upon a debt to the human element in our society. (Williams 1970: vii)

7
Conclusions

I have tried to develop a coherent view of language which takes account of the findings of sociolinguistic research. However, each of the previous chapters has focussed on a different aspect of language, so it may be helpful to bring together some of the more important strands of the argument and show how they fit together. The understanding of language to which the arguments have led is rather different from the established theories of structuralism, and could be characterised as *flexible* and *fragmentary*. It is flexible in that the analytical categories involved are assumed to be prototypes, rather than categories which have clear boundaries and definable necessary-and-sufficient conditions for membership. It is fragmentary in making little or no use of large-scale aggregates of linguistic items or people ('languages', 'dialects', 'registers', 'speech communities') as the basis for generalisations.

It is a truism that *speech occurs in a social context*, which is why the social perspective of sociolinguistics is indispensable to the study of language or speech. The social context in which speech occurs encompasses a large number of factors, including the social group or groups to which the speaker belongs, the social relations between speaker and hearer, the structure of their interaction (in terms of entries, exits, turn-taking, etc.), the type of interaction (a business transaction, a chat, problem-solving, etc.), and the shared knowledge of the participants, which will be both general ('culture') and specific (concerning present interaction). All these aspects of the social context are known when one hears (or reads) any linguistic item, though it is possible, of course, for different people to hear the same bit of speech and disagree about some aspect of the social context. It would consequently be surprising if we did not store such information in our memories along with the linguistic items concerned, and there is every reason to believe that we do so.

Conclusions

Similarly we remember the linguistic contexts in which items occur, but there is no reason why the two kinds of information should be kept quite separate, by treating the latter as part of 'language structure' or 'linguistic competence' and relegating the former to some sort of 'language use', which is excluded from purely linguistic competence.

It might be objected that people could not possibly remember information about all the social contexts for individual linguistic items, given that the term includes lexical items as well as constructions and more general patterns. After all, even a monoglot must know tens of thousands of linguistic items, so the burden on his memory would be intolerable. However, the evidence that we have surveyed suggests that we do in fact remember a vast amount of information concerned with particular lexical as well as other types of item, and that *linguistic items may be related individually to social context*. For example, people in Belfast know that both *pull* and *would* have two pronunciations, one with [ʉ] and the other with [ʌ], but that the [ʌ] pronunciation of *pull* is less 'vernacular' than that of *would* (p. 168).

Given this apparently unlimited capacity for storing information about linguistic items, there is no need to assume in advance that we have to use large-scale constructs like 'language' or 'dialect' in order to relate linguistic items to the social contexts in which they occur. Indeed, the evidence reviewed suggests strongly that such constructs have little or no objective reality, so linguists would be well advised to avoid trying to make generalisations in terms of them. One consequence of this constraint is that linguists should perhaps give up trying to write grammars, unless they are prepared to treat them seriously as descriptions of the competence of an individual, whether monoglot or polyglot. Another consequence for linguistic theory is that we should be seeking a theory which would minimise the differences between different types of linguistic item, since all types seem to be related to social context in the same way. On the other hand, we should perhaps be studying differences between pronunciation, morphology, syntax and lexical items in connection with those social contexts to which they are sensitive.

In common with many other linguists, I believe that the ultimate criterion of success in the study of language is the *psychological reality* of one's descriptions of language structure, and I find this principle just as relevant to sociolinguistics as to descriptive linguistics (not surprisingly, since I have argued that there is no real difference between the two disciplines). We can assume that people's minds contain a vast network of concepts representing what they know about linguistic items and the social contexts in which they occur, and our aim should be to find out more about these concepts and their interrelations. There is no reason to expect different people to have exactly the same concepts, either for linguistic items or social contexts, which makes it all the harder to study the concepts. Methodology becomes a crucial issue. For some time to come we may have to resign ourselves to observing people's behaviour, analysing it quantitatively and statistically where relevant, and hypothesising about the psychological mechanisms which underlie it. Meanwhile there are some perplexing questions to be answered. Why do people in the same community often speak in such a similar way, down to the most minute details of pronunciation? How do they achieve such precise agreement? Why do they differ with regard to some particular variables? We have touched on some of these questions in earlier chapters, but none of them can be considered to have received a wholly satisfactory answer.

One of the most obvious characteristics of both speech and social context is that they consist of many independent variables – they are *multi-dimensional*. We have already listed some of the separate variables involved in social context, but any one of these variables can be broken down still further into a large number of separate variables. For instance, the group membership of the speaker may be defined in terms of region, social status, age, sex and many other factors. Similarly, we might classify the variables in speech according to whether they involve form or content, but each of these may in turn be further divided into a very large number of factors (words, word-classes, constructions, phonemes, semantic features, etc.). As we might expect, the connections between variables in speech and social context are complex and specific, individual linguistic variables being related to individual contextual variables. This allows speakers to use their speech in a remarkably sensitive way to locate themselves and the situation of speaking in a multi-dimensional space, whilst at the same time conveying the message contained in the 'meaning' of their sentences. (Indeed, it is likely that there is no clear difference in principle between the two functions of speech.) In other words, every utterance may be seen as an *act of identity* by its speaker.

Finally we can inquire about the nature of the concepts used in analysing linguistic items and social context, and the answer seems likely to be that they are all *prototypes* – clusters of characteristics that define clear cases, but without any distinction between characteristics

233

that are necessary and those that are not. We have explicitly discussed the relevance of prototypes to several aspects of social context – the speaker's group membership (where the prototypes are called 'stereo-types'), the relations of power and solidarity between speaker and addressee, and the type of interaction (where they are called 'domains'); and other aspects will probably turn out to be the same in this respect. We have also seen that prototypes are needed in the definitions of word-meanings, and recent work on so-called 'non-discrete grammar' suggests strongly that the same may be true of grammatical categories such as 'noun' or 'clause' (see for instance Lakoff 1977, Ross 1973, 1974). Presumably we may expect to find similar evidence from phonology, at least for categories like 'vowel' and 'syllable'. If the conclusion that all such concepts are prototypes is correct, it follows that linguists should give high priority to developing theories which are compatible with prototypes as analytical categories, which is not the case with any of the existing theories. Until this can be done we shall continue to distort language in describing it.

BIBLIOGRAPHY AND
CITATION INDEX

Abercrombie, D. (1968) Paralanguage. *British Journal of Disorders of Communication* 3: 55–9; also in Laver & Hutcheson (1972: 64–70). p. 134

Abrahams, R.D. (1974) Black talking on the streets. In Bauman & Sherzer (1974: 240–62). p. 228

Argyle, M. ed. (1973) *Social Encounters: Readings in social interaction.* Harmondsworth, Middx: Penguin. pp. 108, 131

Argyle, M. & Dean, J. (1965) Eye contact, distance and affiliation. *Sociometry 28*: 289–304; also in Argyle (1973: 173–87). p. 136

Argyle, M. & Kendon, A. (1967) The experimental analysis of social performance. In L. Berkowitz, ed. *Advances in Experimental Social Psychology.* New York: Academic Press, 55–98; also in Laver & Hutcheson (1972: 19–63). p. 113

Austin, J.L. (1962) *How to Do Things with Words.* Cambridge, Mass.: Harvard University Press. p. 110

Bailey, C-J.N. (1972) The integration of linguistic theory: internal reconstruction and the comparative method in descriptive analysis. In R. Stockwell & R. Macaulay, eds. *Linguistic Change and Generative Theory.* Bloomington: Indiana University Press. p. 184

   (1973) *Variation and Linguistic Theory.* Arlington: Center for Applied Linguistics. pp. 41, 184

Bailey, C-J.N. & Shuy, R.W. eds. (1973) *New Ways of Analyzing Variation in English.* Washington: Georgetown University Press. p. 143

Basso, K.H. (1970) 'To give up on words': silence in Western Apache culture. *Southwestern Journal of Anthropology 26*: 213–30; also in Giglioli (1972: 67–86). p. 130

Bates, E. & Benigni, L. (1975) Rules of address in Italy: a sociological survey. *Language in Society 4*: 271–88. p. 124

Bauman, R. & Sherzer, J. eds. (1974) *Explorations in the Ethnography of Speaking.* Cambridge: Cambridge University Press. p. 109

Bell, R. (1976) *Sociolinguistics: Goals, Approaches and Problems.* London: Batsford. pp. 1, 33

Berdan, R. (1978) Multidimensional analysis of vowel variation. In D. Sankoff (1978: 149–60). p. 160

Bereiter, C., Engelman, S., Osborn, J. & Reidford, P.A. (1966) An academically oriented pre-school program for culturally deprived children. In F.M. Hechinger, ed. *Pre-school Education Today.* New York: Doubleday. p. 214

Berger, C.R. (1979) Beyond initial interaction: uncertainty, understanding and the development of interpersonal relations. In H. Giles & R. St Clair, eds. *Language and Social Psychology.* Oxford: Blackwell, 122–44. p. 196

Berger, C.R. & Calabrese, R.J. (1975) Some explorations in initial interaction and beyond: toward a developmental theory of interpersonal communication. *Human Communication Research 1*: 99–112. p. 196

Berko Gleason, J. (1973) Code-switching in children's language. In T.E. Moore, ed. *Cognitive Development and the Acquisition of Language.* London: Academic Press, 159–67. p. 18

Bernstein, B. (1970) A sociolinguistic approach to socialization: with some reference to educability. In Williams (1970: 25–61). p. 226

    (1971) *Class, Codes and Control*, vol. 1: *Theoretical Studies towards a Sociology of Language.* London: Routledge & Kegan Paul. pp. 208, 215, 216

    ed. (1973) *Class, Codes and Control*, vol. 2: *Empirical Studies.* London: Routledge & Kegan Paul. p. 216

Bernstein, B. & Henderson, D. (1969) Social class differences in the relevance of language to socialization. *Sociology 3*: 1–20; also in Fishman (1972b: 126–49) and Argyle (1973: 47–62). p. 100

Bickerton, D. (1971) Inherent variability and variable rules. *Foundations of Language 7*: 457–92. pp. 41, 67, 158, 184, 185

    (1972a) The structure of polylectal grammars. In Shuy (1972: 17–42). p. 184

    (1972b) Quantitative versus dynamic paradigms: the case of Montreal *que.* In Bailey & Shuy (1973: 23–43). p. 184

    (1973) The nature of a creole continuum. *Language 49*: 640–69. pp. 41, 67, 184

    (1975) *The Dynamics of a Creole System.* Cambridge: Cambridge University Press. pp. 41, 67, 68, 148, 184

Blom, J.-P. & Gumperz, J.J. (1971) Social meaning in linguistic structure: code-switching in Norway. In Gumperz (1971: 274–310) and Gumperz & Hymes (1972: 407–34). p. 56

Bloomfield, L. (1933) *Language.* New York: Holt, Rinehart & Winston. pp. 25, 26, 39, 53, 59

Bolinger, D. (1975) *Aspects of Language, 2nd ed.* New York: Harcourt Brace Jovanovich. pp. 16, 23, 28, 37, 40, 53, 61, 64, 92

Brown, P. & Levinson, S. (1978) Universals in language usage. In E.N. Goody, ed. *Questions and Politeness: Strategies in social interaction.* Cambridge: Cambridge University Press, 56–289. pp. 4, 115, 116, 124, 126

Brown, R. (1958a) How shall a thing be called? *Psychological Review 65*: 14–21; also in R.C. Oldfield & J.C. Marshall eds. (1968) *Language.* Harmondsworth, Middx: Penguin, 82–92. p. 92

    (1958b) *Words and Things.* Glencoe, Ill.: Free Press. pp. 92, 103

Brown, R. & Ford, M. (1961) Address in American English. *Journal of Abnormal and Social Psychology 62*: 375–85; also in Hymes (1964a: 234–44) and Laver & Hutcheson (1972: 128–45). pp. 122, 125

Brown, R. & Gilman, A. (1960) The pronouns of power and solidarity. In T.A. Sebeok, ed. *Style in Language.* Cambridge, Mass.: MIT Press, 253–76; also in Fishman (1968), Giglioli (1972: 252–82) and Laver & Hutcheson (1972: 103–27). pp. 122, 124

Burling, R. (1959) Language development of a Garo- and English-speaking child. *Word 15*: 45–68; also in C.A. Ferguson & D.I. Slobin, eds. (1973) *Studies of Child Language Development.* New York: Holt, Rinehart & Winston, 69–90. p. 17

    (1970) *Man's Many Voices: Language in its cultural context.* New York: Holt, Rinehart & Winston. pp. 1, 58, 86, 87, 88, 91, 228

Bynon, T. (1977) *Historical Linguistics.* Cambridge: Cambridge University Press. pp. 37, 40, 41, 47, 58, 60, 148

Cairns, E. & Duriez, B. (1976) The influence of speaker's accent on recall by catholic and protestant school children in Northern Ireland. *British Journal of Social and Clinical Psychology 15*: 441–2. p. 212

Campbell, R. & Wales, R. (1970) The study of language acquisition. In Lyons (1970: 242–60). p. 219

Carroll, J.B. ed. (1956) *Language, Thought and Reality: Selected writings of Benjamin Lee Whorf.* Cambridge, Mass.: MIT Press. p. 103

Carroll, J.B. (1964) *Language and Thought.* Englewood Cliffs: Prentice-Hall. p. 103

Casagrande, J.B. (1948) Comanche baby talk. *International Journal of American Linguistics 14*: 11–14; also in Hymes (1964a: 245–50). p. 122

Cazden, C.B. (1970) The neglected situation in child language research and education. In Williams (1970: 81–101). pp. 225, 228

Cedergren, H.J. (1972) On the nature of variable constraints. In Bailey & Shuy (1973: 13–22). p. 182

Cedergren, H.J. & Sankoff, D. (1974) Variable rules: performance as a statistical reflection of competence. *Language 50*: 333–55. p. 182

Chambers, J.K. & Trudgill, P. (forthcoming) *Modern Dialectology.* Cambridge: Cambridge University Press. p. 39

Chen, M. & Hsieh, H-I. (1971) The time variable in phonological change. *Journal of Linguistics 7*: 1–13. p. 169

Chen, M.Y. & Wang, W. S-Y. (1975) Sound change: actuation and implementation. *Language 51*: 255–81. p. 169

Chomsky, N. (1965) *Aspects of the Theory of Syntax.* Cambridge, Mass.: MIT Press. pp. 7, 22, 69, 192

(1968) *Language and Mind.* New York: Harcourt, Brace & World. p. 69

Chomsky, N. & Halle, M. (1968) *The Sound Pattern of English.* New York: Harper & Row. p. 46

Clark, H.H. & E.V. (1977) *Psychology and Language: An introduction to psycholinguistics.* New York: Harcourt Brace Jovanovich. pp. 77, 78, 82, 88, 92, 93, 94, 98, 102

Cooper, R.L., Fishman, J.A., Lown, L., Scheier, B. & Seckbach, F. (1977) Language, technology and persuasion in the Middle East: three experimental studies. In Giles (1977: 83–98). p. 213

Coulthard, M. (1975) Discourse analysis in English – a short review of the literature. *Language Teaching Abstracts 8.6*: 73–89. pp. 131, 133

(1977) *An Introduction to Discourse Analysis.* London: Longman. pp. 117, 131

Crystal, D. & Davy, D. (1969) *Investigating English Style.* London: Longman. p. 48

DeCamp, D. (1971a) Introduction: The study of pidgin and creole languages. In Hymes (1971a: 13–39). pp. 62, 65

(1971b) Toward a generative analysis of a post-creole continuum. In Hymes (1971b: 349–70). pp. 41, 184

(1972) What do implicational scales imply? In Bailey & Shuy (1972: 141–8). pp. 184, 187

(1977) The development of pidgin and creole studies. In Valdman (1977: 3–20). pp. 61, 65, 66

Denison, N. (1971) Some observations on language variety and plurilingualism. In E. Ardener, ed. *Social Anthropology and Language.* London: Tavistock; also in Pride & Holmes (1972: 65–77). p. 56

De Silva, M.W.S. (1976) *Diglossia and Literacy.* Mysore: Central Institute of Indian Languages. p. 208

(forthcoming) *Vernacularization of Literacy: the Telugu experiment*. Hyderabad: International Telugu Institute. p. 208

Dillard, J.L. (1971) The creolist and the study of Negro non-standard dialects in the continental United States. In Hymes (1971a: 393–408). p. 16

Dittmar, N. (1976) *Sociolinguistics: A critical survey of theory and application*. London: Arnold. pp. 1, 208, 215

Douglas-Cowie, E. (1978) Linguistic code-switching in a Northern Irish village: social interaction and social ambition. In Trudgill (1978: 37–51). p. 164

Edwards, A.D. (1976) *Language in Culture and Class*. London: Heinemann. pp. 215, 226, 228, 229

Elyan, O., Smith, P., Giles, P. & Bourhis, R. (1978) R.P.-accented female speech: the voice of perceived androgyny? In Trudgill (1978: 122–31). p. 121

Ervin-Tripp, S. (1954) Identification and bilingualism. Conference paper in S. Ervin-Tripp (1973) *Language Acquisition and Communicative Choice*. Stanford: Stanford University Press, 1–14. p. 97

(1964) An analysis of the interaction of language, topic and listener. *American Anthropologist 66.6*: 86–102; also in Fishman (1968: 192–211) and Argyle (1973: 65–75). p. 97

Ervin-Tripp, S. & Mitchell-Kernan, C. eds. (1977) *Child Discourse*. London: Academic Press. See Hollos 1977, Watson-Gegeo & Boggs 1977

(1977) *Studies in Language Variation: Semantics, syntax, phonology, pragmatics, social situations, ethnographic approaches*. Washington: Georgetown University Press. p. 143

Fasold, R.W. & Shuy, R.W. eds. (1975) *Analyzing Variation in Language*. Washington: Georgetown University Press. p. 143

(1977) *Studies in Language Variation*. Washington: Georgetown University Press. p. 143

Ferguson, C.A. (1959) Diglossia. *Word 15*: 325–40; also in Hymes (1964a: 429–39) and Giglioli (1972: 232–51). p. 54

(1971) Absence of copula and the notion of simplicity: a study of normal speech, baby talk, foreigner talk and pidgins. In Hymes (1971a: 141–50). p. 122

(1976) The structure and use of politeness formulas. *Language in Society 5*: 137–51. p. 130

Firth, J.R. (1950) Personality and language in society. *The Sociological Review 42.2*: 8–14; also in J.R. Firth (1957) *Papers in Linguistics 1934–1951*. London: Oxford University Press, 177–89. p. 4

(1964) *The Tongues of Men, and Speech*. London: Oxford University Press. p. 4

Fishman, J.A. (1965) Who speaks what language to whom and when? *La Linguistique 2*: 67–88; also in Pride & Holmes (1972: 15–32). p. 80

(1968) *Readings in the Sociology of Language*. The Hague: Mouton. See Brown & Gilman 1960, Ervin-Tripp 1964, Garvin & Mathiot 1956, Geertz 1960, Gumperz 1962, Hymes 1962.

(1971) *Sociolinguistics: A brief introduction*. Rowley: Newbury House. p. 55

(1972a) *The Sociology of Language. An interdisciplinary social science approach to language in society*. Rowley: Newbury House. pp. 1, 5

(1972b) *Advances in the Sociology of Language*, vol. 2: *Selected Studies and Applications*. The Hague: Mouton. p. 5

(1972c) The sociology of language. In Giglioli (1972: 45–58). p. 5

(1972d) Domains and the relationship between micro- and macrosociolinguistics. In Gumperz & Hymes (1972: 435–53). p. 80

Fox, J.J. (1974) 'Our ancestors spoke in pairs': Rotinese views of language, dialect and code. In Bauman & Sherzer (1974: 65–85). p. 117

Friedrich, P. (1972) Social context and semantic feature: the Russian pronominal usage. In Gumperz & Hymes (1972: 270–300). p. 124

Gahagan, D. & G. (1970) *Talk Reform: Explorations in language for infant school children.* Routledge & Kegan Paul. p. 229

Gal, S. (1978) Variation and change in patterns of speaking: language shift in Austria. In D. Sankoff (1978: 227–38). p. 177

Gardener, P. (1966) Symmetric respect and memorate knowledge: the structure and ecology of individualistic culture. *Southwestern Journal of Anthropology 22*: 389–415. p. 116

Garvin, P.L. (1959) The standard language problem: concepts and methods. *Anthropological Linguistics 1*: 28–31; also in Hymes (1964: 521–3). p. 33

Garvin, P.L. & Mathiot, M. (1956) The urbanisation of the Guaraní language: a problem in language and culture. In A.F.C. Wallace, ed. *Men and Cultures.* Philadelphia: University of Pennsylvania Press, 783–90; also in Fishman (1968). pp. 32, 33

Geertz, C. (1960) *The Religion of Java.* Glencoe: The Free Press. Extract in Fishman (1968: 282–96) and Pride & Holmes (1972: 167–79). p. 127

Giglioli, P.P. ed. (1972) *Language and Social Context.* Harmondsworth, Middx: Penguin. p. 5

Giles, H. ed. (1977) *Language, Ethnicity and Intergroup Relations.* London: Academic Press. See Cooper et al. 1977, Parkin 1977

Giles, H., Bourhis, R.Y. & Taylor, D.M. (1977) Towards a theory of language in ethnic group relations. In Giles (1977: 307–48). pp. 197, 198, 223

Giles, H. & Powesland, P.F. (1975) *Speech Style and Social Evaluation.* London: Academic Press. pp. 18, 201, 203, 205, 206, 208, 209, 210, 211, 213

Giles, H., Smith, P.M. & Williams, J.A. (1977) Women speaking: the voices of perceived androgyny and feminism. Mimeo. p. 196

Gimson, A.C. (1962) *An Introduction to the Pronunciation of English.* London: Arnold. p. 40

Goffman, E. (1955) On face-work: an analysis of ritual elements in social interaction. *Psychiatry 18*: 213–31; also in Laver & Hutcheson (1972: 319–46). pp. 115, 129

(1957) Alienation from interaction. *Human Relations 10*: 47–60; also in Laver & Hutcheson (1972: 347–63). p. 116

Goodenough, W.H. (1956) Componential analysis and the study of meaning. *Language 32*: 195–216. p. 86

Goodenough, W.H. (1957) Cultural anthropology and linguistics. In P.L. Garvin, ed. *Report of the 7th Annual Round Table Meeting on Linguistics and Language Study.* Washington: Georgetown University Press, 167–73; also in Hymes (1964: 36–9). pp. 74, 83

Goody, E.N. (1978) Towards a theory of questions. In E.N. Goody ed. *Questions and Politeness: Strategies in social interaction.* Cambridge: Cambridge University Press, 17–43. p. 101

Goody, J. & Watt, I. (1962) The consequences of literacy. *Comparative Studies in Society and History 5*: 304–26, 332–45; also in Giglioli (1972: 311–57). p. 5

Gregory, M. & Carroll, S. (1978) *Language and Situation: Language varieties and their social contexts.* London: Routledge & Kegan Paul. p. 48

Grice, H.P. (1975) Logic and conversation. In P. Cole & J. Morgan, eds. *Syntax and Semantics 3: Speech acts.* London: Academic Press, 41–58. pp. 118, 225

Gumperz, J.J. (1962) Types of linguistic community. *Anthropological Linguistics 4*: 28–40; also in Fishman (1968: 460–72) and Gumperz (1971: 97–113). p. 26

(1968) The speech community. In *International Encyclopedia of the Social Sciences*. London: Macmillan, 381–6; also in Gumperz (1971: 114–28) and Giglioli (1972: 219–31). pp. 5, 26

(1971) *Language in Social Groups*. Stanford: Stanford University Press. See Blom & Gumperz 1971, Gumperz 1962, 1968

(1976) The sociolinguistic significance of conversational code-switching. Mimeo. p. 57

(1977) The conversational analysis of inter-ethnic communication. In E.L. Ross, ed. *Inter-ethnic Communication*. Athens, GA: University of Georgia Press. p. 223

Gumperz, J.J. & Hymes, D.H. eds. (1964) *The Ethnography of Communication* (= *American Anthropologist 66*, special publication). p. 109

(1972) *Directions in Sociolinguistics: The ethnography of communication*. New York: Holt, Rinehart & Winston. See Blom & Gumperz 1971, Fishman 1972d, Friedrich 1972, Hymes 1972, Schegloff 1972

Gumperz, J.J. & Wilson, R. (1971) Convergence and creolization: a case from the Indo-Aryan/Dravidian border in India. In Hymes (1971a: 151–67). p. 47

Haas, M.R. (1944) Men's and women's speech in Koasati. *Language 20*: 142–49; also in Hymes (1964: 228–33). p. 120

Hall, E.T. (1959) *The Silent Language*. Greenwich: Fawcett. p. 135.

Hall, R.A. Jr. (1972) Pidgins and creoles as standard languages. In Pride & Holmes (1972: 142–54). pp. 33, 64

Halliday, M.A.K. (1972) Sociological aspects of semantic change. In *Proceedings of the 11th International Congress of Linguists*. Bologna: il Mulino, 853–88. p. 27

(1973) *Explorations in the Functions of Language*. London: Arnold. p. 4

(1975) *Learning How to Mean: Explorations in the development of language*. London: Arnold. p. 18

(1978) *Language as Social Semiotic*. London: Arnold. p. 49

Halliday, M.A.K., McIntosh, A. & Strevens, P. (1964) *The Linguistic Sciences and Language Teaching*. London: Longman. p. 48

Haugen, E. (1966) Dialect, language, nation. *American Anthropologist 68*: 922–35; also in Pride & Holmes (1972: 97–112). pp. 31, 32

Hawkins, P.R. (1973) Social class, the nominal group and reference. In Bernstein (1973: 81–92). p. 217

Heider, E.R., Cazden, C.B. & Brown, R. (1968) Social class differences in the effectiveness and style of children's coding ability. In *Project Literacy Report 9*. Ithaca: Cornell University, 1–10. p. 225

Hess, R.D. & Shipman, V. (1965) Early experience and the socialization of cognitive modes in children. *Child Development 36*: 869–86. pp. 100, 225

Hill, J.H. & K.C. (1978) Honorific usage in modern Nahuatl. The expression of social distance and respect in the Nahuatl of the Malinche Volcano area. *Language 54*: 123–55. pp. 127, 128

Hockett, C.F. (1950) Age-grading and linguistic continuity. *Language 26*: 449–59. p. 16

(1958) *A Course in Modern Linguistics*. New York: Macmillan. pp. 16, 26, 39.

Hollos, M. (1977) Comprehension and use of social rules in pronoun selection by Hungarian children. In Ervin-Tripp & Mitchell-Kernan (1977: 211–24). p. 124

Holm, J.A. (1978) The Creole English of Nicaragua's Miskito Coast: its sociolinguistic history and a comparative study of its lexicon and syntax. London University PhD thesis. p. 69

Hsieh, H.-I. (1972) Lexical diffusion: evidence from child language acquisition. *Glossa 6*: 89–104. p. 169

(1975) How generative is phonology? In E.F.K. Koerner, ed. *The Transformational–*

Generative Paradigm and Modern Linguistic Theory. Amsterdam: Benjamins,
   109–44. p. 169
Hudson, R.A. (1976) *Arguments for a Non-transformational Grammar.* Chicago:
   University of Chicago Press. p. 190
Hughes, A. & Trudgill, P. (1979) *English Accent and Dialects: An introduction to
   social and regional variation in British English.* London: Arnold. p. 39
Hymes, D.H. (1962) The ethnography of speaking. In T. Gladwin & W.C. Sturtevant,
   eds. *Anthropology and Human Behavior.* Washington: Anthropological
   Society of Washington, 13–53; also in Fishman (1968: 99–138). p. 109
   ed. (1964) *Language in Culture and Society.* New York: Harper & Row. p. 109
   ed. (1971a) *Pidginization and Creolization of Language.* Cambridge: Cambridge
   University Press. See DeCamp 1971a, 1971b, Dillard 1971, Ferguson 1971,
   Gumperz & Wilson 1971, Labov 1971
   (1971b) Competence and performance in linguistic theory. In R. Huxley &
   E. Ingram, eds. *Language Acquisition: Models and methods.* London: Academic
   Press, 3–28. pp. 116, 219, 220
   (1972) Models of the interaction of language and social life. In Gumperz &
   Hymes (1972: 35–71). pp. 27, 49, 120
   (1974) *Foundations of Sociolinguistics: An ethnographic approach.* Philadelphia:
   University of Pennsylvania Press. p. 109
Inglehart, R.F. & Woodward, M. (1967) Language conflicts and political
   community. *Comparative Studies in Society and History 10*: 27–45; also in
   Giglioli (1972: 358–78). p. 5
Irvine, J.T. (1974) Strategies of status manipulation in the Wolof greeting. In
   Bauman & Sherzer (1974: 167–91). p. 136
Jackson, J. (1974) Language identity of the Colombian Vaupés Indians. In Bauman
   & Sherzer (1974: 50–64). p. 8
**Jahangiri, N. (1980) A sociolinguistic study of Tehrani Persian. London University
   PhD thesis. p. 124, 126, 165, 170**
Johnson-Laird, P. & Wason, P.C. (1977) *Thinking: Readings in cognitive science.*
   Cambridge: Cambridge University Press. p. 77
Kay, P. (1978) Variable rules, community grammar and linguistic change. In D.
   Sankoff (1978: 71–83). p. 184
Keenan, E.O. (1977) The universality of conversational implicatures. In Fasold &
   Shuy (1977: 255–68). p. 118
Kempson, R.M. (1977) *Semantic Theory.* Cambridge: Cambridge University Press.
   pp. 82, 86, 110, 115
Kendon, A. (1967) Some functions of gaze-direction in social interaction. *Acta
   Psychologica 26*: 22–47; also in Argyle (1973: 76–92). p. 136
Knowles, G.O. (1978) The nature of phonological variables in Scouse. In Trudgill
   (1978: 80–90). pp. 145, 159
Kroch, A. & Small, C. (1978) Grammatical ideology and its effect on speech. In
   D. Sankoff (1978: 45–55). p. 158
Labov, W. (1971) The notion of system in creole studies. In Hymes (1971a: 447–72).
   p. 57
   (1972a) *Sociolinguistic Patterns.* Philadelphia: University of Pennsylvania Press,
   and Oxford: Blackwell. pp. 16, 27, 139, 143, 144, 148, 152, 164, 174, 182, 184,
   192, 199, 200, 202, 203, 205
   (1972b) *Language in the Inner City.* Philadelphia: University of Pennsylvania
   Press, and Oxford: Blackwell. pp. 143, 156, 158, 167, 168, 173, 182, 184, 214,
   215, 227

Bibliography and citation index

Lakoff, G. (1977) Linguistic gestalts. *Proceedings of the Annual Regional Meeting of the Chicago Linguistic Society 13*: 236–87. pp. 73, 82, 234

Lambert, W.E. (1967) A social psychology of bilingualism. *Journal of Social Issues 23*: 91–108; also in Pride & Holmes (1972: 336–49). pp. 205, 210

Lambert, W.E. (1974) Culture and language as factors in learning and education. In F.E. Aboud & R.D. Meade, eds. *Cultural Factors in Learning and Education.* Bellingham: Western Washington State College. p. 223

Laver, J. & Hutcheson, S. (1972) *Communication in Face to Face Interaction.* Harmondsworth, Middx: Penguin. See Argyle & Kendon 1967, Brown & Ford 1961, Brown & Gilman 1960, Goffman 1955, 1957, Malinowski 1923, Schegloff 1968

Lawton, D. (1968) *Social Class, Language and Education.* London: Routledge & Kegan Paul. p. 217

Leech, G.N. (1974) *Semantics.* Harmondsworth, Middx: Penguin. p. 92

Le Page, R.B. (1968a) Problems of description in multilingual communities. *Transactions of the Philological Society:* 189–212. pp. 27, 181

   (1968b) Problems to be faced in the use of English as the medium of education in four West Indian territories. In J.A. Fishman, C.A. Ferguson & J. Das Gupta, eds. *Language Problems of Developing Nations.* New York: Wiley. pp. 67, 210

   (1972) Preliminary report on the sociolinguistic survey of Cayo District, British Honduras. *Language in Society 1*: 155–72. p. 148

   (1977a) De-creolization and re-creolization: a preliminary report on the socio-linguistic survey of multilingual communities. Stage II: St. Lucia. *York Papers in Linguistics 7*: 107–28. pp. 14, 158

   (1977b) Processes of pidginization and creolization. In Valdman (1977: 222–55). p. 70

Le Page, R.B., Christie, P., Jurdant, B., Weekes, A.J. & Tabouret-Keller, A. (1974) Further report on the sociolinguistic survey of multilingual communities: survey of Cayo District, British Honduras. *Language in Society 3*: 1–32. pp. 14, 146, 148, 158, 164

Linde, C. & Labov, W. (1975) Spatial networks as a site for the study of language and thought. *Language 51*: 924–39. p. 134

Local, J.K. (1978) Studies towards a description of the development and functioning of linguistic variability in young children. University of Newcastle upon Tyne PhD thesis. p. 210

Lounsbury, F.G. (1969) Language and culture. In S. Hook, ed. *Language and Philosophy.* New York: New York University Press, 3–29. p. 88

Lyons, J. (1970) *New Horizons in Linguistics.* Harmondsworth, Middx: Penguin. p. 25

Lyons, J. (1977) *Semantics.* 2 vols. Cambridge: Cambridge University Press. pp. 82, 108, 110f, 115

Macaulay, R.K.S. (1973) Double standards. *American Anthropologist 75*: 1324–37. p. 33

   (1975) Negative prestige, linguistic insecurity and linguistic self-hatred. *Lingua 36*: 147–61. p. 200

   (1978) Variation and consistency in Glaswegian English. In Trudgill (1978: 132–43). p. 164

McCawley, J.D. (1977) Acquisition models as models of acquisition. In Fasold & Shuy (1977: 51–64). p. 13, 189

Maclaren, R. (1976) The variable (ʌ), a relic form with social correlates. *Belfast Working Papers in Language and Linguistics 1*: 45–68. p. 168

Malinowski, B. (1923) The problem of meaning in primitive languages. In C.K. Ogden & I.A. Richards *The Meaning of Meaning*. London: Routledge & Kegan Paul; also in Laver & Hutcheson (1972: 146–52). p. 109

Mandelbaum, D.G. ed. (1949) *Selected Writings of Edward Sapir in Language, Culture and Personality*. Cambridge: Cambridge University Press. p. 103

Martin, L.W., Bradac, J.J. & Elliott, N.D. (1977) On the empirical basis of linguistics: a multivariate analysis of sentence judgments. *Proceedings of the Annual Regional Meeting of the Chicago Linguistic Society 13*: 357–71. p. 19

Martin, S.E. (1964) Speech levels in Japan and Korea. In Hymes (1964a: 407–15). p. 126

Matthews, P.H. (1974) *Morphology: An introduction to the theory of word-structure*. Cambridge: Cambridge University Press. p. 92

(1979) *Generative Grammar and Linguistic Competence*. London: Allen & Unwin. pp. 37, 40, 184

Miller, S. (1975) *Experimental Design and Statistics*. London: Methuen. p. 147

Milroy, J. (1978) Lexical alternation and diffusion in vernacular speech. *Belfast Working Papers in Language and Linguistics 3*: 101–14. pp. 155, 168, 169

Milroy, J. & L. (1978) Belfast: change and variation in an urban vernacular. In Trudgill (1978: 19–36). pp. 155, 156, 160, 180

Milroy, L. (1976) Phonological correlates to community structure in Belfast. *Belfast Working Papers in Language and Linguistics 1*: 1–44. p. 155

Milroy, L. & J. (1977) Speech and context in an urban setting. *Belfast Working Papers in Language and Linguistics 2*: 1–85. p. 155

Milroy, L. & Margrain, S. (1978) Vernacular language loyalty and social network. *Belfast Working Papers in Language and Linguistics 3*: 1–58. pp. 155, 178, 184

Mitchell, A.G. & Delbridge, A. (1965) *The Speech of Australian Adolescents*. Sydney: Angus & Robertson. p. 177

Mitchell, T.F. (1975) *Principles of Firthian Linguistics*. London: Longman. pp. 4, 126

Naro, A.J. (1978) The social and structural dimensions of a syntactic change. Mimeo. p. 171

O'Connor, J.D. (1973) *Phonetics*. Harmondsworth, Middx: Penguin. p. 46

Omondi, L. (1976) Paralinguistics: a survey of non-verbal communication. Mimeo. p. 137

Opie, I. & P. (1959) *The Lore and Language of School-children*. London: Oxford University Press. p. 16

Parkin, D. (1977) Emergent and stabilized multilingualism: polyethnic peer groups in urban Kenya. In Giles (1977: 185–210). p. 56

Pellowe, J., Nixon, G., Strang, B. & McNeany, V. (1972) A dynamic modelling of linguistic variation: the Urban (Tyneside) Linguistic Survey. *Lingua 30*: 1–30. p. 141

Platt, J.T. & H.K. (1975) *The Social Significance of Speech*. Amsterdam: North Holland. p. 1

Pride, J.B. (1971) *The Social Meaning of Language*. London: Oxford University Press. p. 1

Pride, J.B. & Holmes, J. eds. (1972) *Sociolinguistics*. Harmondsworth, Middx: Penguin. See Denison 1971, Fishman 1965, Geertz 1960, Hall 1972, Haugen 1966, Lambert 1967, Sankoff 1972, Sorensen 1971

Reid, E. (1978) Social and stylistic variation in the speech of children: some evidence from Edinburgh. In Trudgill (1978: 158–71). p. 164

Reisman, K. (1974) Contrapuntal conversations in an Antiguan village. In Bauman & Sherzer (1974: 110–24). p. 117

Robinson, W.P. (1972) *Language and Social Behaviour*. Harmondsworth, Middx: Penguin. pp. 1, 100, 110, 225

Romaine, S. (1978) Postvocalic /r/ in Scottish English: sound change in progress? In Trudgill (1978: 144–57). p. 162

Ronjat, J. (1913) *Le Développement du Langage Chez un Enfant Bilingue*. Paris. p. 17

Rosch, E. (1974) Linguistic relativity. In A. Silverstein, ed. *Human Communication: Theoretical perspectives*. Hillsdale: Lawrence Erlbaum; also in Johnson-Laird & Wason (1977: 501–19). p. 88

    (1976) Classification of real-world objects: origins and representations in cognition. In S. Ehrlich & E. Tulving, eds. *La Mémoire Sémantique*. Paris: Bulletin de Psychologie; also in Johnson-Laird & Wason (1977: 212–22). pp. 78, 92, 94

Rosen, H. (1972) *Language and Class: A critical look at the theories of Basil Bernstein*. Bristol: Falling Wall Press. p. 227

Rosenthal, M. (1974) The magic boxes: pre-school children's attitudes towards black and standard English. *Florida F.L. Reporter*: 55–93. p. 210

Rosenthal, R. & Jacobson, L. (1968) *Pygmalion in the Classroom: Teacher expectations and pupils' intellectual development*. New York: Holt, Rinehart & Winston. p. 209.

Ross, J.R. (1973) A fake NP squish. In Bailey & Shuy (1973: 96–140). p. 234

    (1974) There, there, (there, (there, (there . . .))). *Proceedings of the Annual Regional Meeting of the Chicago Linguistic Society 10*: 569–87. p. 234

Sachs, J. & Devin, J. (1976) Young children's use of age-appropriate speech styles in social interaction and role-playing. *Journal of Child Language 3*: 81–98. p. 18

Sankoff, D. (1978) *Linguistic Variation: Models and Methods*. New York: Academic Press. pp. 143, 147, 182

Sankoff, D. & Thibault, P. (1978) Weak complementarity: tense and aspect in Montreal French. Mimeo. p. 159

Sankoff, G. (1969) Mutual intelligibility, bilingualism and linguistic boundaries. In *International Days of Sociolinguistics*. Rome: Baldassini, 839–48. p. 35

    (1971) Quantitative analysis of sharing and variability in a cognitive model. *Ethnology 10*: 389–408. p. 75

    (1972) Language use in multilingual societies: some alternative approaches. In Pride & Holmes (1972: 33–51). p. 57

    (1973a) Dialectology. *Annual Reviews of Anthropology 2*: 165–77. pp. 39, 40

    (1973b) Above and beyond phonology in variable rules. In Bailey & Shuy (1973: 44–61). pp. 158, 168

    (1976) Political power and linguistic inequality in Papua New Guinea. in W. & J. O'Barr, eds. *Language and Politics*. The Hague: Mouton, 283–310. pp. 198, 199

    (1977) Creolization and syntactic change in New Guinea Tok Pisin. In B.G. Blount, ed. *Social Dimensions of Language Change*. New York: Academic Press, 119–30. p. 67

Sankoff, G. & Brown, P. (1976) The origins of syntax in discourse. *Language 52*: 631–66. p. 69

Sankoff, G. & Thibault, P. (1977) L'alternance entre les auxiliaires *avoir* et *être* en français parlé à Montréal. *Langue Française 34*: 81–108. p. 158

Sankoff, G. & Vincent, D. (1977) L'emploi productif du *ne* dans le français parlé à Montréal. *Le Français Moderne 45*: 243–56. p. 158

Sapir, E. (1915) Abnormal types of speech in Nootka. *Canada Geological Survey Memoir 62, Anthropological Series 5*. Ottawa: Government Printing Bureau; also in Mandelbaum (1949: 179–96). p. 122

(1929) Male and female forms of speech in Yana. In S.W.J. Teeuwen, ed. *Donum Natalicum Schrijnen.* Nijmegen: Dekker & Van de Vegt, 79–85; also in Mandelbaum (1949: 206–12). p. 120

Saussure, F. de (1916/1959) *Course in General Linguistics.* New York: McGraw-Hill. p. 106

Schank, R. & Abelson, R. (1977) *Scripts, Plans, Goals and Understanding: An inquiry into human knowledge structures.* Hillsdale: Lawrence Erlbaum. pp. 133, 221

Schegloff, E.A. (1968) Sequencing in conversational openings. *American Anthropologist 70:* 1075–95; also in Gumperz & Hymes (1972: 346–80) and Laver & Hutcheson (1972: 374–405). p. 132

Schneiderman, E. (1976) An examination of the ethnic and linguistic attitudes of bilingual children. *I.T.L. Review of Applied Linguistics 33:* 59–72. p. 212

Scribner, S. (1977) Modes of thinking and ways of speaking: culture and logic reconsidered. In Johnson-Laird & Wason (1977: 483–519). p. 222

Searle, J. (1965) What is a speech act? In M. Black, ed. *Philosophy in America.* London: Allen & Unwin; also in Giglioli (1972: 136–54). p. 110

Shuy, R.W. (1970) The sociolinguists and urban language problems. In Williams (1970: 335–50). p. 211

   ed. (1972) *Sociolinguistics: Current trends and prospects.* Washington: Georgetown University Press. See Bickerton 1972a

Shuy, R.W. & Fasold, W. eds. (1973) *Language Attitudes: Current trends and prospects.* Washington: Georgetown University Press. See Taylor 1973, Williams 1973

Sinclair, J.M. & Coulthard, R.M. (1975) *Towards an Analysis of Discourse: The English used by teachers and pupils.* London: Oxford University Press. p. 132

Slobin, D.I. (1971) *Psycholinguistics.* London: Scott, Foresman. p. 103

Smith, G. (1979) Attitudes to language in a multilingual community in East London. London University PhD thesis. p. 204

Smith, P.M. & Giles, H. (1978) Sociolinguistics: a social psychological perspective. Paper presented to the 9th World Congress of Sociology, Uppsala. p. 196

Sorensen, A.P. Jr. (1971) Multilingualism in the Northwest Amazon. *American Anthropologist 69:* 670–84; also in Pride & Holmes (1972: 78–94). p. 8

Stross, B. (1974) Speaking of speaking: Tenejapa Tzeltal metalinguistics. In Bauman & Sherzer (1974: 213–39). p. 111

Tajfel, H. (1974) Social identity and intergroup behaviour. *Social Science Information 13:* 65–93. p. 197

Taylor, D.M. (1951) *The Black Carib of British Honduras.* New York: Wenner-Gren Foundation for Anthropological Research. p. 121

Taylor, O.L. (1973) Teachers' attitudes toward black and nonstandard English as measured by the Language Attitude Scale. In Shuy & Fasold (1973: 174–201). p. 208

Traugott, E.C. (1977) Pidginization, creolization and language change. In Valdman (1977: 70–98). p. 38

Trubetzkoy, N.S. (1931) Phonologie und Sprachgeographie. *Travaux du Cercle Linguistique de Prague 4:* 228–34. p. 46

Trudgill, P. (1974a) *The Social Differentiation of English in Norwich.* Cambridge: Cambridge University Press. pp. 143, 152, 154, 155, 159, 175

   (1974b) *Sociolinguistics: An introduction.* Harmondsworth, Middx: Penguin. pp. 1, 33, 40, 120

   (1975a) *Accent, Dialect and the School.* London: Arnold. pp. 34, 215

(1975b) Linguistic change and diffusion: description and exploration in socio-linguistic dialect geography. *Language in Society* 2: 215–46. pp. 171, 172

(1978) *Sociolinguistic Patterns in British English*. London: Arnold. pp. 5, 138, 143, 158

Turner, G.J. & Pickvance, R.E. (1973) Social class differences in the expression of uncertainty in five year old children. In Bernstein (1973: 93–119). p. 225

Valdman, A. ed. (1977) *Pidgin and Creole Linguistics*. Bloomington: Indiana University Press. See Le Page 1977b, Traugott 1977

Wakelin, M.F. (1972) *English Dialects: An introduction*. London: Athlone. p. 39

(1978) *Discovering English Dialects*. Aylesbury: Shire. pp. 23, 40

Wang, W.S-Y. (1969) Competing changes as a cause of residue. *Language 45*: 9–25. p. 169

Wang, W.S-Y. & Cheng, C-c. (1970) Implementation of phonological change: the Shuāng-fēng Chinese case. *Proceedings of the Annual Regional Meeting of the Chicago Linguistic Society 6*: 552–9. p. 169

Wardhaugh, R. (1976) *The Contexts of Language*. Rowley: Newbury House. p. 1

Watson, O.M. & Graves, T.D. (1966) Quantitative research on proxemic behavior. *American Anthropologist 68*: 971–85; also in Argyle (1973: 34–46). p. 135

Watson-Gegeo, K.A. & Boggs, S.T. (1977) From verbal play to talk story: the role of routines in speech events among Hawaiian children. In Ervin-Tripp & Mitchell-Kernan (1977: 67–90). p. 114

Weeks, T.E. (1971) Speech registers in young children. *Child Development 42*: 1119–31. p. 18

Weinreich, U. (1953) *Languages in Contact*. New York: Linguistic Circle and The Hague: Mouton. p. 17

Wells, G.G. (1979a) Variation in child language. In P. Fletcher & M. Garman, eds. *Language Acquisition: Studies in first language development*. Cambridge: Cambridge University Press, 377–95. p. 217

(1979b) Language development in pre-school children. Final Report to SSRC. Unpublished. p. 217

Wells, J.C. (1970) Local accents in England and Wales. *Journal of Linguistics 6*: 231–52. p. 46

Whorf, B.L. (1940) Science and linguistics. *Technological Review 42*: 229–31, 47–8; also in J.B. Carroll, ed. (1956) *Language, Thought and Reality*. Cambridge, Mass: MIT Press, 207–19. p. 104

Williams, F. ed. (1970) *Language and Poverty: Perspectives on a theme*. Chicago: Markham. pp. 229, 230

Williams, F. (1973) Some research notes on dialect attitudes and stereotypes. In Shuy & Fasold (1973: 113–28). p. 207

Winograd, T. (1975) Frame representation and the declarative-procedural controversy. In D.G. Bobrow, & A. Collins, eds. *Representation and Understanding*. New York: Academic Press, 185–210. p. 114

Wolfram, W.A. (1969) *A Sociolinguistic Description of Detroit Negro Speech*. Washington: Center for Applied Linguistics. p. 45

(1971) Black–white speech differences revisited. *Viewpoints: Bulletin of the School of Education, Indiana University, 47*; also in W.A. Wolfram & N.H. Clarke, eds. (1971) *Black–white Speech Relationships*. Washington: Center for Applied Linguistics, 139–61. p. 66

INDEX

Index

Sapir–Whorf hypothesis 96, 103–5
schemata 221–30
schools, language in 132f, 194, chapter 6
  passim
semantics *see* meaning
Seminole Indians 88
Senegal 136
sex 43, 120f, 165, 171, 179f
slang 53
social class 43, 100f, 124f, 148–55,
  165f, 171, 173–7, 200, 211, 214–19,
  224–30
social dialect 43, 216; *see also* social
  distribution
social distribution 23f, 39f, 53, 83, 108,
  171–81, 189
socialisation 99–105, 117, 225f
social structure 124, 152, 166f, 173–7,
  179–81, 199f, 226
social variables 142f; *see also* social
  distribution
socio-economic status *see* social class
sociolect *see* social dialect
sociolinguistics 1, 138
  and linguistics 3f, 19
  and the sociology of language 4f
sociology 109, 115
sociology of language 5, 32–4
solidarity *see* power
Somerset 213
Spanish 55, 57
speech 2, 106; *see also* functions of
  speech
  as skilled work 113–16, 193
speech acts 110–12
speech community 9, 25–30, 41f, 54,
  184
standard deviation 164f
standard languages 15, 32–7, 54, 64, 180
statistics 146f, 160, 163–7, 178
stereotypes 202–14, 219, 227, 229
structural(ist) linguistics 3f, 14, 25, 73,
  191, 193, 220, 231
structured interviews 152–5
subjective inequality 193f
subjective reaction tests 202–6
subtractive bilingualism 223
swearing 53
syntax, as influence on variables 168
  lack of variability in 46–8, 57f, 62
  variability in 45, 67–9, 121f, 141, 158,
  184–8, 216–18

taboo, linguistic 53
Tanzania 60
teaching, of foreign languages 3
  of native languages 33, 53f, 67, 102,
  193, 196, 200, 223
Tehran *see* Persian
television *see* mass media
Tok Pisin 58, 64, 69, 168
topic 132–4; *see also* code-switching,
  metaphorical
trade languages 61
transformational-generative linguistics
  3, 22, 139, 144, 182–4, 190, 192, 220
translation 85
Trobriand Islands 88
Tukano 8, 10, 61
Turkish 62
turn-taking 131f, 136
Tyneside 210
typology 55
Tzeltal 111f

United States 34, 42–4, 55, 96f, 103,
  117, 122f, 130, 135, 137, 143, 158,
  197, 199, 201, 210f, 218, 224;
  see also Black English
universals 57f, 84, 125, 128, 135, 137,
  189; *see also* relativity
Urdu 47

variables *see* linguistic variables
variable rules 181–4
variant 139f
varieties of language chapter 2 *passim*;
  see also lect
vocabulary *see* lexical item

Wales 213
wave theory 41f, 169–72, 184–8;
  see diffusion
Welsh 88
West Indian English 67, 204, 210, 219
Wolof 136
word-formation 92
writing 32f, 44, 132, 193, 216; *see also*
  reading

Yana 120

Zuni 88